Racial Issues in Criminal Justice

Racial Issues in Criminal Justice

The Case of African Americans

EDITED BY MARVIN D. FREE, JR.

Criminal Justice, Delinquency, and Corrections
Marilyn D. McShane and Frank Williams, Series Editors

Westport, Connecticut
London

70.95

Library of Congress Cataloging-in-Publication Data

Racial issues in criminal justice: The case of African Americans / edited by Marvin D. Free, Jr.
    p. cm.—(Criminal justice, delinquency, and corrections, ISSN 1535–0371)
    ISBN 0–275–97562–2 (alk. paper)
    1. Discrimination in criminal justice administration—United States. 2. Race discrimination—United States. 3. African Americans—Civil rights. 4. African Americans—Legal status, laws, etc. 5. United States—Race relations. 6. United States—Politics and government. I. Free, Marvin D. II. Series.
    HV9950.R33   2003
    364'.089'96073—dc21   2002044541

British Library Cataloguing in Publication Data is available.

Library of Congress Catalog Card Number: 2002044541
ISBN: 0–275–97562–2
ISSN: 1535–0371

First published in 2003

Praeger Publishers, 88 Post Road West, Westport, CT 06881
An imprint of Greenwood Publishing Group, Inc.
www.praeger.com

Printed in the United States of America

The paper used in this book complies with the Permanent Paper Standard issued by the National Information Standards Organization (Z39.48–1984).

10 9 8 7 6 5 4 3 2

Copyright Acknowledgments

"'Driving While Black': Corollary Phenomena and Collateral Consequences," Katheryn K. Russell, *Boston College Law Review*, volume 40, number 3, 1999, pp. 717–731. Reprinted by permission.
"The Myth of Black Juror Nullification: Racism Dressed Up in Jurisprudential Clothing," Elissa Krauss and Martha Schulman, *Cornell Journal of Law & Public Policy*, volume 7, number 1, 1997, pp. 57–75. Reprinted by permission.

Contents

Series Foreword

Once again, we are delighted to be working with Marvin Free and assisting in the publication of a timely and provocative work. In our view, the challenge for scholarship on race and crime lies in the way that issues rapidly evolve in dynamic social environments. Today's discussions are unique in their context, with distinct political, legal, and economic features. The rhetoric and parameters of the dialogues of the 1960s, 1970s, and 1980s now present us with new frameworks, regardless of the seemingly perpetual nature of many of the debates.

Though some may counter that the racial aspects of social conflict are so fundamental as to transcend time and community context, certainly most would agree that we continue to find different ways to measure, address, and theorize about them. Academicians and researchers play a very important role in that process. As you will see, Professor Free has worked diligently to produce a work that demonstrates how issues of race have evolved and how they affect us now. We think readers will be pleased with the end product. Above all, it reinforces the need to ensure that the objective nature of scholarly research in this and in all areas of crime and justice are reported and disseminated without the filters of political spin.

Marilyn D. McShane
Frank Williams
Series Editors

Preface

Shortly after the release of my first book (*African Americans and the Criminal Justice System*), the Sentencing Project released its findings of African Americans under the control of the criminal justice system. Their findings, that 32.2 percent of all African American men in their twenties in the United States during 1995 were either in jail, prison, or on probation or parole, provided a particularly poignant example of the importance of race. Now, seven years later, as I finish another book about African Americans and the criminal justice system, the Justice Policy Institute has released *Cellblocks or Classrooms? The Funding of Higher Education and Corrections and Its Impact on African American Men*. Again, the news is bleak. In 2000 there were 188,500 more African American men in prison or jail than enrolled in higher education. Between 1980 and 2000 thirty-eight states added more African American men to their prison systems than were added to their respective higher education systems. What these numbers suggest is that race continues to be a defining feature of American society and its criminal justice system.

The fact that the Sentencing Project's 1995 report was soon eclipsed by other news stories left me feeling uncomfortable. Had there been a report that almost one-third of all *white* males in their twenties were in some way involved with the criminal justice system, I am confident that there would have been a public outcry and demand for answers to the "problem," yet nothing of substance emerged from that report. That the Justice Policy Institute's results in 2002 are not even deemed newsworthy only serves to heighten my concern. These feelings (and a wealth of other data showing substantial black/white differences in various areas of criminal processing) were the impetus behind this reader.

To facilitate a discussion of race and criminal justice, each chapter offers the reader a critical analysis of some aspect of criminal justice and African Americans that is designed to question racial equality. Through this approach it is hoped that the book will serve to document the significance of race in criminal justice and to provide a vigilant reminder that the criminal justice system is not a value-neutral system that operates without regard to the race or ethnicity of its participants.

A number of individuals and institutions were instrumental in the preparation of this book. First, I would like to thank the University of Wisconsin—Whitewater for awarding me a sabbatical for this project. Second, I would like to thank Marilyn McShane, editor of the Praeger series, Criminal Justice, Delinquency, and Corrections, who saw the merits of my book proposal. Though we did not always agree on everything throughout the process, we always respected the professional integrity of the other. To the extent that the book provides a more thorough account of the major issues, she deserves much of the credit. Third, I would like to thank Suzanne Staszak-Silva at the Greenwood Publishing Group. Her expeditious replies to my numerous queries provided me with much needed assistance. Fourth, I would like to thank the indulgence shown by my family. Without their tolerance, this project would not have been successful. And finally, I would like to acknowledge the role of my contributors. My requests for revisions and modifications were always met with enthusiasm that is indicative of a true community of scholars. Without the thoughtful professionalism exhibited by my contributors this book would not have reached fruition.

CHAPTER 1

Race and Criminal Justice in the United States: Some Introductory Remarks

Marvin D. Free, Jr.

INTRODUCTION

Despite their shortcomings,[1] the *Uniform Crime Reports* (UCR) disclose some important facets of crime and the criminal justice system. Most apparent, perhaps, is the decline in crime in recent years. Total crime in the United States decreased 22 percent between 1991 and 2000 (Federal Bureau of Investigation, 2001, p. 6). The decline in crime was not accompanied by a decline in total arrests, however. A further analysis of that ten-year period reveals that arrests vacillated by offense type. Arrests for Part I offenses (murder and nonnegligent manslaughter, forcible rape, robbery, aggravated assault, burglary, larceny-theft, motor vehicle theft, and arson) plummeted 25.3 percent. Concomitantly, arrests for Part II offenses rose, particularly drug abuse violations, which grew 49.4 percent (Federal Bureau of Investigation, 2001, p. 215). Also apparent from the UCR data is the overrepresentation of people of color. Although comprising less than 13 percent of the general population, African Americans made up 27.9 percent of the persons arrested in 2000. In the ubiquitous War on Drugs, African Americans accounted for 34.5 percent of drug abuse arrests (Federal Bureau of Investigation, 2001, table 43).

Youths in juvenile institutions are also disproportionately African American. According to a recent report sponsored by the Department of Justice and six leading foundations, African American youths without a previous juvenile incarceration record were over six times more likely than similarly situated white youths to be sentenced to juvenile prison by juvenile courts. The disparity was especially prominent for violent and

drug crimes, where African American teenagers were 9 and 48 times, respectively, more likely than white teenagers to be sentenced to juvenile
prison (Butterfield, 2000).

Nor are sanctioning disparities confined to youthful offenders. Adult
African Americans are frequently subjected to harsher penalties than their
white counterparts. An analysis of the first six months of the implementation of California Assembly Bill 971, which established a mandatory 25-
year-to-life sentence upon conviction for a third felony, reveals racial
differences. In Los Angeles County, where African Americans comprise
10 percent of the general population, they constituted 30.5 percent of the
felony cases and 57.3 percent of the "third-strike" cases. Conversely,
whites, who represent 36.6 percent of the general population, accounted
for only 19.7 percent of the felony cases and only 12.6 percent of the third-
strike cases (Schiraldi & Godfrey, 1994, p. 3).

Incarceration statistics for jails and prisons further display racial disparities. At midyear 2000, non-Hispanic African Americans represented
44.6 percent of all male inmates in state or federal prisons or local jails.
The comparable figure for non-Hispanic African American females was
44.5 percent. When comparing number of inmates per 100,000 residents
of each group, the disparity becomes even more stark. Non-Hispanic African American males were almost seven times more likely than their non-
Hispanic white counterparts to be incarcerated, whereas non-Hispanic
African American females were six times more likely than their non-
Hispanic white counterparts to be incarcerated (Beck & Karberg, 2001,
tables 12 & 13).

Once in prison, African Americans remain incarcerated longer than
whites. A review of discretionary parole (determined by a parole board)
and mandatory parole (determined by statute) discloses substantial black/
white differences in the mean time served in prison for first releases to
state parole. Non-Hispanic African Americans average three months
longer in prison than non-Hispanic whites for discretionary parole releases. The largest racial disparity appears in forcible rape, in which non-
Hispanic African Americans average 42 months longer than their
non-Hispanic white counterparts. For mandatory parole releases, there is
an average 7-month differential favoring non-Hispanic whites. Again,
forcible rape represents the largest racial disparity. Non-Hispanic African
Americans are, on average, incarcerated for 16 more months than non-
Hispanic whites. Interestingly, the next two largest differentials are drug-
related offenses. For drug possession and drug trafficking the mean time
served in prison for non-Hispanic African Americans is 14 months and
11 months, respectively, greater than that for non-Hispanic whites
(Hughes, Wilson, & Beck, 2001, table 8).

Capital punishment represents another area where racial disparities exist. African Americans in 2000 made up 39.6 percent of the new admis-

sions to state prison death rows (Snell, 2001, table 5). Whereas the federal system has few death-certified cases, over 70 percent of those awaiting death in federal prison on April 1, 2001 were non-Hispanic African Americans (Maguire & Pastore, 2001, table 6.80).[2]

Although these statistics collectively seem to provide prima facie support for a racial bias argument, Petersilia and Turner (1988) contend that racial disparity can be present without racial discrimination. They argue that the former exists "when legitimate standards are applied but have different results for different racial groups," whereas the latter is present "if system officials make ad hoc decisions based on race rather than clearly defined standards" (Petersilia & Turner, 1988, p. 92). Their distinction, nonetheless, is problematic on at least two counts. First, they assert that different outcomes for different groups is not indicative of racial discrimination if "legitimate standards" have been applied. This raises an important question: if proposed legislation that will knowingly have a more adverse impact on people of color is passed, does the uniform application of this standard reflect racial disparity or racial discrimination? A second problem with their distinction is that their definition of racial discrimination glosses over the less blatant forms of racial discrimination that occur when race interacts with other variables (legal and extralegal) in ways to produce a disadvantage for people of color.[3]

To facilitate a better comprehension of the role of race in the criminal justice system, two offenses for which African Americans are disproportionately arrested are now examined. The first crime category analyzed is drug abuse violations. This is followed by an investigation of violent Index crimes (murder, forcible rape, aggravated assault, and robbery).

THE WAR ON DRUGS AND AFRICAN AMERICANS

That African Americans have been disproportionately affected by the War on Drugs is indisputable. Arrest statistics from 2000 show that, excluding the catch-all category "all other offenses (except traffic)," drug abuse violations represented the largest single crime category for which African Americans were arrested. As previously noted, African Americans constituted over a third of all drug abuse violation arrests in that year (Federal Bureau of Investigation, 2001, table 43).

Two opposing interpretations of this disparity may be proffered. One interpretation contends that arrest statistics mirror the extensive involvement of African Americans in drug offenses. In other words, racial disparities in arrests reflect actual behavioral differences in offending. An alternative interpretation argues that arrest statistics are a product of selective drug legislation aimed primarily at the poor and people of color and the selective enforcement of such laws. To ascertain the impact of race on drug arrests let us now proceed to an assessment of these discordant positions.

Interpretation 1: African Americans Are Extensively Involved in Drug Offenses

To adequately address this issue one must go beyond the crimes known to the police. Admittedly open to criticisms themselves, self-reported measures of drug use, nonetheless, remain an important source of information, since the data are not influenced by potentially selective enforcement of the drug laws. The National Household Survey on Drug Abuse, an annual probability sample of Americans age 12 and older, reports some interesting information on African American and white drug use. The top of Table 1.1 displays the percentage of each group that has ever used any of the seven drug categories listed. Since this is a lifetime measure, the percentage for each drug is higher than the bottom half of the table, which depicts the percentage of each group that has used the drug within the past year. The column on the far right shows the difference in the percentages for non-Hispanic African Americans and non-Hispanic whites. An analysis of the data discloses that (1) a small percentage of both groups have used drugs; (2) there are few differences in reported drug use by these two groups; and (3) when one analyzes most recent drug use (i.e., within the past year), the largest percentage difference is 1 percent. Nowhere in Table 1.1 are there large differences that support an assumption that African Americans are more extensively involved in drug use than whites.

Still, there remains the possibility that arrest disparities are a reflection of the overrepresentation of African Americans in drug trafficking. Yet data on youthful drug sellers suggest otherwise. According to the 1999 National Household Survey on Drug Abuse, white adolescents ages 12–17 are over one-third more likely than their African American counterparts to have sold drugs (Substance Abuse & Mental Health Services Administration, 2000, table G71). Furthermore, even *if* African Americans were more likely than whites to sell drugs, it is inconceivable that this could fully account for the racial disparity because only 19 percent of drug arrests in 2000 were for the sale or manufacturing of illegal substances (Federal Bureau of Investigation, 2001, table 4.1).

Interpretation 2: African Americans Are the Recipients of Selective Drug Legislation and Law Enforcement

An alternative interpretation of the data suggests that racial disparities in drug violations are the result of selective drug legislation as well as selective law enforcement. This argument is buttressed by the fact that

Table 1.1

Self-Reported Drug Use for African Americans and Whites by Drug Type, 1998

	Lifetime Measure		
	Non-Hispanic African American	Non-Hispanic White	
Drug	Ever Used	Ever Used	Difference[1]
Cocaine[2]	8.5%	11.4%	-2.9%
Crack	4.2%	1.8%	+2.4%
Heroin	1.9%	1.0%	+0.9%
LSD	4.0%	9.2%	-5.2%
PCP	2.8%	3.9%	-1.1%
Inhalants	2.2%	6.6%	-4.4%
Stimulants	2.9%	5.0%	-2.1%
	Most Recent Use		
	Non-Hispanic African American	Non-Hispanic White	
Drug	Within Past Year	Within Past Year	Difference[1]
Cocaine[2]	1.9%	1.7%	+0.2%
Crack	1.3%	0.3%	+1.0%
Heroin	0.2%	0.1%	+0.1%
LSD	0.1%	1.0%	-0.9%
PCP	0.1%	0.2%	-0.1%
Inhalants	0.3%	1.0%	-0.7%
Stimulants	0.6%	0.7%	-0.1%

[1]A positive sign means that African Americans report higher rates; a negative sign means that whites report higher rates.
[2]Includes crack.
Source: Maguire & Pastore (2001, Tables 3.99 & 3.100).

not until the late 1980s and the passage of drug legislation focusing on cocaine use and trafficking did large racial differentials in drug offending appear. In 1986, for example, 7 percent of all African Americans and 8 percent of all whites in state prisons were incarcerated for drug offenses. By 1991, however, 25 percent of all African Americans in state prisons had been convicted of drug offenses. And while 12 percent of all whites in state prisons were incarcerated for drug offenses in 1991, the 4 percent increase for whites pales in comparison to the 18 percent increase for African Americans (U.S. Department of Justice, 1993, Figure 4). What apparently was responsible for much of the African American increase was drug legislation and law enforcement aimed at controlling crack cocaine.

During the mid-1980s the news media was quick to exploit the dangers of this new drug. With the first stories about crack cocaine appearing in November 1984 in the *Los Angeles Times,* drug coverage soon expanded to other parts of the country. In 1985 the *New York Times* reported on the growing problem of crack cocaine. By 1986 drug coverage of the "coke plague" suggested that its use had spread to the suburbs and the Midwest and that crack use was now a "national crisis" (Berger, Free, & Searles, 2001, p. 14). Further fueling the drug scare was the media's equating crack cocaine use with violence. A *Time* magazine article exemplifies this sense of urgency. In it Attinger and Cronin (1990, p. 36) write that "[a] growing sense of vulnerability has been deepened by the belief that deadly violence, once mostly confined to crime-ridden ghetto neighborhoods that the police once wrote off as free-fire zones, is now lashing out randomly at anyone, even in areas once considered relatively safe."

Legislators responded by passing drug laws that were aimed primarily at crack cocaine, a less expensive form of cocaine. The 1986 Anti-Drug Abuse Act represented the first time that a distinction was drawn between powder cocaine and crack cocaine for purposes of sentencing in federal court. For an individual possessing powder cocaine to receive the same minimum sentence as an individual possessing crack cocaine, the former had to possess a quantity that was 100 times greater than the latter (McDonald & Carlson, 1993). African Americans, being more likely to be charged with possession of crack cocaine than whites (see *State v. Russell,* 1991), were consequently more adversely affected by the stiffer sentences imposed for crack cocaine possession. The get tough on crime mentality is revealed by the fact that only 14 percent of the funding was allocated for the treatment and prevention of drug abuse (Johnson, Golub, & Fagan, 1995, p. 288). In 1988, five-year mandatory minimum sentences were established in federal courts for first-time offenders with five grams of crack cocaine. Prior to this act, federal judges typically placed first-time offenders on probation (Alschuler, 1991). The 1988 Omnibus Drug Abuse Act additionally provided for mandatory minimum five-year sentences for three grams of crack for second-time offenders and mandatory minimum five-year sentences for one gram of crack for third-time offenders (Wallace, 1993). As with the earlier legislation, law enforcement was stressed over treatment and prevention. It is no coincidence that by 1993 drug offenses represented the single largest crime category in federal trials (Miller, 1995).

Whereas it might be tempting to dismiss this legislation as a benign, albeit misdirected, reaction to a perceived threat, Tonry (1995) posits that legislators were aware of the probable repercussions of their actions.

The . . . officials of the Office of National Drug Control Policy understood the arcane intricacies of NIDA [National Institute on Drug Abuse], DUF [Drug Use Forecasting], and DAWN [Drug Abuse Warning Network] better than anyone else in the United States. They knew that drug abuse was falling among the vast majority of the population. They knew that drug use was not declining among disadvantaged members of the urban underclass. They knew that the War on Drugs would be fought mainly in the minority areas of American cities and that those arrested and imprisoned would disproportionately be young blacks and Hispanics. . . . If the criminal law's mens rea equivalence between purpose and knowledge were applied to the decision to launch the war, knowing its likely effects on black Americans, the indictments would be unanswerable: The war's planners knew exactly what they were doing. (Tonry, 1995, p. 104)

The 1986 and 1988 federal acts are not isolated incidents of drug legislation that disproportionately affects people of color. In 1985 the Illinois Safe School Zone Act mandated that youths as young as 15, who sold illegal drugs within 1,000 feet of a school, were to be tried as adults. Four years later these safe zones were expanded to public housing projects, thereby increasing the probability that inner-city drug offenses would occur in one of the two protected areas ("Drugs and Disparity," 2002). The impact of this legislation on African Americans was swift and inevitable. By 1992 *all* youths who were automatically transferred for drug offenses within 1,000 feet of public housing in Illinois were African American (Karp, 2000). And between 1995 and 1999 in Cook County, Illinois, 95 percent of the youths charged with selling illegal drugs within 1,000 feet of a safe zone were African American. The gravity of these drug-trafficking charges is somewhat suspect, however, since only 14 percent of the youths charged with selling illegal drugs were remanded to the Illinois Department of Corrections ("Drugs and Disparity," 2002). Adult African Americans in Illinois have been additionally disproportionately affected by that state's drug laws. A study released by Human Rights Watch in 2000 revealed that Illinois had the highest ratio of African Americans-to-whites for inmates serving prison sentences for drug offenses among the 37 states surveyed. Fifty-seven African American males were incarcerated for every white male in that state ("Blacks Target in Drug War," 2000, p. 15).

Information on police operations in Los Angeles and New York City further corroborate the extent to which the bulk of the War on Drugs has been shouldered by people of color. During the so-called cocaine epidemic, police in Los Angeles arrested large numbers of suspected gang members on the flimsiest of evidence as part of Operation Hammer. That people of color were singled out is evidenced by the fact that during one

October weekend in 1989, of the more than 1,000 persons arrested, all were African American or Hispanic (Walker, Spohn, & DeLone, 1996, p. 100). Previously, in 1984, over 240 additional police officers on Manhattan's Lower East Side had been deployed in Operation Pressure Point. According to Zimmer (1990, p. 56), "many of the buyers were white, and many appeared to be middle class—men with briefcases, wearing business suits, and women with babies, in back-pack carriers." To discourage drug purchasing, police harassed "suspicious people . . . by stopping them, questioning them, searching them, and telling them to 'move on' " (p. 53). Police also relied on parking tickets and arrests for misdemeanor possession, albeit the latter infrequently led to incarceration. In contrast, much harsher measures were imposed upon the non-white drug sellers. To maximize the penalty for drug trafficking, once a week all drug arrests were processed through federal court where sanctions were harsher. Moreover, police concentrated much of their operation in the poorest areas where gentrification by middle-class whites had not occurred.

National data document that the racial composition of the city influences drug arrest rates independent of poverty, region, and percentage of males in their crime-prone years. Mosher (2001), who examined data from 159 U.S. cities with populations greater than 100,000 and used variables from social disorganization and conflict theories, looked separately at drug possession and drug-trafficking arrests. His research disclosed that the racial composition of the city (percentage black) was significantly related to drug possession and drug-trafficking arrests even after controlling for a number of other relevant factors. Furthermore, the racial composition of the city was the strongest predictor of arrest rates for all four models that employed trafficking arrests as the dependent variable. These findings lead Mosher (2001, p. 100) to conclude "that, consistent with its historical legacy, drug legislation continues to be used to control minority populations in the United States."

VIOLENCE AND AFRICAN AMERICANS

That African Americans are disproportionately arrested for violent Part I offenses is readily apparent in the UCR. African Americans accounted for 37.8 percent of arrests for murder, forcible rape, robbery, and aggravated assault in 2000 (Federal Bureau of Investigation, 2001, table 43).[4] Of the four offenses, aggravated assault constitutes the largest arrest category, with 107,494 arrests involving African Americans (Federal Bureau of Investigation, 2001, table 43). Although arrest statistics portray African Americans as disproportionately violent, police discretion in arrest decisions raises the question whether African Americans are as violent as official data indicate. Because 68.6 percent of the black arrests for violent Part I crimes in 2000 consisted of aggravated assaults, our discussion begins with an analysis of this offense.

Over three decades ago Wolfgang and Ferracuti (1967) advanced a theoretical argument to explain the presumed greater proclivity of African Americans (and other minority groups) to engage in violent behavior that continues to influence much of the research. They posit that certain segments of society subscribe to a value system that supports the use of physical force in daily human interaction. Though sharing some of the values of the larger culture, members of this subculture condone the use of violence to resolve individual differences to a measurably greater degree than do members of the dominant culture. Moreover, failure to engage in aggressive behavior when subcultural expectations dictate such behavior can lead to peer group rejection.

To assess the accuracy of the suppositions of the subculture of violence thesis, one must go beyond aggregate-level data that usually accompany empirical tests of this theory. Individual-level data are necessary to determine the interpersonal setting in which conflict emerges, as well as to assess the psychological processes behind the behavior (Luckenbill & Doyle, 1989). While no such body of research exists, investigators that have examined the perceived appropriateness of aggressive behavior in hypothetical situations suggest that whites—not African Americans—are more likely to approve of interpersonal violence. Using data from seven years of General Social Surveys, Shoemaker and Williams (1987) analyzed responses to five hypothetical questions regarding the use of violence against an adult male stranger in a variety of circumstances. The researchers report that African Americans were less tolerant of violence than the general population. In fact, after controlling for age, sex, income, region, and residence, race explained less than 0.2 percent of the variance in attitudes toward violence. Similarly, Ellison (1991, p. 1229), using a more elaborate model that encompassed 14 variables from the 1983 General Social Survey, concluded that "whites are substantially more likely than nonwhites to endorse interpersonal violence in defensive situations."

More direct evidence that arrest statistics exaggerate the amount of black violence is also available. In *Search and Destroy: African American Males in the Criminal Justice System,* Jerome Miller (1996) presents data that intimate that police routinely overcharge African Americans with violent crime. Following the criminal processing of police arrests for aggravated assault over a three-month period in Duvall County (Jacksonville), Florida, Miller discovered that over three-fourths of the initial charges of aggravated assault were either downgraded to simple assault or to a misdemeanor.

Another way to approach the issue of violence is to examine the *pattern* of offending for African Americans and whites. If UCR data reveal few differences in their pattern of offending, this would reinforce the notion that, on average, African Americans are no more prone toward violence than whites. Table 1.2 displays the ten most common offenses for which African Americans and whites were arrested in 2000, as well as the ten least common offenses for which African Americans and whites were arrested that same year. The table thus includes 20 of the 29 offenses contained in UCR arrest data. An examination of the top of the table discloses that there are nine matches between the two groups. Burglary, which is the ninth most common crime for which African Americans were arrested, is not among the top ten crimes for which whites were arrested.[5] Conversely, only vandalism, the tenth most common crime for which whites were arrested, does not appear among the top ten crimes for African Americans.

When attention is directed to the ten least common offenses (bottom of Table 1.2) we see that eight out of ten offenses appear on both lists. Runaways (number nine) and forgery/counterfeiting (number ten), on the least-common crimes list for African Americans, are not replicated among the least-common crimes for whites. For whites, robbery (number eight) and prostitution (number nine) are not found among the list of least-common offenses resulting in arrest for African Americans. Hence, the UCR data, when examined in terms of pattern of offending, paint a different picture than when only the violent Part I offenses are examined. The importance of looking at the big picture is further evidenced by the fact that, collectively, Part I offenses comprised only 16.4 percent of the total arrests in 2000 (Federal Bureau of Investigation, 2001, table 43).

Although, comparatively speaking, arrests for forcible rape are relatively low, this offense has traditionally affected African Americans to a much greater extent than whites. Before the *Coker v. Georgia* (1977) decision, in which the U.S. Supreme Court ruled that it was unconstitutional to award a death sentence in cases involving the nonlethal rape of an adult female, African Americans were grossly overrepresented among those executed for forcible rape. Between 1930 (when the UCR originated) and 1964 (the last year anyone was executed for rape), 405 of the 455 persons executed for rape (89 percent) were African American (Maguire and Pastore, 2001, table 6.92). Given the considerable racial disparity that has existed historically, an examination of forcible rape seems justified.

According to the UCR, there were 6,089 black arrests for forcible rape in 2000. This figure represents 34.1 percent of all arrests for that offense (Federal Bureau of Investigation, 2001, table 43). Stated somewhat differently, African Americans were arrested for forcible rape at a rate that exceeds 2.5 times their representation in the general population. UCR data are particularly suspect, however, since rape frequently goes unreported. A more accurate portrait of rape appears in the *National Crime Victimization Survey* (NCVS), which obtains its data directly from crime victims.

Given the disproportionate number of African Americans arrested for

Table 1.2
Most and Least Common Offenses Based on Arrests for African Americans and Whites in 2000

10 Most Common Offenses[1]

	African Americans (number of arrests)	Whites (number of arrests)
1.	Drug abuse violations (358,571)	DUI (793,696)
2.	Other assaults (269,736)	Drug abuse violations (667,485)
3.	Larceny-theft (236,801)	Other assaults (564,571)
4.	Disorderly conduct (136,573)	Larceny-theft (519,671)
5.	Aggravated assault (107,494)	Liquor laws (371,186)
6.	DUI (86,194)	Drunkenness (357,283)
7.	Fraud (66,672)	Disorderly conduct (273,884)
8.	Drunkenness (57,806)	Aggravated assault (200,634)
9.	Burglary (53,573)	Fraud (142,684)
10.	Liquor laws (46,107)	Vandalism (139,662)

10 Least Common Offenses[1]

	African Americans (number of arrests)	Whites (number of arrests)
1.	Suspicion (1,086)	Gambling (2,195)
2.	Arson (2,305)	Suspicion (2,535)
3.	Murder (4,238)	Murder (4,231)
4.	Embezzlement (4,281)	Embezzlement (7,975)
5.	Gambling (4,607)	Arson (8,121)
6.	Forcible rape (6,089)	Forcible rape (11,381)
7.	Vagrancy (9,524)	Vagrancy (11,772)
8.	Sex offenses (14,149)	Robbery (31,921)
9.	Runaways (16,726)	Prostitution (35,567)
10.	Forgery & counterfeiting (21,227)	Sex offenses (45,317)

[1]Excludes "all other offenses (except traffic)."
Source: Federal Bureau of Investigation (2001, Table 43).

forcible rape, and given that rape tends to be an intraracial crime, one would surmise that substantial black/white victimization differentials in the NCVS should be present. Yet the rate of victimizations per 1,000 persons age 12 or older for rape/sexual assault is virtually the same for African Americans and whites. In 2000 the figure for African Americans was 1.2, whereas the figure for whites was 1.1 (Bureau of Justice Statistics, 2001, table 2). If African Americans and whites are about equally likely to be victimized, then perhaps the disparity in the UCR data can be accounted for by racial differences in reporting, since rape is primarily intraracial. Again, data from the NCVS suggest no significant difference in the reporting habits of African Americans and whites. In 1999 the police were notified 25.7 percent of the time in cases involving the rape/sexual assault of African Americans and 27.7 percent of the time in cases involving the rape/sexual assault of whites (U.S. Department of Justice, 2001, table 94). Ergo, African Americans and whites have similar reporting habits when victimized by rape/sexual assault. Although it is possible that racial differences exist in the ability of the victim to identify her assailant, evidentiary strength, and the presence of credible eyewitnesses—all of which could produce racial disparity in arrests—victimization data seem to raise the specter of police bias in arrests for forcible rape.

SUMMARY AND CONCLUSION

This brief excursion into race and criminal justice highlights several important issues. First, African Americans are overrepresented in both juvenile justice and criminal justice statistics. They are more likely than their white counterparts to be arrested, incarcerated, and sentenced to death in capital-eligible cases. Second, sentencing reforms and drug legislation has disproportionately affected people of color. Third, although racial disparity may exist without racial discrimination, discussions of the War on Drugs and violent Part I offenses generate uncertainties about the race neutrality of the American criminal justice system. And finally, when attention is turned from specific crimes to the pattern of offending, one finds that African Americans and whites are arrested for many of the same crimes.

To facilitate an understanding of the intricacies of the relationship between race and criminal justice, this book is divided into three major parts. In part 1, "The Significance of Race in American Society: Past and Present," three chapters focus on the marginalization of African Americans, the role of race in incarceration and the privatization of prisons, and the portrayal of African Americans in the media. Part 2, "Criminal Justice Responses to Crime and African Americans," includes discussions of racial profiling, hate crime scholarship and the underrepresentation of African Americans in victimization research, race and presentencing, waivers of juvenile African Americans into adult court, and racism and capital punishment. The book concludes with "Seeking Solutions," in which there are discussions of the impact of African American police officers on policing, jury nullification, affirmative action for jury selection, and the role of race in restorative justice.

NOTES

1. Official crime data (such as that found in the UCR and in other government-sponsored publications) pose significant problems for researchers studying the effect of race on criminal processing. Particularly problematic are the racial/ethnic classification schemes employed by the various agencies. In the Harris County (Houston, Texas) jail system, for instance, only two racial designations—black and white—are used. For purposes of statistical analysis, Hispanics (who may be of any race) are counted as white (M. McShane, personal communication, May 24, 2002). Yet the use of such classification schemes may result in the reduction or elimination of black/white differences in criminal processing (Lynch, 1990). Consequently, official statistics may understate the actual amount of racial disparity present in the criminal justice system.

2. Of the 24 inmates on federal death row, 17 were non-Hispanic African Americans (Maguire & Pastore, 2001, table 6.80).

3. See Zatz (1987) for a discussion of subtle bias. For an excellent discussion of the importance of interaction terms see Miethe and Moore (1986).

4. Their overrepresentation is even greater when arrests involving minors are examined. African Americans comprised 42.1 percent of arrests of persons under the age of 18 (Federal Bureau of Investigation, 2001, table 43).

5. Although not appearing in the table, burglary was the 11th most common offense for which whites were arrested in 2000.

CASES CITED

Coker v. Georgia, 97 S. Ct. 2861 (1977)
State v. Russell, 477 N.W. 2d 886 (Minn. 1991)

REFERENCES

Alschuler, A. (1991). The failure of sentencing guidelines: A plea for less aggregation. *University of Chicago Law Review, 58*, 901–951.

Attinger, J., & Cronin, M. (1990, September 17). The decline of New York. *Time, 136* pp. 36–41, 44.

Beck, A., & Karberg, J. (2001). *Prison and jail inmates at midyear 2000.* Washington, DC: Bureau of Justice Statistics.

Berger, R., Free, M., & Searles, P. (2001). *Crime, justice, and society: Criminology and the sociological imagination.* Boston: McGraw Hill.

Blacks target in drug war. (2000, June 8). *Daily Jefferson County Union* (Fort Atkinson, Wisconsin), p. 15.

Bureau of Justice Statistics. (2001). *Criminal victimization 2000: Changes 1999–2000 with trends 1993–2000*. Washington, DC: U.S. Department of Justice.

Butterfield, F. (2000, April 26). Racial disparities are pervasive in justice system, report says. *The New York Times*. Retrieved April 26, 2000, from http://www.nytimes.com/yr/mo/day/news/national/juvenile-prison.html.

Drugs and disparity: The racial impact of Illinois' practice of transferring young drug offenders to adult court. (2002). *Building blocks for youth*. Retrieved January 14, 2002, from http://www.buildingblocksfor youth.org/illinois/illinois.html.

Ellison, C. (1991). An eye for an eye? A note on the southern subculture of violence thesis. *Social Forces, 69,* 1223–1239.

Federal Bureau of Investigation. (2001). *Crime in the United States 2000*. Washington, DC: U.S. Department of Justice.

Hughes, T., Wilson, D., & Beck, A. (2001). *Trends in state parole, 1990–2000*. Washington, DC: Bureau of Justice Statistics.

Johnson, B., Golub, A., & Fagan, J. (1995). Careers in crack, drug use, drug distribution, and nondrug criminality. *Crime & Delinquency, 41,* 275–295.

Karp, S. (2000, May). State drug law hits city, teens, minorities. *The Chicago Reporter*. Retrieved August 2, 2002, from http://www.chicago reporter.com/2000/5–2000/TJ/TJ1.htm.

Luckenbill, D., & Doyle, D. (1989). Structural position and violence: Developing a cultural explanation. *Criminology, 27,* 419–436.

Lynch, M. (1990). Racial bias and criminal justice: Definitional and methodological issues. In B. MacLean & D. Milovanovic (Eds.), *Racism, empiricism and criminal justice* (pp. 35–42). Vancouver, Canada: Collective Press.

Maguire, K., & Pastore, A. (Eds.). (2001). *Sourcebook of criminal justice statistics—2000*. Retrieved January 17, 2002, from http://www .albany.edu/sourcebook.

McDonald, D., & Carlson, K. (1993). *Sentencing in the federal courts: Does race matter? The transition to sentencing guidelines, 1986–90 (summary)*. Washington, DC: U.S. Government Printing Office.

Miethe, T., & Moore, C. (1986). Racial differences in criminal processing: The consequences of model selection on conclusions about differential treatment. *Sociological Quarterly, 27,* 217–237.

Miller, J. (1996). *Search and destroy: African American males in the criminal justice system*. New York: Cambridge University Press.

Miller, M. (1995). Rehabilitating the federal sentencing guidelines. *Judicature, 78,* 180–188.

Mosher, C. (2001). Predicting drug arrest rates: Conflict and social disorganization perspectives. *Crime & Delinquency, 47,* 84–104.

Petersilia, J., & Turner, S. (1988). Minorities in prison: Discrimination or disparity? *Corrections Today, 50,* 92–94.

Schiraldi, V., & Godfrey, M. (1994). *Racial disparities in the charging of Los Angeles County's third "strike" cases.* San Francisco: Center on Juvenile & Criminal Justice.

Shoemaker, D., & Williams, J. (1987). The subculture of violence and ethnicity. *Journal of Criminal Justice, 15,* 461–472.

Snell, T. (2001). *Capital punishment 2000.* Washington, DC: Bureau of Justice Statistics.

Substance Abuse & Mental Health Services Administration. (2000). *National household survey on drug abuse, 1999.* Washington, DC: Office of Applied Studies.

Tonry, M. (1995). *Malign neglect—race, crime, and punishment in America.* New York: Oxford University Press.

U. S. Department of Justice. (1993). *Survey of state prison inmates, 1991.* Washington, DC: Bureau of Justice Statistics.

U. S. Department of Justice. (2001). *Criminal victimization in the United States, 1999: Statistical tables.* Washington, DC: Bureau of Justice Statistics.

Walker, S., Spohn, C., & DeLone, M. (1996). *The color of justice: Race, ethnicity, and crime in America.* Belmont, CA: Wadsworth.

Wolfgang, M., & Ferracuti, F. (1967). *The subculture of violence: Towards an integrated theory in criminology.* London: Tavistock.

Zatz, M. (1987). The changing forms of racial/ethnic biases in sentencing. *Journal of Research in Crime & Delinquency, 24,* 69–92.

Zimmer, L. (1990). Proactive policing against street-level drug trafficking. *American Journal of Police, 9,* 43–74.

PART I

The Significance of Race in American Society: Past and Present

Almost six decades have passed since the Swedish sociologist Gunnar Myrdal (1944) authored *An American Dilemma: The Negro Problem and Modern Democracy*, a critique of black–white relations in the United States. With the impending sixtieth anniversary of this seminal publication, it is appropriate that we update the progress made by African Americans in the United States. And though it would be misleading to suggest that African Americans have not posted some substantial gains in their positions vis-à-vis whites, it would be equally misleading to argue that African Americans have achieved parity with their white counterparts. In numerous aspects African Americans remain subordinate to whites in American society. Let us now turn to some of those areas.

One area where African Americans continue to trail whites is income. In 1999 only 4.4 percent of all white families had incomes under $10,000. That same year 14.6 percent of all African American families had incomes under $10,000. This difference is also manifested in 1999 poverty rates, where 7.3 percent of all white families were below the poverty line, but 21.9 percent of all African American families were similarly situated. More revealing perhaps is a black–white comparison using median family income, since this figure encompasses all income ranges. Using this as a gauge of parity we find that the family income of whites continues to outpace that of African Americans. More specifically, the 1999 median family income of whites exceeded that of African Americans by $19,446 (U.S. Census, 2001, table 37).

African Americans additionally lag behind whites in education and employment. In 2000 over one-fourth of all whites twenty-five years old and over had a baccalaureate degree or higher. For African Americans this figure was 16.5 percent (U.S. Census Bureau, 2001, table 215). Unemployment mirrors the racial differences in education. The black unemployment rate was over twice as high as that of whites in 2000 (7.6 percent versus 3.5 percent) (U.S. Census Bureau, 2001, table 569). However, not all of the difference can be attributed to educational disparities. Regardless of level of education, African Americans were more likely than whites to be unemployed in 2000. For instance, whereas only 3.3 percent of all whites with a high school diploma were unemployed, 6.3 percent of all African

Americans who were high school graduates were unemployed. Similarly, the unemployment rate for white college graduates was 1.4 percent, compared with 2.5 percent for black college graduates (U.S. Census Bureau, 2001, table 604).

Two particularly telling measures of marginality are infant mortality rates and life expectancy. Based on figures for 1998, the U.S. Census Bureau (2001, table 102) reports that there were 6 infant deaths per 1,000 live births among whites and 14.3 deaths per 1,000 live births among African Americans. Life expectancy also varies by race and gender. Although white males at birth can expect to live an average of 74.5 years, black males can expect to live 67.6 years. White females, on the other hand, can expect to live to be 80 years old. Though black females outlive their male counterparts, with a life expectancy of 74.8 years, they more closely resemble white males than white females (U.S. Census Bureau, 2001, table 98).

Another way of ascertaining the relative position of a group in society is through an analysis of their inclusion in the power structure of that society. Again, the data disclose a subordinate status for African Americans. Although 12.8 percent of the U.S. population is African American (U.S. Census Bureau, 2001, table 10), less than 9 percent of the House of Representatives of the 106th Congress was African American. Even more abysmal was black representation in the Senate, where there were no African American senators (U.S. Census Bureau, 2001, table 390). That African Americans have additionally made few inroads into the judicial system is revealed by the fact that African Americans comprise only 5.7 percent of all lawyers and judges in the United States (U.S. Census Bureau, 2001, table 593). As these statistics demonstrate, African Americans remain substantially underrepresented in America's power structure.

Given their inadequate representation in the legislative and judicial branches of government, it should perhaps come as no surprise that African Americans are disproportionately found in the criminal justice system. As disclosed in chapter 1, African Americans are overrepresented in both the juvenile and criminal justice systems. Furthermore, they are more likely than their white counterparts to be sentenced to death and to be the targets of drug crackdowns. African Americans are, nevertheless, no more likely than whites to be consumers of controlled substances, nor do they necessarily engage in different types of offending than whites. Instead, their overrepresentation in these statistics tends to parallel their subordinate status in the larger society.

Robert Engvall examines the issue of African American marginality in chapter 2. Beginning with an overview of African American marginality in the criminal justice system, he then analyzes African American marginality within the academic discipline of criminal justice, itself a marginalized discipline. He concludes that the legitimacy of the discipline and the academic quality of instruction are contingent upon the greater diversification of criminal justice faculty and the abolition of collegiate boundaries based on tradition, oppression, and fear that have been used to exclude criminal justice (and women's studies and ethnic studies) from full inclusion into the academic community.

The issue of African American marginality is further addressed in chapter 3, in which Michael Hallett notes similarities between the large concentration of African Americans in private (and public) prisons today and the post–Civil War convict lease system used to control the freed slaves. He contends that the mass imprisonment of people of color that began in the 1980s can be best understood by using a culturalist perspective to reveal the racialized nature of U.S. criminal justice policy.

Part 1 concludes with "The Color of Prime-Time Justice: Racial Characteristics of Television Offenders and Victims" by Sarah Eschholz. In chapter 4 Eschholz reports the results of a content analysis of twenty-six regular evening network television programs over an eight-week period in 1996. She examines the extent to which African Americans and Hispanics are overrepresented among televised criminals and the extent to which criminals are overrepresented among African Americans and Hispanics who appear on television. The implications of these findings are then discussed in terms of Blalock's (1967) racial threat hypothesis.

REFERENCES

Blalock, H., Jr. (1967). *Toward a theory of minority group relations*. New York: Wiley.

Myrdal, G. (1944). *An American dilemma: The negro problem and modern democracy*. New York: Harper Brothers.

U.S. Census Bureau. (2001). *Statistical abstract of the United States: 2001* (121st ed.). Washington, DC: U.S. Government Printing Office.

CHAPTER 2

Marginalization and Racial Stratification in the Academic Discipline of Criminal Justice

Robert Engvall

INTRODUCTION

That the criminal justice system plays a significant role in the lives of African Americans and that African Americans are disproportionately impacted by that system is amply documented. This chapter also addresses this impact but does so by focusing upon whether academia has played a role in the continued diminishment of individuals and the continued marginalization of groups of persons. Also examined is the place of the criminal justice discipline within the larger academy and the status of African Americans within this discipline. The invisibility of certain groups, traditionally those of minority status, from positions of power within society has done much to shape justice policy. Such invisibility can transcend traditionally considered avenues of power and can be traced to assumptions made within the academy as well.

This chapter, then, is organized into three fairly distinct parts: an examination of the marginalization of African Americans within society and within the discipline of criminal justice, an examination of the marginalization of criminal justice as a discipline more generally, and finally, a conclusion that ties these concepts together.

RACIAL STRATIFICATION WITHIN THE CRIMINAL JUSTICE SYSTEM AND ACADEME

Racism. The fear of otherness is an unattractive but constant human trait, and one that we social meliorists like to say education and peaceful commingling will do away with in, as always, time. There is some truth in this.

(Vidal, 2001, p. 372)

That there is but *some* truth in the belief that the fear of "otherness" will dissipate, rather than *complete* truth, is, no doubt, sobering. The fact that race continues to be a polarizing feature in American society is evidenced in many areas of society. Perhaps nowhere is this more apparent than in the criminal justice system.

Differential Treatment of African Americans within the Criminal Justice System

African Americans comprise roughly 12 percent of the U.S. population, yet account for 29.7 percent of all arrests (Pastore & Maguire, 2000, p. 352), 47 percent of felony convictions, and 54 percent of prison admissions (Donohue & Levitt, 2001). The per capita incarceration rate of African Americans is seven times that of whites (Cole, 1999). Statistics such as these allude to the marginalization of African Americans, a recurring theme of this book.

Race remains a crucial site of social struggles over power in the United States (Artz & Murphy, 2000). But is race a site of social struggles over power within the academy? If struggles about race per se have been removed from our most polite academy discussions, what about marginalization? Has the white side of the line been so long the dominant side that recognition of that dominance has been lost? Dominant groups tend not to negotiate away their dominance nor, in many cases, even acknowledge their dominant status. The dominant group comforts itself with the rationale, if you deserved it, you would have it.

When we consider the underrepresentation of African Americans within the discipline of criminal justice while we acknowledge their overrepresentation among official arrest statistics, there is a stark contrast. It is perhaps beyond argument that African Americans, if not purposely discriminated against by law enforcement and our court systems, are at a minimum disproportionately impacted by criminal justice policy. Wacquant (2002, pp. 59–60) viewed the prison and the criminal justice system broadly as contributing to an ongoing reconstruction of the imagined community of Americans around the polar opposites of praiseworthy working families—implicitly white, suburban, and deserving—and a despicable underclass of criminals, loafers, and leeches—by definition dark-skinned, urban, and undeserving. If Wacquant is correct, then the academy must bear its share of the blame for such reconstruction, or at a minimum, it must share the blame for our collective inability to have prevented it.

If statistics tell some of the story, our symbolic institutions tell us more.

Given that the U.S. Supreme Court sits at the top, both conceptually and symbolically, of our system of criminal justice, it is worth examining how that Court has historically viewed African Americans. Since the Court's inception, African Americans have been afforded fewer rights and privileges than their white counterparts. For instance, in *Scott v. Sanford* (1857) the majority opined: "We think . . . [African Americans] . . . are not included, and were intended not to be included, under the word 'citizens' in the Constitution, and can therefore claim none of the rights and privileges which that instrument provides for and secures to citizens of the United States." In sum, the infamous *Dred Scott* decision stood for the proposition that slaves were merely the property of their owner and nothing more. If we fast-forward to 1896, long after the conclusion of the Civil War and more than thirty years after the Emancipation Proclamation, the rhetoric of the Justices becomes no less offensive. The case of *Plessy v. Ferguson* (1896) included within its affirmation of the "separate but equal" doctrine the following words: "If one race be inferior to the other socially, the Constitution of the United States cannot put them upon the same plane." The fiction that was "separate but equal" and the holding of *Plessy* existed as good law for the next fifty-eight years and was only rejected by the Supreme Court (at least in the area of public education) in the case of *Brown v. Board of Education* (1954).

Less than fifty years have passed since the holding and the rhetoric contained within *Plessy* controlled the day. Other Supreme Court cases confirm the disparate treatment of African Americans, with the most notable, and arguably the most notorious, being *McCleskey v. Kemp* (1987). *McCleskey* involved the application of the death penalty in the state of Georgia. The gist of the *McCleskey* case was that despite overwhelming statistical evidence collected from more than 2,000 murder cases in Georgia in the 1970s, in which it was found, among other racial disparities, that defendants charged with killing whites were 4.3 times as likely to receive the death penalty as those charged with killing African Americans, the Supreme Court declined to find such evidence of racial prejudice to be "an unacceptable risk" to be taken in capital sentencing cases. In essence, the value placed upon the life of a white person in Georgia was significantly greater than the value placed upon the life of an African American. That such devaluing of African Americans was taking place in the nineteenth century cannot be in dispute. That such devaluing was taking place within the U.S. Supreme Court in recent years speaks volumes of the distance yet to be traveled on the road toward equality. Whereas students of history might, perhaps, attempt to rationalize Supreme Court decisions of the nineteenth and early twentieth centuries as the natural consequences of the context of the times, understanding the racial implications of the relative recent case of *McCleskey v. Kemp* presents the student with a more contemporary and, therefore, even more troubling look into the practices and beliefs of the members of the U.S. Supreme Court.

Perhaps the best example of the extreme disparity between Supreme Court rhetoric and the realistic application of players within the justice system can be found in the case of *Batson v. Kentucky* (1986). *Batson* overruled *Swain v. Alabama* (1965), which had held that, without violating equal protection, a prosecutor may use peremptory challenges to strike all African Americans from the jury pool in a particular case. *Batson* held that equal protection forbade the prosecutor from using race as the sole factor in eliminating prospective jurors from serving. While *Batson* appears to be a step toward racial parity, the reality was that prosecutors simply used other reasons for eliminating potential jurors (Cole, 1999). Prosecutors could no longer openly admit race was the reason for exclusion, but African American jurors continued to be excised from jury pools through the use of peremptory challenges for such "racially neutral" reasons as the length and/or curl of their hair or the presence of facial hair. *Purkett v. Elem* (1995) presents a classic, albeit contemporary, tale of a prosecutor who used his discretion to remove African Americans from the jury pool based on such seemingly transparent racially neutral grounds. That case involved the exclusion of a potential juror because he had "shoulder length, curly, unkempt hair, a mustache and . . . a goatee-type beard." The prosecution argued, successfully, that such an exclusion based upon physical appearance, without more, was "not a characteristic of a particular race." Though *Purkett* may be the best-known example, it is far from the only example of such conduct. Cole (1999) describes several scenarios in the late 1980s and 1990s in which entire groups of African Americans were removed from jury pools based on such racially neutral and, of course, wholly discretionary (and therefore practically unassailable), criteria. *Batson*, it seemed, held no more real weight than did the founding fathers' eighteenth century proclamations that "all men are created equal."

Donohue and Levitt (2001) conclude that the addition of police officers of a given race is associated with an increase in the number of arrests of suspects of a different race but has little impact on same-race arrests. In other words, white officers (by far the largest number) tend not to shy away from arresting black suspects for whatever reasons. Black officers, like their white counterparts who show little reluctance when it comes to arresting black suspects, tend to show an equal affinity for arresting white suspects. It appears then, that were more nonwhite police officers hired, more whites would be arrested; just as it explains the propensity of white-dominated police agencies to arrest nonwhite suspects. These findings suggest that race tends to influence arresting decisions.

Differential treatment within the criminal justice system is, of course, not confined to policing. Given the fact that whites dominate the numbers at every level of the system from prison guards to probation officers and lawyers to judges, how race is portrayed in our larger society tends to be how race is portrayed within our criminal justice system. Moffitt (2000–2001) writes about his experiences as an African American defense attorney and the many instances of marginalization that came his way. Mistaken identity based upon Moffitt's race led to one particularly memorable incident in which Moffitt was attacked by the sheriff as he approached the bench for a sidebar. Sheriffs, however, were no more or less likely to mistake Moffitt for the defendant he represented than were other court officers, including a propensity on the part of many judges he appeared before to mistake his role with that of his (usually) white client, the defendant. The assumption was quite clear: the black man was the defendant; the white man, his counsel.

Polls conducted by the Gallup Organization consistently reveal a perception by the general public that African Americans are treated less equitably than whites in the criminal justice system ("Black–White Relations," 2001). Still, despite poll results, there seems to be little consensus toward any sort of program that might systematically decrease such unfairness. Ostensibly, dominant group members are largely unburdened by their knowledge of the unfairness that surrounds them since it does not directly impact them.

But why should those of us in academia care? The critical element seems to be the correlation between searching for things and finding those things. According to Department of Justice statistics, blacks do not use drugs any more than do whites. Yet, despite such knowledge, roughly 75 percent of the people incarcerated for drug use are black (Drucker, 1999).[1] Remember when presidential candidate Michael Dukakis urged a reduction in our national deficit, merely by enforcing existing tax laws? In essence, if we hired more Internal Revenue Service agents to look into our tax returns, more of us would be getting into trouble, and taxes actually owed would be paid. Perhaps not surprisingly, the majority denounced such a plan. Because society has chosen to concentrate its efforts on substance abuse and trafficking primarily in inner city, urban areas heavily populated with people of color rather than on tax law violations, African Americans are overrepresented in arrest and incarceration statistics.

Differential Treatment of African Americans in Academe

What about the ivory tower? Is justice more accessible there, or is marginalization just as present within the walls of academia? U.S. Department of Education statistics, as reported in the *Chronicle of Higher Education* ("Number of Full-Time Faculty", 2001, p. 28), reveal that of 420,223 full-time professors (assistant, associate, and full) in the United States in 1997, less than 5 percent (19,333) were African American. Though racial breakdowns are not available (at least beyond voluntary self-reporting questionnaires) for membership in the Academy of Criminal Justice Sciences and the American Society of Criminology (the two most common disciplinary organizations in which professors of criminal justice hold membership), anecdotal evidence suggests that a presumption that 5 percent of the members of these organizations are African American is overly optimistic. Because criminal justice is a discipline in which many professors have had past careers as police officers, lawyers, and/or judges in a white-dominated criminal justice system, the number of African American criminal justice professors is likely to lag behind even the low percentages of African American professors found in the other disciplines.

Numbers alone, however, do not prove that marginalization of African Americans exists even in marginalized academic fields. Nonetheless, several qualitative studies lend credence to the quantitative data. Heard and Bing (1993) report feelings of alienation and high levels of mistrust at a majority of educational institutions among African American faculty members, whereas del Carmen and Bing (2000) report that African Americans may be at a disadvantage in research productivity as well. Young and Sulton (1991) further observe that African Americans are conspicuously absent when it comes to conducting empirical research on crime and delinquency, recommending policy, and serving on editorial boards of journals and in the faculties of colleges and universities in criminology and criminal justice departments. Ross and Edwards (1998) additionally assert that there is a generalized devaluation of African American scholarship.

Devaluation is a theme that seems to equally describe treatment of African Americans within textbooks. Free (1999) concludes that not only are there more negative than positive images of African Americans within criminology textbooks, coverage of African American scholarship and issues generally tend to be inadequate. Greene, Gabbidon, and Ebersole (2001) similarly observe inadequate coverage of African American scholarship in juvenile delinquency textbooks. Such findings seem wholly consistent with the devaluation of marginalized groups within the university.

Unfortunately, improvement in the numbers of African Americans participating in university criminology and criminal justice programs may be far away. Although more African Americans attend college now than thirty years ago, fewer finish and fewer still pursue postgraduate degrees (Artz & Murphy, 2000). In fact, there are more African American men in their twenties in prison than in school. Biased practices in law enforcement ensure that the war on drugs and crime is disproportionately focused on the poor and people of color living in the inner city. Prosecuting decisions tend to reflect police discretion, as more African Americans face prosecution and similarly situated whites often go unprosecuted. If African American men are devalued in society, are they also devalued in academia? The same type of denial that allows many the belief that African Americans are overrepresented in prison because they are the ones committing the crimes can be seen in academia, where the pervasive belief seems to be that few are hired and few comprise disciplines other than ethnic studies solely because of a lack of qualified applicants and nothing more.

The Anointed

What about our societal response to crime? Might it be connected to the marginalization of criminal justice within the academy?[2] The real work of the university is to enhance the powers of the mind (Anderson, 1993, p. 59). The difficulty comes into play when it appears that many disciplines seek to enhance the powers of the mind only in directions that they themselves have deemed worthy. Rather than a true liberal education, such closure within and among a group of established disciplines, is conservatism at its finest. *Merriam Webster's Collegiate Dictionary* (1993) defines conservative as "opposed to change; desiring the preservation of the existing order of things; moderate; cautious; wanting to conserve." Many of our finest liberal arts–minded individuals, so openly liberal in their personas, are conservative in their views toward liberal education.

Sowell (1995) describes what he calls the "vision of the anointed" as that vision that has become self-contained and self-justifying, which, in his view, makes it a vision independent of empirical evidence. This is what makes it problematic, not because a particular set of policies may be flawed or counterproductive, but because "insulation from evidence virtually guarantees a never-ending supply of policies and practices fatally independent of reality" (p. 241). At many colleges, it would seem as if many of our more entrenched faculty are the anointed. Phipps (1995) referred to the academy of higher education faculty as a "bona fide and authentic religion . . . deriving its legitimacy through a set of historical values and beliefs" (p. 20). These historical values and beliefs seem to have a foundation set in faith rather than stone.

If, indeed, faculty are both anointed and members of the faith, change is daunting. "A challenge to the core values and beliefs of the academy will elicit a negative response" (Phipps, 1995, p. 23). Why would we expect professors to be different from other members of society who recoil and defend themselves when their core values and beliefs are challenged? Many faculty members who might "know" that adding criminal justice, women's studies, and/or ethnic studies to the general education requirements is not appropriate, cannot empirically express why. It has thus become among the most dangerous of facts, that which is simply accepted because it has been accepted for a long period of time. Havel (1985) told us that "reality does not shape theory, but rather the reverse" (p. 33). The theory behind the traditional liberal arts curriculum has shaped the reality that has become entrenched. Academics who seek an alternative reality often have their critical acuity severely questioned, even while they question the analysis of those quite comfortable in the present reality. Martinez and Martinez (1997) wrote: "acceptance of diversity connotes intellectual enlightenment." Academe's acceptance of diversity in race, culture, and lifestyle must, with exceptions, of course, be reviewed favorably in comparisons with the world outside of college campuses. Still, celebrations and acceptance notwithstanding, diversity is not always welcome, whether that diversity concerns individual traits or the traits of disciplines within the academy.

If inclusion within the liberal arts is the goal of many existing outside of the margins of traditional academia, why is it so important? The answer lies in the belief that the achievement of full inclusion is necessary less for faculty members' self-esteem (although there are benefits to be sure in increases in that) than it is necessary as a method of creating a truly inclusive college campus in which disciplines deemed worthy enough to exist are given the status that makes that existence fully worthwhile.

Professor Derrick A. Bell, Jr., wrote of "interest convergence," a principle in which "the interest of blacks in achieving racial equality will be accommodated only when it converges with the interests of whites" (Bell, 1980, p. 523). Perhaps the convergence of the disciplines within academia will likewise occur only when the interests of those in marginalized disciplines converge with the interests of those in more powerful ones.

Challenging long-held assumptions is threatening to those challenged, even those who are capable of making well-reasoned arguments in favor of the status quo. Still, however threatening, "every professional intellectual bent on theoretical innovation must at some point challenge the assumptions implicit in the 'conventional wisdom' " (Berger, 1995, p. 32). Challenging conventional wisdom means having the courage to openly proclaim that conventional wisdom is often merely conventional and wise because it has not been subjected to the scrutiny of critical reason. Sometimes when intellectuals disagree, it is easier to label the opposition as second rate, either in mind or in morality.

Following this examination of the racial stratification and marginalization of African Americans inside and outside of academia, it is time to turn toward a discussion of the marginalization of criminal justice as a discipline within the academy. To be doubly marginalized is an historical way of life for African American women and others facing oppression (some more obviously than others) on more than one front. To understand such marginalization, one might consider the opposite, which I shall call *double dominance*. To be white and male outside the academy, is to be white and a professor of economics, psychology, or another favored discipline within the academy. To be black and female outside of the academy, is to be black and a professor of criminal justice or ethnic studies or women's studies within the academy. Double marginalization exists when the combination of race and the status of the discipline combine to provide diminishment and marginalization on more than one front.

THE MARGINALIZATION OF THE DISCIPLINE OF CRIMINAL JUSTICE

> By and large, the academic world is tolerant. But it tends toward passivity, and tolerance and passivity are a deadly combination. Together they allow us to tolerate the intolerable, to ignore the power of anger in the words of love; for if you lessen your anger at the structures of power you lower your love for the victims of power.
>
> (Coffin, 1999, p. 5)

Academia has long organized knowledge along disciplinary boundaries. Where a discipline fits in the academy determines much about the resources that will or will not be devoted to that discipline. Thus, disciplines may be conceptualized into those that have attained a favored status within the collegiate hierarchy and those that are less favored and have a marginal status within that hierarchy. Many within academia have "lessened their anger at the structures of power," at least those structures within the academy, and have grown increasingly tolerant and passive when it comes to inequality within academia. As comforting as it may be to claim that those within academia merely educate others about social ordering, while doing none of it themselves, it is surely a denial of their genuine roles, both individually and collectively.

Having assessed the historical position of marginalized groups, it is time to more fully assess the impact that history has upon the future position of marginalized disciplines within the larger academy. A preface to that discussion, however, must involve a recognition of the position of African Americans within our larger society, surely both a reflection of and a reflection for academia. In 1989, the National Research Council (NRC) released *A Common Destiny: Blacks and American Society* (Jaynes & Williams, 1989), a comprehensive study based on the research of over one hundred social scientists. The NRC concluded that despite major gains, blacks continued to face major inequality, not just by some, but by every indicator studied. For instance, black and white disparities in infant mortality, poverty, and access to quality education and health care persisted. Despite overwhelming statistical evidence supporting the conclusions reached by the NRC, many influential commentators, and even many academics, denied the existence of such inequality. It is hoped that an examination of marginalization, more so than race and racism, might lend itself to reasoned and informed dialogue that might actually move the academy forward so that our reality might more realistically match our

rhetoric. Its purpose is to search for a place in which difference is celebrated not as "difference" in the traditional limiting sense, but as diversity
in a truly intellectually expansive sense. If education is about learning to
see the world in new ways, it is bound, at least occasionally, to leave us
somewhat discomfited.

Social justice requires moral commitment. Social justice within the academy requires an increased awareness of minority issues (in every sense of
that word). Gordon (1999) asserted that social justice is a necessary condition for education, that without it, optimal educational outcomes are
impossible.

Attaining an optimal educational outcome will mean overcoming institutional history and politics that have often played perhaps the most
significant role in keeping some disciplines out of the mainstream curriculum. It will mean overcoming some of the same history and politics that
have long kept African Americans outside the mainstream academy. A
lack of inclusion of new and emerging disciplines brings with it a sort of
second-class citizenship that limits the contributions of both students and
faculty alike who toil in marginalized programs. Being an active partici-
pant in the discourse of the academy differs significantly from merely
being an observer.

Dominance of one or more groups over others, even though rhetorically
denounced, is a very real part of the hidden curriculum. The rigid structure and mechanisms in place to ensure that meaning is not somehow
"de-formed" or recontextualized, can be every bit as marginalizing to
those on the outside looking in, as it is comforting to those already on the
inside and who, it may seem, seldom bother to look out. Are colleges
merely highly controlled instructional sites wherein the official ideology
of those in power is reproduced? If this is so, then how might faculty
members credibly encourage students to embrace change and multicul-
turalism and reject oppression and dominance when they are acting as
agents (unwitting or otherwise) in the reproduction of the official ideology
of power. Some are inside the corridors of power, others are left out. It is
perhaps academia's dirty little secret that while many marginalized programs gain enough standing to be a part of the university, they are often
barely accepted, if at all, by more mainstream and traditional faculty
members.

During this writing, I was stung by the words of a colleague in another
academic discipline, who, in proofreading my work, offered the following
criticism: "If the academic substance of the program is sound, if students
are held to solid academic standards, and the faculty is productive in
teaching, research, and service, then the academic standing of the program
will be respected." In essence, the argument against greater mainstream
status for marginalized programs is shockingly simple: if you deserved
it, you would have it. It is not altogether different from the perceptions of

many concerning inequality in our greater society. Unfortunately, for those outside academia and those within, many people believing that one gets what one deserves are those who have gotten a lot. Such beliefs, whether valid or not, tend to stifle consideration of the place of others, since, after all, the conclusion is so simple: if you deserved it, you would have it.

Perhaps the best definition of *mainstream* comes from those outside looking in. Similarly, and most surely, the very best definitions of discrimination and/or inequality can be given by those who face it, not by those who best understand it from an academic viewpoint. Definitions of mainstream necessarily sort us into classes: those who belong and those are deemed less worthy of belonging. In a discussion of social justice, we cannot avoid a discussion of class, even though "any serious discussion has been banished from polite company" (Zweig, 2000, p. 4). Class, in academia and out, has strengthened the hand of the powerful, whereas it has diminished the role of the powerless. Interestingly, if not ironically, whether class distinctions exist in America or not, seems largely to be a matter of the class to which one belongs. At the bottom and middle, there is little doubt that class distinctions exist. At the top, however, it is often simple: if you deserved it, you would have it.

In a capitalist economy, one's position at birth is undoubtedly a significant factor in determining one's position at death, but that truism notwithstanding, does the accident of academic birth have to determine the position of a discipline within the academy? If new and emerging disciplines are not born to royal positions within academia can they fight their way in?

Stephan (1999) provided an excellent analysis of the concept of stereotyping, a concept that has been largely ignored in descriptions of academia. Even in academics, the most open-minded people around must confess to a certain level of expectation based on stereotyping that is attached to given professions, if not certain races, ethnic groups, and one or both genders. As a white male, my own experiences with stereotyping have been limited. As a college professor, I have encountered some instances in which people have viewed me as consisting of the traits of others they have known in similar circumstances. As a criminal justice professor, I have encountered what I perceive to be classic stereotyping: a belief that I must be like others who possess similar traits. If stereotyping has, among its other functions, the role of allowing people to justify their own worldviews and their own social status, then surely stereotyping is present within the corridors of academia.

Classes . . . in Every Meaning of That Word

There continues to be an ongoing debate within the literature and within the hallways of academia concerning the appropriate makeup of the general education curriculum. Which programs and which courses need to be included in order to ensure that undergraduate students receive a well-rounded education have consistently bewildered many of academia's best minds. The reasons for decisions that ultimately are made are often mysterious to both seasoned and unseasoned academic observers.

The difficulty for criminal justice, as for other marginalized disciplines, lies in how to gain academic credibility, long reserved for traditional mainstream disciplines, without presently being a member of the liberal arts mainstream. Such a dilemma is exacerbated by the powerful forces of tradition that make high-quality departments able to use their status on campus to command greater resources, thus further solidifying their reputation and that of their members (Baldi, 1997). There is no doubt that criminal justice, women's studies, and ethnic studies (as marginalized examples) can be and often are every bit as high quality as other departments; however, perceptions and tradition often combine to impede their forward progress. These limitations within academia often create an environment that parallels our larger society in which the rich get richer while the poor struggle to make ends meet.

Real communities of learning must be founded on concepts of justice and equality. If colleges are to avoid becoming complacent and/or to prevent disciplinary enclaves from lessening our communities of learning, we need to give open and honest consideration to changes within our curriculum that might promote our larger community of learning. Many of the issues that concern criminal justice scholars on a daily basis blend together elements such as racism, sexism, and class bias and the impact these have upon the social system.

If those in divergent disciplines and with divergent interests can agree about anything, they should agree that the purpose of general education within the liberal arts curriculum is to expose students to a variety of disciplines, a variety of viewpoints, a variety of fields of knowledge, to ensure their introduction to the arts, the sciences, the social sciences, and literature. The purpose is to ensure that all students have some breadth of knowledge aside from the depth that they might obtain by picking out a single discipline as a major.

History suggests that genuine agents of change must have a certain passion for their cause, whether that cause is as far-reaching as that of civil rights or the much narrower cause of a more inclusive and open-minded college curriculum. The passion must allow for arguments that persist over time and gradually make inroads against strongly held opinions that are not often swayed despite what may seem to be overwhelming evidence that they should be. Fighting the good fight for curriculum reform becomes increasingly difficult against the pressures exerted both overtly by those against change and covertly by those who simply do not care.

Credibility and Inclusion (Which Came First, the Chicken or the Egg?)

A lack of experience as a stumbling block is not only the bane of job-hunting college graduates, it is symbolic of the very institutions from which they come. Institutions have sometimes shut out new ideas and innovations, severely hampering, if not entirely stunting, the growth of curriculum and other program changes, in the name of experience in the form of academic tradition.

Perhaps it isn't as simple as self-protection on the part of those doing the excluding. Perhaps there is some merit to their claims that criminal justice really does have little to offer in support of liberal education for undergraduates and/or that the discipline has been poor at communicating its contributions to liberal education. This chapter and the thoughts contained herein are evidence that our discipline has poorly communicated our contributions, both real and perceived. The first premise, however, that criminal justice has little to offer undergraduates' understanding of the world around them and their place in it—seemingly one of the goals of a liberal arts education—surely cannot withstand even low-level scrutiny or analysis. Flanagan (2000), for example, examined the connections between liberal education and criminal justice and arrived at the conclusion that the integration of criminal justice into the curriculum provides for a rigorous and intellectually broadening undergraduate experience. The challenge of criminal justice educators to make the case for inclusion continues unabated, although perhaps the events of September 11, 2001, might again make the value of an understanding of the broad concept of justice generally, and our criminal justice system, particularly, seem both worthy and necessary as academe prepares well-rounded undergraduates.

Social systems, such as undergraduate education programs, must continually seek ways in which to meet the changing demands of an ever more complicated society. To resist changes that might enhance present curricula structure is antithetical to the existence of academia. Indeed, part of the role of college professors is to examine ways in which the delivery of undergraduate education might be improved. Adaptation to the changing demands of the student marketplace has been a key to the advent of criminal justice, women's studies, and ethnic studies programs on campuses across America.

Farmer (1996) describes many of the barriers involved in the initiation of a criminal justice major on campus. Among the obstacles is the inherent difficulty of convincing noncriminal justice faculty members of the liberal arts value of the criminal justice major beyond its perceived vocational significance. Such perceptions, however outdated, cannot be summarily dismissed, given the criminal justice discipline's less than glorious history and its humble beginnings at many colleges and universities as a grouping of vocationally oriented courses under the label of police science. Attempts to overcome this history merely need address the merits of present programs in an attempt to make inroads into some widely held and strongly held perceptions. (Making inroads into some widely held and strongly held perceptions has been the challenge of marginalized peoples for generations. Overcoming historical practice has required much more than merely winning on the merits of one's argument. Indeed, for many it has required civil disobedience and other radical approaches as a means of garnering enough attention to not simply advocate change, but to demand change.) Despite criminal justice programs' popularity and hence their ability to serve as cash cows for many colleges and universities, correlations between the money brought into the university and the funding for various programs are not always present. Although disciplines such as philosophy and sociology may continue to exist with student-major/faculty ratios of less than 10:1, many criminal justice programs exist with ratios of as many as 50:1, or in extreme cases, even 80:1.

CONCLUSIONS: I, TOO, HAVE A DREAM (THOUGH MUCH LESS IMPORTANT)

The obligation to move beyond rhetoric toward creating an environment of genuine inclusion depends upon the recognition of the identities of criminal justice faculty members particularly and other marginalized disciplinarians more generally. What is done with these identities depends upon the ability, individually and collectively, to align with disciplines in the social sciences. Differences, though real, are fewer than similarities, and the place of criminal justice lies within the margins of academia, rather than outside. The boundaries that have repelled criminal justice educators as being different need to go the way of other archaic boundaries that prevented racial minorities and females from fully participating in a democracy. Boundaries that have been based on tradition, oppression, and fear, need to give way to more reasonable collaborations based on similarities in design and in purpose. The inclusion, ultimately, of more diverse groups within the discipline of criminal justice will enhance the legitimacy of the discipline and further the academic quality of instruction. A better understanding of racial disparities within the system might best come from a more racially diverse faculty within the criminal justice discipline. Given the importance of justice issues within American society, as well as the global community, greater inclusion within the academy would be a logical starting point for curriculum improvement.

It is not my intention to compare the vastly less-significant plight of marginalized academics with those of racial minorities in the 1960s, but I, like Martin Luther King, Jr., have a dream, and someday I hope that we academics can live and work together and be judged on the content of our academic characters rather than the "color" of our academic "skins."

NOTES

1. The racial imbalance apparently cannot be attributed to racial differences in drug trafficking, since less than 20 percent of drug arrests are for the sale or manufacture of illegal substances (Federal Bureau of Investigation, 2001, table 4.1). Furthermore, whites may actually be more likely than African Americans to sell illegal substances. According to the Substance Abuse and Mental Health Services Administration (2000, table G71), white adolescents are over one-third more likely than their African American counterparts to sell illegal drugs.

2. The marginalization of the discipline of criminal justice is perhaps most apparent by its conspicuous absence among the curricula of the most prestigious universities of America. There are no criminal justice departments in any of the Ivy League universities, nor are there criminal justice departments at the University of Chicago, Stanford University, Duke University, or Vanderbilt University. Moreover, criminal justice departments are not present in many of the more respected state universities. In the Big Ten, for instance, only Michigan State University and Indiana University have criminal justice departments.

CASES CITED

Batson v. Kentucky, 476 U.S. 79 (1986)
Brown v. Board of Education, 347 U.S. 483 (1954)
McCleskey v. Kemp, 481 U.S. 279 (1987)
Plessy v. Ferguson, 163 U.S. 537 (1896)
Purkett v. Elem, 115 S.Ct. 1769 (1995)
Scott v. Sanford, 60 U.S. 393 (1857)
Swain v. Alabama, 380 U.S. 202 (1965)

REFERENCES

Anderson, C. W. (1993). *Prescribing the life of the mind: An essay on the purpose of the university, the aims of liberal education, the competence of citizens, and the cultivation of practical reason.* Madison: University of Wisconsin Press.

Artz, L., & Murphy, B. O. (2000). *Cultural hegemony in the United States.* Thousand Oaks, CA: Sage.

Baldi, S. (1997, Spring). Departmental quality ratings and visibility: The advantages of size and age. *The American Sociologist, 28,* 28–43.

Bell, D. A., Jr. (1980, January). *Brown v. Board of Education* and the interest convergence dilemma. *Harvard Law Review, 93,* 518–533.

Berger, B. M. (1995). *An essay on culture: Symbolic structure and social structure.* Berkeley, CA: University of California Press.

Black-white relations in the United States 2001 update. (2001). *Gallup Poll Special Reports*. Retrieved July 10, 2001, from http://www.gallup .com/poll/specialreports/pollsummaries/sr010711.asp?Version = p

Coffin, W. S. (1999). *The heart is a little to the left: Essays on public morality*. Hanover, NH: University Press of New England.

Cole, D. (1999). *No equal justice: Race and class in the American criminal justice system*. New York: The New Press.

del Carmen, A., & Bing, R. L. (Fall 2000). Academic productivity of African Americans in criminology and criminal justice. *Journal of Criminal Justice Education, 11*, 237–249.

Donohue, J. J., III, & Levitt, S. D. (2001, October). The impact of race on policing and arrests. *Journal of Law and Economics, 44*, 367–394.

Drucker, E. (1999). Drug prohibition and public health: 25 years of evidence, U.S. Department of Health and Human Services. *Public Health Reports, 114*, 14.

Farmer, J. F. (1996, September/October). Wrestling with what to include in a new criminal justice curriculum. *ACJS Today, 15*, 1, 3, 9.

Federal Bureau of Investigation. (2001). *Crime in the United States 2000*. Washington, DC: U. S. Department of Justice.

Flanagan, T. J. (2000, Spring). Liberal education and the criminal justice major. *Journal of Criminal Justice Education, 11*, 1–13.

Free, M. D., Jr. (1999). Racial issues in contemporary criminology textbooks: The case of African Americans. *Contemporary Justice Review, 1*, 429–466.

Gordon, E. W. (1999). *Education and justice: A view from the back of the bus*. New York: Teachers College Press.

Greene, H. T., Gabbidon, S. L., & Ebersole, M. (2001). A multi-faceted analysis of the African American presence in juvenile delinquency textbooks published between 1997 and 2000. *Journal of Crime and Justice, 24*, 87–101.

Havel, V. (1985). *The power of the powerless*. Armonk, NY: M.E. Sharpe.

Heard, C., & Bing, R. (1993). African American faculty and students on predominantly white university campuses. *Journal of Criminal Justice Education, 4*, 1–15.

Jaynes, G. D., & Williams, R. M. (Eds.). (1989). *A common destiny*. Washington, DC: National Academy Press.

Martinez, J. G. R., & Martinez, N. C. (1997, Winter). Academe's secret problem: The tug of war between privilege and equal opportunity. *Journal of Thought, 32*, 73–84.

Merriam Webster's Collegiate Dictionary. (10th ed.). 1993. Ashland, OH: Landall.

Moffitt, W. (2000–2001). Race and the criminal justice system. *Gonzaga Law Review, 36*, 305–313.

Number of full-time faculty members by sex, rank, and racial and ethnic group, fall 1997. (2001, August 31). *Chronicle of Higher Education Almanac Issue 2001–02, 48*, 28.

Pastore, A. L., & Maguire, K. (Eds.) (2000). *Sourcebook of criminal justice statistics 1999.* U. S. Department of Justice, Bureau of Justice Statistics. Washington, DC: Author.

Phipps, R. A. (1995, Fall). The theology of faculty: A religion of higher education. *Colleges and Universities, 71*, 20–24.

Ross, L. E., & Edwards, W. J. (1998). Publishing among African American criminologists: A devaluing experience. *Journal of Criminal Justice, 26*, 29–40.

Sowell, T. (1995). *The vision of the anointed.* New York: Times Books.

Stephan, W. (1999). *Reducing prejudice and stereotyping in schools.* New York: Teachers College Press.

Substance Abuse & Mental Health Services Administration. (2000). *National household survey on drug abuse, 1999.* Washington, DC: Office of Applied Studies.

Vidal, G. (2001). *The last empire: Essays 1992–2000.* New York: Doubleday.

Wacquant, L. (2002, January/February). From slavery to mass incarceration. *New Left Review, 13*, 41–60.

Young, V., & Sulton, A. T. (1991). Excluded: The status of African American scholars in the field of criminology and criminal justice. *Journal of Research in Crime & Delinquency, 28*, 101–116.

Zweig, M. (2000). *The working class majority: America's best kept secret.* Ithaca, NY: Cornell University Press.

CHAPTER 3

Slavery's Legacy?
Private Prisons and
Mass Imprisonment

Michael A. Hallett

> Disregarding evidence that the levels of drug use were already in decline, that drug use is not responsive to criminal penalties, that criminalization brings its own pathologies (notably street violence and disrespect for authorities), and that declaring a war against drugs is, in effect, to declare a war against minorities, the U.S. government proceeded to declare such a war and to persist in pursuing it, despite every indication of its failure. Why? Because the groups most adversely affected lack political power and are widely regarded as dangerous and undeserving; because the groups least affected could be assured that something is being done and lawlessness is not tolerated; and because few politicians are willing to oppose a policy when there is so little political advantage to be gained by doing so.
>
> (Garland, 2001a, p. 132)

According to the U.S. Bureau of Justice Statistics, "A black male in the United States today has a greater than 1 in 4 chance of going to prison during his lifetime . . . and a white male has a 1 in 23 chance of serving time" (Bonczar & Beck, 1997, p.1). To emphasize this point in yet another way, the incarceration of young African American men in the United States "has escalated to heights experienced by no other group in history, even under the repressive authoritarian regimes and in Soviet-style societies" (Wacquant, 2001, p. 105). When certain segments of the population become the focus of such disproportionately high rates of imprisonment

Thanks to Marvin Free and Marilyn McShane for a helpful critique of an early draft of this chapter.

and incarceration becomes a common characteristic of their experience as a social group, a new social phenomenon of mass imprisonment has emerged (Garland, 2001b): "Imprisonment becomes mass imprisonment when it ceases to be the incarceration of individual offenders and becomes the systematic imprisonment of whole groups of the population. . . . Imprisonment ceases to be the fate of a few criminal individuals, and becomes a shaping institution for whole sectors of the population" (Garland 2001b, p. 2). High rates of victimization, incarceration, and criminality in the African American community have thus become normalized to the point of becoming a social *expectation* (Davis, 1998; Garland, 2001a). Targeting inner-city minority males, particularly for nonviolent drug-related crimes, the drug war undertaken over the past twenty-five years fights only a limited type of crime and targets only a narrow spectrum of offender (young black men).

The mass incarceration of young African American men in the United States today, and the renewed use of privatized prisons to house them, is socially meaningful for reasons separate from concerns about criminality alone. As prison historian Alex Lichtenstein recently queried:

Imagine what the results would be if the impact of mass incarceration on whites was comparable to its effects on blacks. If nearly 10 percent of all white people were placed under correctional control tomorrow, would there be a national outcry? Of course there would. But today's penal policies are not likely to produce this kind of nonracialized police state. Their character is instead to be found in America's intertwined histories of prisons, penal reform, and racism. (2001, p. 176)

Would today's system of incarcerating predominantly African American men in both state-run and private, for-profit prisons be as acceptable without the legacy of slavery that preceded it? In the pages that follow, I wish to persuade readers that the clear answer to this question is "No." As Bosworth and Carrabine (2001, p. 509) recently concluded, "Given the overrepresentation of people of color in British and U.S. prisons as inmates, and the fact that they are typically guarded by white prison officers, it seems that color and culture are indices of certain positions within a power hierarchy."

In this chapter, I document the re-emergence of private prisons in the United States, arguing that private prisons reveal truths about our current culture and social system that have little to do with crime control, but have much to do, instead, with the often racist and exploitative character of our capitalistic economic system. The mass incarceration of African American men, for example, is now so ubiquitous that it has become an accepted social fact—crime is seen largely as a racial problem, rather than the complex and multidimensional phenomenon it actually is (Davis, 1998; Garland 2001b; Sampson & Wilson, 2000). When we declare "wars" on crime, do we do so against corrupt accounting firms that cost thousands of jobs, as with Arthur Anderson in the recent Enron scandal, or do we declare war against lower-class, uneducated, and already largely condemned street offenders? If punishment is targeted primarily at specific types of criminals (e.g., politically powerless, young, black, urban males), rather than protecting or changing society for the better, the criminal justice system functions to order social life along lines of preexisting power much more so than to protect society from social harm.

PRIVATE PRISONS AGAIN?

It is perhaps surprising to realize that the Thirteenth Amendment to the U.S. Constitution, which ended slavery, is also the very legal instrument that authorized the "involuntary servitude" of prisoners as a punishment for crime: "Neither slavery nor involuntary servitude, except as a punishment for crime whereof the party shall have been duly convicted, shall exist within the United States, or any place subject to their jurisdiction." In the aftermath of the Civil War, freed slaves often had nowhere to go. Being designated trespassers on their former owners' plantations, "several laws were passed that helped keep the African American population in its place, including vagrancy, loitering, disturbing the peace, and Jim Crow laws. One result of this practice was the shift in prison populations to predominantly African American following the war" (Shelden, 2001, p. 170). As Shelden's (2001, p. 171) data from Tennessee's Main Prison at Nashville indicate, blacks sent to prison increased dramatically after the Civil War, whereas the proportion of whites sent to prison decreased. For instance, in October of 1855, Shelden's data from Tennessee's Main Prison at Nashville indicate that the institution had 200 inmates—134 white and 66 black. In November 1867, after the Civil War had ended, the prison had a total of 485 inmates—202 white and 283 black. And by October 1869, the Nashville prison had 551 inmates, of which 198 were white and 353 were black (64 percent) (see Shelden, 2001, p. 171).

Once imprisoned, inmates were leased to private vendors as low-cost laborers (below free-market value) to become the foundation of lucrative, profit-driven, white-owned businesses. Early industries using convict labor included logging, coal mining, turpentine production, railroad construction, and farm work (Lichtenstein, 1996; Mancini, 1996). Emerging in the context of the abolition of slavery, the convict-lease system in the United States engendered a highly racialized but legal form of coercive labor practice, through criminalizing the activities of newly freed slaves for being vagrants or paupers or migrants and sending them in large numbers into prisons (Lichtenstein, 1996). As such, the convict-lease system kept alive a racially disproportionate system of involuntary servitude—and a slavery-era understanding of captives as legitimately exploitable commodities. Not until organized free labor gained voice enough to remove cheap convict labor from the marketplace was the convict-lease system transformed into strictly public works chain gang road crews, which helped build the roads of the new South (Hallett, 1996; Mancini, 1978, 1996; Oshinsky, 1996). As Mark Colvin (1997, p. 218) well documents, "The white South was convinced that only coercive force could keep blacks tied to agricultural production. Planters turned to the state to create the mechanisms for this coercion."

THE WAR ON DRUGS, DISPROPORTIONATE MINORITY CONFINEMENT, AND CONTEMPORARY PRISON PRIVATIZATION

As depicted in Figure 3.1, a rapid increase in the rate of incarceration took place during the latter part of the twentieth century. Particularly during the years 1980–2000, under the auspices of an officially sanctioned War on Crime, the American incarceration rate roughly quadrupled and, as reflected in Table 3.1, in 2000 stood at unprecedented levels. As a result of this dramatic increase in the level of incarceration, correctional administrators at all three levels of government (federal, state, and local) increas-

Figure 3.1
Sentenced Prisoners under Jurisdiction of State and Federal Correctional Authorities, United States, 1925–2000[a]

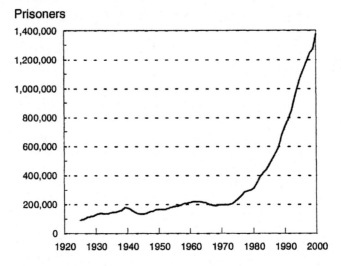

[a]Data for 2000 are as of June 30.
Source: Pastore & Maguire (2001, figure 6.1).

Table 3.1

Adults on Probation, in Jail or Prison, and on Parole, United States, 1980–2000

	Total estimated correctional population[a]	Probation	Jail	Prison	Parole
1980	1,840,400	1,118,097	182,288[b]	319,598	220,438
1981	2,006,600	1,225,934	195,085[b]	360,029	225,539
1982	2,192,600	1,357,264	207,853	402,914	224,604
1983	2,475,100	1,582,947	221,815	423,898	246,440
1984	2,689,200	1,740,948	233,018	448,264	266,992
1985	3,011,500	1,968,712	254,986	487,593	300,203
1986	3,239,400	2,114,621	272,735	526,436	325,638
1987	3,459,600	2,247,158	294,092	562,814	355,505
1988	3,714,100	2,356,483	341,893	607,766	407,977
1989	4,055,600	2,522,125	393,303	683,367	456,803
1990	4,350,300	2,670,234	405,320	743,382	531,407
1991	4,535,600	2,728,472	424,129[c]	792,535	590,442
1992	4,762,600	2,811,611	441,781[c]	850,566	658,601
1993	4,944,000	2,903,061	455,500[c]	909,381	676,100
1994	5,141,300	2,981,022	479,800	990,147	690,371
1995	5,342,900	3,077,861	507,044	1,078,542	679,421
1996	5,490,700	3,164,996	518,492	1,127,528	679,733
1997	5,734,900	3,296,513	567,079	1,176,564	694,787
1998	6,134,200	3,670,441	592,462	1,224,469	696,385
1999	6,349,800	3,779,922	605,943	1,287,172	714,457
2000[d]	6,467,200	3,839,532	621,149	1,312,354	725,527
Percent change					
1999 to 2000	2.0%	1.6%	2.5%	2.0%	1.5%
1990 to 2000	48.7	43.8	53.2	76.5	36.5

Note: Counts for probation, prison, and parole populations are for December 31 of each year; jail population counts are for June 30 of each year. Counts of adults held in jail facilities for 1993–1996 were estimated and rounded to the nearest 100. Data for jail and prison are for inmates under custody. Totals for 1998–2000 exclude probationers reported to have been in jail or prison. These data have been revised by the *Sourcebook* based on the most recently reported counts and may differ from previous editions of *Sourcebook*.

[a]A small number of individuals have multiple correctional statuses; consequently, the total number of persons under correctional supervision is an overestimate. The total is rounded to the nearest 100.

[b]Estimated.

[c]Includes an unknown number of persons supervised outside jail facilities.

[d]Excludes 20,4000 probationers in jail and 10,985 probationers in prison.

Source: Pastore & Maguire (2001, table 6.1)

ingly turned to private, for-profit corporations to manage the burgeoning
number of inmates in privately operated correctional facilities. A disproportionate number of the offenders sent to prison during this time of dramatic increase were inner-city minority males incarcerated for nonviolent
drug crimes, a pattern that continues today. As Rose and Clear recently
put it:

> Growth in imprisonment has disproportionately affected the poor and people of
> color. The residential segregation of African Americans in urban communities
> means that some of their neighborhoods have suffered war-level casualties in
> parenting-age males during the increase of imprisonment since 1973, when far
> fewer African American males were incarcerated. (1998, pp. 450–451)

According to the most recent data, 66 percent of inmates currently held
in private prisons are racial minorities, with African Americans consti-
tuting the single largest group (43.9 percent black) (Austin & Coventry,
2001, p. 41). As Waquant (1999, p. 215) points out, it is only recently (1989)
that blacks began again to dominate American prison populations in the
twentieth century, as the drug war reached full implementation. Even
though African Americans constitute less than 13 percent the American
population, African American men today represent 46.5 percent of prisoners in state and federal prisons.[1]

The renewed *commodification* of disproportionately black human beings
in American private prisons, even though distinct certainly from the
convict-lease system itself, bears profound similarities to the social regu-
lation of poor blacks in the aftermath of the Civil War (Hallett, 2002).[2] Not
surprisingly, the largest proportion of inmates in today's private prisons
are African American (Austin & Coventry, 2001, p. 41). As William Julius
Wilson points out, while the economic recovery of the mid-1990s helped
many people, and arguably helped reduce the crime rate overall, African
American men trapped in inner cities found themselves more thoroughly
disenfranchised than ever before—and simultaneously became the targets
of hyperincarceration (Sampson & Wilson, 2000; Wilson, 1996).

It is important to note that a disproportionate number of the offenders
sent to prison during the dramatic upswing in incarceration since 1980
were inner-city minority males, incarcerated for nonviolent drug crimes.
Jerome Miller (1996), tracking black versus white admissions to American
state and federal prisons in the 1900s, traces the re-emerging racial disparity between blacks and whites by the early 1990s directly to the drug
war (see Miller's data in Table 3.2). Though, according to many indexes,
the American economy was at its strongest ever during the year 2000—
with the lowest rates of unemployment in generations—another, less-
widely cited index clouded this picture of societal health: the American
incarceration rate was at an all-time high, 682 per 100,000 citizens—higher

Table 3.2
Racial Percentages of U.S. Prison Populations

Year	% White	% Black	% Other
1926	79	21	1
1930	77	22	1
1935	74	25	1
1940	71	28	1
1945	68	31	1
1950	69	30	1
1960	66	32	2
1964	65	33	2
1974	59	38	3
1978	58	41	1
1981	57	42	2
1986	40	45	15
1993	27	55	18

Source: Miller (1996, p. 55).

even than China or the former Soviet Union (Freeman, 2001). The association between the all-time low in unemployment rates and the corresponding all-time high in incarceration rates is indeed cause for suspicion. Combined with the fact that the highest concentrations of *unemployment* in the United States are found among urban, African American males, and the fact that the highest rates of *incarceration* are found among this same population—there is not yet cause to celebrate the success of welfare reform policy (Beckett, 1997; Sampson & Wilson, 2000; Wilson, 1996)! The low unemployment rate of the 1990s was artificially low because of the unprecedented number of people in prison (Western & Beckett, 1999). In this context, reduced spending on welfare assistance due to seemingly high employment is not an indication of less governmental intervention in people's lives, because it was accompanied by an incarceration rate so high as to constitute a means of regulating the poor (Beckett & Sasson, 2000).

FROM LOCAL TO NATIONAL CONCERN: UNDERSTANDING RACE AND CONTEMPORARY MASS IMPRISONMENT

To gain popular support for getting tough on crime, conservative U.S. politicians successfully employed a racialized strategy associating public disorder with perceptions of individual morality, rather than with macro-level shifts in economic well-being or opportunity (Beckett & Sasson, 2000; Clear, 1997; Parenti, 2000; Wilson, 1996, 1999). These moral entrepreneurs shifted public resources away from ameliorative and preventative social programs (the welfare state) and directed them, instead, toward crime control and the building of a security state (Beckett & Sasson, 2000). The welfare state was undermined, in particular, by a racialized change in the moral status of the poor from deserving to undeserving. According to Beckett and Sasson (2000, p. 68), "this transformation of the moral status of the poor was predicated on a change in the identity of the prototypical poor person from white and rural (in the imagery of the Great Depression and the war on poverty) to black and urban (in the iconography of the wars on crime and drugs)."

Starting especially with Barry Goldwater in 1964, and later with the administration of Richard Nixon, conservative political activists recognized the value of the so-called crime problem as a vehicle for winning votes, particularly from alienated Southern white Democrats (Beckett, 1997; Epstein, 1977; Parenti, 2000). Coming out of the turbulent 1960s, policy changes revealing the success of this strategy, such as those put forward in the insightfully titled Omnibus Crime Control and Safe Streets Act of 1968, were already apparent. "At the heart of this new type of politics was a very old political trope: crime meant urban, urban meant black, and the war on crime meant a bulwark built against the increasingly political and vocal racial 'other' by the predominantly white state" (Parenti, 2000, p. 7).

In the process of orchestrating the War on Crime, conservative activists successfully had to recharacterize crime control from being a primarily local and preventative enterprise, to one necessitating federal government involvement in a war against individual offenders deserving of punishment. "Suddenly, the debate about crime was galvanized into camps—the liberals and conservatives. Was a person in favor of the criminal or the victim? Did someone believe in rehabilitation or punishment?" (Clear, 1997, p. 139). Crime, in other words, became a moral issue, much more so than one of policy design, economy, or law. In this context, punishment soon became the dominant and most frequently prescribed solution, even by otherwise liberal politicians.

Whereas past poverty and public order discussions focused on jobs, employment training, and worker placement, the new conservative paradigm focused on implementing wider use of punishment and reducing the size of government (Tonry & Petersilia, 2000; Wilson, 1996, 1999). Indeed, by the presidency of Ronald Reagan, conservatives were promoting mandatory sentencing as the greatest means of improving life in poor communities (Clear, 1997). By the 1990s, the conservative paradigm for crime and punishment was so firmly in place that incarceration rates increased *faster* during the presidency of Democrat Bill Clinton than during that of either conservative Republican Reagan or Bush (Justice Policy Institute, 2001).

The harshness and corresponding ineffectiveness of our current punishment schemes leads many to ask if punishment is really about control (Garland, 1990; Simon, 1993). Many critics of the modern criminal justice system argue that its workings are devoted less to reducing crime than to providing politicians and other social entrepreneurs a symbolic means of justifying their *own* existence. By identifying suitable enemies deserving of social action, entrepreneurs of this sort develop and implement reactive policies inadequate to the task of affecting real change, thereby perpetuating the need for action and fueling public outrage (Beckett, 1997; Chambliss, 2001; Sherman, 1983; Christie, 1993; Gusfield, 1963).

Today we face a situation in many states where spending on incarceration is greater than spending on *education*—with state department of corrections' budgets frequently being the single largest expenditure of state resources (Hallett, 2002; Petersilia, 1994). Despite decades of research demonstrating that increased spending on expanded prison systems and hiring more police officers have little impact on crime, public spending on just these activities has dominated criminal justice policy over the past thirty years (Kelling, Pate, Dieckman, & Brown, 1974; RAND, 1997; Rose & Clear, 1998).

A HOUSE THE DRUG WAR BUILT: FOR-PROFIT IMPRISONMENT

A key strategy in the War on Crime was the implementation of a *determinate* or *mandatory minimum* sentencing scheme, which sought both to lengthen the duration of time served by offenders as well as to limit the ability of judges and parole boards to reduce the actual amount of time they served (Clear & Cole, 1994, p. 81). Drug-related crimes, of course, were the particular target of mandatory sentencing, including even nonviolent drug crimes such as possession of marijuana (Cloud, 1999, pp. 48–51; Donziger, 1996, pp.15, 25). The increase in the incarceration rate itself, and a corresponding increase in the lengths of sentences imposed, resulted in overcrowding and an increase in the costs of operating the swelling prisons. By the late 1980s prisons were extremely overcrowded and dangerous, with roughly two-thirds of U.S. correctional facilities under federal court order to reduce overcrowding for violations of inmates' Eighth Amendment rights under the Constitution (Bohm & Haley, 1997, p. 327). As a result of the overcrowding crisis generated by mandatory sentencing schemes, jurisdictions looked to private vendors to fill the incarceration breach.

By 1999 there were thirteen private contractors operating adult correctional facilities in the United States, with a total bed space approaching 140,000 prisoners (Pastore & Maguire, 2000, p. 82). The two largest of these—Corrections Corporation of America (CCA) and Wackenhut Corrections Corporation—together held 80 percent of the total U.S. prisoners housed in private facilities. As documented in Table 3.3, it is also worth noting that CCA continues to dominate the prison privatization market, holding 52 percent of the available contracts, whereas Wackenhut holds roughly 20 percent (Abt Associates, 1998, p. 18). By comparison, then, Corrections Corporation of America's inmate population is larger than that of most state prison systems. In the late 1990s, for example, the state of Tennessee had an inmate population of roughly 17,000. Wackenhut's total inmate population for 1999 was 39,565 (Pastore & Maguire, 2000, p. 82). In total, over 150 private correctional facilities were operational in the United States in 1999 and housed roughly 5 percent of the total inmate population in the country (Abt Associates, 1998, Appendix 1, p. 2; Pastore & Maguire, 2000, p. 82). A breakdown of privately controlled bed space by state for 2000 is found in Table 3.4.

Ninety-five percent of inmates in private facilities are minimum or medium security classification, with only four percent of privately held inmates having a maximum security designation (Abt Associates, 1998, p. 25). At the end of 1997, only one private prison facility in operation was designated exclusively for maximum security inmates—the South Bay Correctional Facility in Florida operated by Wackenhut (Abt Associ-

Table 3.3
Private Adult Correctional Facility Management Firms by Capacity of Facilities under Contract, United States, December 31, 1997–2000 and September 4, 2001

Management firm	Capacity of all facilities under contract[a]				
	1997	1998	1999	2000	2001
Total	97,062	116,932	122,871	119,453	119,023
Alternative Programs, Inc.	340	340	340	340	340
Avalon Correctional Services, Inc.[b]	150	350	350	350	710
The Bobby Ross Group	2,825	464	464	464	464
CiviGenics, Inc.	3,563	3,563	2,791	2,795	2,243
Cornell Corrections, Inc.	3,882	5,916	7,138	8,464	8,424
Correctional Services Corporation	2,629	6,891	6,517	4,241	3,891
Correctional Systems, Inc.	170	272	272	272	272
Corrections Corporation of America	50,866	67,286	68,256	62,431	62,231
Dominion Correctional Services, Inc.	NA	NA	NA	2,064	2,064
The GRW Corporation	362	362	362	614	614
Management & Training Corporation	4,259	6,447	9,177	10,214	10,566
Maranatha Production Company	500	500	500	500	500
U.S. Corrections Corporation	5,259	NA	NA	NA	NA
Wackenhut Corrections Corporation[c]	22,257	24,541	26,704	26,704	26,704

[a]Includes operational facilities, facilities under construction, and planned expansions of existing facilities.
[b]Formerly Avalon Community Services, Inc.
[c]The Wackenhut Corrections Corporation did not respond to the survey by the Private Corrections Project at the Center for Studies in Criminology and Law at the University of Florida; data were estimated by the *Sourcebook of Criminal Justice Statistics*.
Source: Pastore & Maguire (2002, table 1.92).

ates, 1998, p. 25). As the recently released Federal Bureau of Prisons (2000) study, *Private Prisons in the United States, 1999: An Assessment of Growth, Performance, Custody Standards, and Training Requirements* (Camp & Gaes, 2000b), concludes, "Compared to all prisoners held by state and federal prisons operated by public employees, the private sector has a disproportionate number of minimum security prisoners and few maximum security ones" (pp. 109–110). Targeting nonviolent minimum security inmates, then, who typically require less discipline, lower rates of medical care, and who have less elaborate criminal histories, is the clear pattern of the industry (Hallett, 2001). As Todd Clear and George F. Cole conclude:

Most privatization plans call for skimming off the best of the worst—the nonserious offenders who can be efficiently processed. Thus the government-run part of the correctional system faces the possibility of having to manage only the most costly, most intractable offenders on a reduced budget, and with the worsened

Table 3.4
Number and Rated Capacity of Private Adult Correctional Facilities by Jurisdiction, December 31, 1997–2000 and September 4, 2001

Jurisdiction	Number of facilities					Rated capacity				
	1997	1998	1999	2000	2001	1997	1998	1999	2000	2001
Arizona	5	6	6	6	6	4,748	6,860	6,860	6,860	6,860
Arkansas	2	2	2	2	2	1,200	1,200	1,885	1,885	1,885
California	19	24	24	22	22	10,292	11,294	11,462	10,470	10,470
Colorado	8	9	6	6	6	3,444	4,644	3,824	3,824	3,824
District of Columbia	1	1	1	1	1	866	866	866	866	866
Florida	10	10	9	8	8	6,223	6,255	5,465	5,561	5,561
Georgia	3	5	7	4	4	1,566	6,409	9,457	6,197	6,197
Idaho	1	1	1	1	1	1,250	1,250	1,250	1,250	1,250
Illinois	1	1	NA	1	1	220	220	NA	200	200
Indiana	1	1	1	1	1	670	670	670	670	670
Kansas	2	2	2	2	2	529	529	685	687	687
Kentucky	4	4	4	3	3	1,973	2,631	2,631	2,268	2,268
Louisiana	2	2	2	2	2	2,948	2,948	3,012	3,012	3,012
Michigan	1	1	1	1	1	480	480	480	480	480
Minnesota	1	1	1	1	1	1,338	1,338	1,338	1,338	1,338
Mississippi	5	6	6	6	6	3,176	4,650	4,700	4,700	4,700
Missouri	2	2	1	1	1	660	660	60	60	60
Montana	NA	1	1	1	1	NA	512	512	512	512
Nevada	1	1	1	1	1	500	500	500	500	500
New Jersey	1	1	1	1	1	300	300	300	300	300
New Mexico	6	7	7	8	8	3,836	4,864	5,322	5,508	5,508
New York	1	1	1	1	1	200	200	200	200	200
North Carolina	2	2	3	1	1	2,000	2,112	2,256	1,200	1,200
Ohio	2	2	4	4	4	2,256	2,256	4,140	4,140	4,140
Oklahoma	6	8	8	8	8	7,068	9,716	10,436	10,436	10,796
Pennsylvania	1	1	1	2	3	1,200	1,200	1,562	2,762	3,222
Puerto Rico	4	4	4	4	4	3,000	3,000	3,000	3,000	3,000
Rhode Island	1	1	1	1	1	302	302	302	302	302
Tennessee	5	6	6	6	6	5,628	7,326	7,326	7,326	7,326
Texas	41	43	42	43	42	27,139	29,690	29,820	30,389	30,039
Utah	1	1	2	2	NA	400	400	900	900	NA
Virginia	1	1	1	1	1	1,500	1,500	1,500	1,500	1,500
Washington	1	1	1	1	1	150	150	150	150	150

Note: The geographic location of facilities does not necessarily indicate contracting decisions made by agencies in those jurisdictions; some states contract for the housing of their prisoners in other jurisdictions and some states provide sites only for federal facilities. Data include facilities in operation and those under construction.
Source: Pastore & Maguire (2002, table 1.93).

fiscal and personnel situations that would result from such a development. (1994, p. 513)

CRIME CONSCIOUSNESS: PUNISHMENT AS CULTURALLY REVEALING

To deliver up bodies destined for profitable punishment, the political economy of prisons relies on racialized assumptions of criminality—such as images of black welfare mothers reproducing criminal children—and on racist practices in arrest, conviction, and sentencing patterns. Colored bodies constitute the main human raw material in this vast experiment to disappear the major social problems of our

time. The prison industrial system materially and morally impover-
ishes its inhabitants and devours the social wealth needed to address
the very problems that have led to spiraling numbers of prisoners.
(Davis, 1998)

It is uncomfortable, certainly, to ponder the notion of *racist* law, as distinct from *neutral* law or *fair* law. Though few would deny that race has
played a central role in the creation of American social classes or the existing social order, people are still often very reluctant to extend their racial
consciousness to law itself. Denying the fairness of law throws everything
else out of whack: solving the crime problem might be more complex than
simply hiring more police officers or building more prisons. As the RAND
Corporation has repeatedly found with its statistical analyses of mandatory sentencing, getting tough on crime without addressing the underlying causes of crime might ultimately be a waste of taxpayer money (1997).
Finally, if law—as it is actually enforced—disproportionately targets one
group versus another, what socially harmful effects of law itself are being
ignored? What social damage is law itself causing?

The renewed appearance of private prisons at this point in our history
cannot be explained by charges of exploding crime rates (which are down
dramatically over the past 15 years), or the proven effectiveness of incarceration as a response to crime (long-term incarceration is both destructive
to offenders and expensive to society), or the compelling cost-effectiveness
of private-sector prisons (privatization of prisons does not save money).
Market-based business logic has not radically transformed the operation
of prisons to make them more rehabilitative, socially just, or secure.

If, as the U.S. General Accounting Office (and many others) point out,
large-scale savings have not been generated by prison privatization, why
does it continue to be considered? (Abt Associates, 1998; Austin & Irwin,
2001; U.S. General Accounting Office, 1996). Moreover, since privatized
control over prisons re-emerged in the mid-1980s, numerous prison contracts between private companies and jurisdictions of all sizes (federal,
state, and local) have been terminated for either lack of performance or
outright abuse (Abt Associates, 1998; Camp & Gaes, 2000a). Nevertheless,
at this writing, at least eleven states and the federal government are considering or have recently enacted expansive prison privatization contracts,
with the number of prisoners in private prisons today at an all-time high
of 87,369 inmates.

To understand the re-emergence of privatized prisons, one must dig
deeper than the contemporary justifications put forward on their behalf
(that private prisons save money, that private prisons are better run than
state prisons, that market forces and competition order the social world
in healthy ways). The profoundly high rate of imprisonment of young
African American men from the inner city, the lack of regulatory oversight

that characterizes the private prisons industry despite an elaborate history of abuses, combined with the mere fact that the racial imbalances characterizing U.S. prisons today are hardly ever mentioned during legislative discussions of reinstituting private prisons—all speak to *race* as the dominant but tellingly unspoken subtext of American criminal justice policy.

CONCLUSION

> In designing penal policy we are not simply deciding how to deal with a group of people on the margins of society—whether to deter, reform, or incapacitate them and if so how. Nor are we simply deploying power or economic resources for penological ends. We are also and at the same time defining ourselves and our society in ways which may be quite central to our cultural and political identity.
>
> (Garland, 1990, p. 276)

A well-established tradition of viewing punishment—and imprisonment in particular—as serving agendas other than crime control has long existed in criminology. This tradition includes the work of Emile Durkheim (1933) (who argued punishment enhances social solidarity), George Herbert Mead (1918) (who argued punishment releases inhibited social aggression), Georg Rusche and Otto Kirchheimer (1968) (who argued incarceration rates fluctuate with labor and economic demand), Michel Foucault (1977) (who viewed punishment strategies as part of a larger disciplinary strategy of social control), and David Garland (1990) (who views punishments as cultural expressions involving economic, moral, political, and functional aims).

The fact that our "crime wars" center almost exclusively on the behaviors of inner-city minorities also sends a socially revealing signal about our crime consciousness. As Garland (1991, p. 195) states, "[P]enality communicates meaning not just about crime and punishment but also about power, authority, legitimacy, normality, morality, personhood, social relations and a host of other tangential matters." Putting large numbers of black men once again into private prisons reveals something about today's prevailing social order: that inflicting punishment for the crimes of inner-city minority males is our highest criminal justice priority.

The culturalist perspective on incarceration argues that systems of punishment always reflect and reinforce preexisting social relations (Garland, 1990). Pondered in this way, one comes to realize the truth of Durkheim's (1933) argument that certain segments of society both need and benefit from crime—and that criminality itself, in surprising ways, is an exploitable social resource for many in our society (see also Beckett, 1997; Chambliss, 2001). It is meaningful that we are sending large numbers of black men, once again, into private, for-profit prisons: it says that race is (still) very much part of our criminal justice and relational social world.

Under the auspices of the convict-lease system, this country first instituted privatized control over inmates in the context of the abolition of slavery. As such, a racialized population of inmates soon emerged in the private prisons of the time.[3] Today, in the era of welfare reform and less government, large numbers of African American men find themselves once again in private prisons. Arguably, the same forces of social dislocation are at work.

Prisons, when viewed outside of the modern instrumentalist/social engineering formulae so often attached to them, become more socially revealing institutions. What kinds of political and even economic interests help keep prisons expanding—even in the face of long-term falling crime rates? What kinds of symbolic things are accomplished by prisons, regardless of whether or not they actually control crime? Prisons give people jobs, provide labor for high-tech production and information technology firms, enhance tax-base stability, and convince people that something is being done about crime, despite decades of research indicating the opposite.

When examined closely, one realizes that there is much more going on with the use of prisons than the simple attempt to control crime. Indeed, the vast number of stakeholders with life-sustaining ties to prison facilities (i.e., labor unions, consumers, politicians, voters, communities desperate for tax-base stability, citizens hungry for jobs, private manufacturing and information-technology firms, lobbyists, academics, and, not least, prisoners and their families) make prisons complex social institutions. Many peoples' lives and livelihoods are tied to the continuation and expansion of incarceration as a social policy. Moreover, that prisons are used disproportionately against one particular group is socially meaningful, not just in terms of the obvious power imbalance between groups, but also for what it says about the culture itself.

NOTES

1. An examination of the racial composition of the larger state prison population discloses that 52 percent of all state inmates are African American (Seigel, 2001). Thus, the racial disparity is even greater in the state system than in the federal system.

2. Although prisoners today are no longer profitable solely for their labor, as was the case during the convict-lease period, their commodity value has been enhanced by their ability to produce per diem payments for the providers of private prisons (Hallett, 2002).

3. For instance, Myers and Massey's account of postbellum Georgia suggests that primarily black convicts were deemed suitable for the harsh environment of the convict-lease system.

"Destitute of pride of character," blacks were considered unintelligent, incapable of reform, and inherently able to perform only the "simplest and roughest" tasks (Principal Keeper of the Penitentiary, 1873, 1876). As was the case in other Southern states, there appeared to be *little demand for the labor of white convicts,* and courts were reluctant to sentence whites to work for lessees (italics added). (1991, p. 270)

Moreover, Rabinowitz (1976) argues that the desire to maintain racial segregation played a role in the disproportionate singling out of blacks for leasing. He contends that "As a result of the influx of black prisoners [after the Civil War], racial contact became as much of a problem within the correctional institutions as in the outside world" (p. 339). Because "segregation was seen as the ideal solution for regulating contact between the races once exclusion became unfeasible" (p. 339), the leasing out of black prisoners made racial segregation possible even within the limitations of the small penitentiaries typical of southern states.

REFERENCES

Abt Associates, Inc. (1998). *Private prisons in the United States: An assessment of current practice.* Cambridge, MA: Author.

Austin, J., & Coventry, G. (2001). *Emerging issues on privatized prisons.* Washington, DC: National Council on Crime & Delinquency.

Austin, J., & Irwin, J. (2001). *It's about time: America's imprisonment binge* (3rd ed.). Belmont, CA: Wadsworth.

Beckett, K. (1997). *Making crime pay: Law and order in contemporary American politics.* New York: Oxford University Press.

Beckett, K., & Sasson, T. (2000). The war on crime as hegemonic strategy. In S. Simpson (Ed.), *Of crime and criminality: The use of theory in everyday life* (pp. 61–84). Thousand Oaks, CA: Pine Forge.

Bohm, R., & Haley, K. (1997). *Introduction to criminal justice.* New York: Glencoe/McGraw Hill.

Bonczar, T., & Beck, A. (1997). *Lifetime likelihood of going to state or federal prison.* Washington, DC: U.S. Department of Justice.

Bosworth, M., & Carrabine, E. (2001). Reassessing resistance: Race, gender and sexuality in prison. *Punishment & Society, 3,* 501–515.

Camp, S., & Gaes, G. (2000a). Private adult prisons: What do we really know and why don't we know more? In D. Shichor & M. Gilbert (Eds.), *Privatization in criminal justice: Past, present, and future* (pp. 283–298). Cincinnati: Anderson.

Camp, S., & Gaes, G. (2000b). *Private prisons in the United States, 1999: An assessment of growth, performance, custody standards, and training requirements.* Washington, DC: Federal Bureau of Prisons.

Chambliss, W. (2001). *Power, politics and crime.* Boulder, CO: Westview.

Christie, N. (1993). *Crime control as industry: Gulags western style.* New York: Routledge.

Clear, T. (1997). Societal responses to the President's Crime Commission: A thirty-year retrospective. In *The challenge of crime in a free society:*

Looking back, looking forward. Washington, DC: National Institute of Justice.

Clear, T., & Cole, G. (1994). *American corrections.* Boston: Wadsworth.

Cloud, J. (1999, February 1). A get-tough policy that failed. *Time,* pp. 48–51.

Colvin, M. (1997). *Penitentiaries, reformatories, and chain gangs: Social theory and the history of punishment in nineteenth-century America.* New York: St. Martin's.

Davis, A. (1998). Reflections on the prison industrial complex. *ColorLines* 1(2), 1–8. Available: http://www.arc.org/C_Lines/CLArchive/story1–2-01.html.

Donziger, S. (Ed.). (1996). *The real war on crime: The report of the National Criminal Justice Commission.* New York: Harper Collins.

Durkheim, E. (1933). *The Division of Labor in Society.* Glencoe, IL: Free Press.

Epstein, E. (1977). *Agency of fear: Opiates and political power in America.* New York: Putnam.

Foucault, M. (1977). *Discipline and punish: The birth of the prison.* London: Pantheon.

Freeman, R. (2001). Does the booming economy help explain the fall in crime? In *Perspectives on crime and justice: 1999–2000 lecture series* (pp. 23–50). Washington, DC: U.S. Department of Justice.

Garland, D. (1990). *Punishment and modern society: A study in social theory.* Chicago: University of Chicago Press.

Garland, D. (1991). Punishment and culture: The symbolic dimension in criminal justice. *Studies in Law, Politics, & Society, 11,* 191–224.

Garland, D. (2001a). *The culture of control: Crime and social order in contemporary society.* Chicago: University of Chicago Press.

Garland, D. (2001b). Introduction: The meaning of mass imprisonment. In D. Garland (Ed.), *Mass imprisonment: Social causes and consequences.* Thousand Oaks, CA: Sage.

Gusfield, J. (1963). *Symbolic crusade: Status politics and the American temperance movement.* Urbana, IL: University of Illinois Press.

Hallett, M. (1996). The social dimensions of prison labor laws: The Hawes-Cooper Act. In M. McShane & F. Williams, III (Eds.), *The encyclopedia of American prisons.* New York: Garland.

Hallett, M. (2001). An introduction to prison privatization: Issues for the 21st century. In R. Muraskin & A. Roberts (Eds.), *Visions for change: Criminal justice in the 21st century* (pp. 371–389). Upper Saddle River, NJ: Prentice Hall.

Hallett, M. (2002). Race, crime and for-profit imprisonment: Social disorganization as market opportunity. *Punishment & Society, 4,* 369–393.

Justice Policy Institute. (2001). Too little too late: President Clinton's prison legacy. Washington, DC: Author.

Kelling, G., Pate, T., Dieckman, D., & Brown, C. (1974). *The Kansas City preventive patrol experiment: A technical report.* Washington, DC: Police Foundation.

Lichtenstein, A. (1996). *Twice the work of free labor: The political economy of convict labor in the new South.* New York: Verso.

Lichtenstein, A. (2001). The private and the public in penal history. In D. Garland (Ed.), *Mass imprisonment: Social causes and consequences* (pp. 171–178). Thousand Oaks, CA: Sage.

Maguire, K., & Pastore, A. (Eds.). (2002). *Sourcebook of criminal justice statistics.* Retrieved June 23, 2002, from http://www.albany.edu/sourcebook.

Mancini, M. (1978). Race, economics, and the abandonment of convict leasing. *Journal of Negro History, 63,* 339–352.

Mancini, M. (1996). *One dies, get another: Convict leasing in the American South, 1866–1928.* Columbia, SC: University of South Carolina Press.

Mead, G. H. (1918). The psychology of punitive justice. *American Journal of Sociology, 23,* 577–602.

Miller, J. (1996). *Search and destroy: African American males in the criminal justice system.* New York: Cambridge University Press.

Myers, M., & Massey, J. (1991). Race, labor, and punishment in postbellum Georgia. *Social Problems, 38,* 267–286.

Oshinsky, D. (1996). *Worse than slavery: Parchman Farm and the ordeal of Jim Crow justice.* New York: Free Press.

Parenti, C. (2000). *Lockdown America: Police and prisons in the age of crisis.* New York: Verso.

Pastore, A., & Maguire, K. (Eds.). (2000). *Sourcebook of criminal justice statistics—1999.* Washington, DC: U.S. Government Printing Office.

Pastore, A., & Maguire, K. (Eds.). (2001). *Sourcebook of criminal justice statistics—2000.* Washington, DC: U.S. Government Printing Office.

Petersilia, J. (1994). Debating crime and imprisonment in California. *Evaluation & Program Planning, 17,* 165–177.

Rabinowitz, H. (1976). From exclusion to segregation: Southern race relations, 1865–1890. *Journal of American History, 63,* 325–350.

RAND. (1997). *Mandatory minimum drug sentences: Throwing away the key or the taxpayers' money?* Santa Monica, CA: Author.

Rose, D., & Clear, T. (1998). Incarceration, social capital, and crime: Implications for social disorganization theory. *Criminology, 36,* 441–479.

Rusche, G., & Kirchheimer, O. (1968/1939). *Punishment and social structure.* New York: Russell & Russell.

Sampson, R., & Wilson, W. (2000). Toward a theory of race, crime and urban inequality. In R. Crutchfield, G. Bridges, J. Weis, & C. Kubrin (Eds.), *CRIME: Readings* (2nd ed.) (pp. 126–137). Thousand Oaks, CA: Pine Forge.

Seigel, L. (2001). *Criminology* (7th ed.). Belmont, CA: Wadsworth.

Shelden, R. (2001). *Controlling the dangerous classes: A critical introduction to the history of criminal justice.* Boston: Allyn & Bacon.

Sherman, M. (1983). Prisons in the theater of American justice. In K. Feinberg (Ed.), *Violent crime in America* (pp. 54–67). Washington, DC: National Policy Exchange.

Simon, D. (1993). *Poor discipline: Parole and the social control of the underclass, 1890–1990.* Chicago: University of Chicago Press.

Tonry, M., & Petersilia, J. (2000). *Prisons research at the beginning of the 21st century.* Washington, DC: National Institute of Justice.

U. S. General Accounting Office. (1996). *Private and public prisons.* Report to Subcommittee on Crime, Committee on Judiciary, House of Representatives. Washington, DC: Author.

Waquant, L. (1999). "Suitable enemies": Foreigners and immigrants in the prisons of Europe. *Punishment & Society, 1,* 215–222.

Waquant, L. (2001). Deadly symbiosis: When ghetto and prison meet and mesh. In D. Garland (Ed.), *Mass Imprisonment: Social causes and consequences* (pp. 82–119). Thousand Oaks, CA: Sage.

Western, B., & Beckett, K. (1999). How unregulated is the U.S. labor market? The penal system as a labor market institution. *American Journal of Sociology, 104,* 1030–1053.

Wilson, W. (1996). *When work disappears: The world of the new urban poor.* New York: Alfred Knopf.

Wilson, W. (1999). *The bridge over the racial divide: Rising inequality and coalition politics.* Berkeley, CA: University of California Press.

CHAPTER 4

The Color of Prime-Time Justice: Racial Characteristics of Television Offenders and Victims

Sarah Eschholz

INTRODUCTION

Television helps to define our world and is a major source of information for the average individual. The typical American spends one-third of his/her leisure time watching television (Stossel, 1997). Television offers viewers vicarious experiences of numerous events that one would not normally encounter. With television it is possible to get live news around the clock, see the ruins of ancient cultures, experience the music of the hippest new bands, and glimpse into the lives of both fictional and nonfictional criminals and victims. In short, television and other forms of media have created a new "electronic space" in our society (Manning, 1996). Though this space is remarkably different from actual experience, in many ways it presents the appearance of reality.

Scholars, politicians, criminal justice professionals, and members of the general public frequently implicate the media in the United States crime problem (Drummond, 1990; Surette, 1998; Van Dijk, 1991). Whereas most public discussion focuses on the impact of the media on violent behavior, scholars also hypothesize that the media has a more general impact on public perceptions, such as fear of crime (Gerbner & Gross, 1976; Heath & Gilbreth, 1996). Additionally, several media events such as the Amadou

The author would like to thank Ted Chiricos for his valuable assistance and guidance in developing the idea for the project and Kimberly Martin for her editing work.

Diallo shooting in New York, the beating of Reginald Denny in Los Angeles, and the O.J. Simpson case have renewed longstanding discussions over the media's role in perpetuating racism (Davis & Gandy, 1999; Entman, 1992; Gilens, 1996; Oliver, 1994).

As people spend increasing amounts of time consuming the media (U.S. Bureau of the Census, 1997; Stossel, 1997), this electronic space, with its appearance of reality, helps define and color viewers' reality (Barak, 1996), much like interactions with friends, neighbors, and coworkers shape perceptions. Understanding television space as an important instrument of social definition, it is possible that viewing television may impact an individual's perceptions of race relations, especially if minorities are portrayed in a negative light. This chapter will explore television portrayals of crime in terms of race in the context of Blalock's (1967, p. 104) "power-threat" and Liska's (1992) "social-threat" argument, that "a high percentage of non-whites produces an emergent property, 'perceived threat of crime.'" Many scholars reference the presence of a stereotypical image of a young black male criminal, both in the media and among members of the general public (Anderson, 1995; Barak, 1996; Skogan, 1995), but few studies have explored the racial makeup of television offenders and victims.

To the extent that television programming is racialized, a case could be made for the role of the media as an ideological instrument that reinforces the dangers of African Americans, particularly young black males. In addition, the chapter will examine how Hispanics[1] are shown on television, given they are the fastest growing minority population in the United States (Marin & Marin, 1991). The racial content of television crime shows will be explored in two ways: (1) the racial typification of crime, or the proportion of all offenders and victims that are black[2] or Hispanic, and (2) the criminal typification of race, or the ratio of offenders to victims within racial categories. Before analyzing data from a content analysis of twenty-six popular evening television programs with a crime theme in 1996, I will examine the theoretical significance of the symbolic race–crime connection that television may be perpetuating.

THEORETICAL BACKGROUND

Ideology has been described as discourse based on reports about a particular situation or problem. These reports justify commands that call for (either directly or indirectly) a unified public response.

Ideologies, then, are belief-systems distinguished by the centrality of their concern for What Is and by their world-referencing "reports." Ideologies are essentially public doctrines offering publicly inscrutable evidence and reasoning on their behalf; they are never offered as *secret* doctrines. (Gouldner, 1976, p. 33)

Through its frequent portrayal of crime in both the news and entertainment broadcasting, television reports that crime is one of the biggest problems facing our country. When crime is seen as a large problem, individuals may be more likely to support politicians who demand more punitive responses to crime.

Ideology is also partisan discourse, so it necessarily presents a one-sided view of reality as if it were reality in its entirety, often distorting at the same time the interests that it supports (Gouldner, 1976). Larrain characterizes negative ideology[3] in two ways that are useful in the present context:

(1) Ideology is a particular form of consciousness, which gives an inadequate and distorted picture of contradictions, either by ignoring them, or by misrepresenting them. (2) Ideology refers to a limited material practice which generates ideas that misrepresent social contradictions in the interest of the ruling class. (1983, p. 27)

These distortions are hegemonic when the majority of individuals in a society accept this consciousness to be natural and do not question the source of this information (Gramsci, 1971). Television is an ideal way to reinforce hegemony because most viewers are unaware that they are being manipulated by the persistent reproduction of one-dimensional images of social life (Marcuse, 1964).

Ideological discourse always serves particular interests, but almost as often, is presented in terms that claim universality as a basis or grounding. If television is ideological discourse, then it is important to try to identify the interests served by the presentation of material concerning crime. Often overlooked is the fact that television's primary function in the United States is not to inform the public, but rather to make profit for its owners (Gitlin, 1980, 1986). As a private industry, television targets specific audiences and will do more to meet their needs than the needs of other viewers. Advertisers pay more for programming when they can be assured that *consumers* between the age of eighteen and forty-nine will be watching a program (Gitlin, 1983; Krajicek, 1998). Regardless of whether the program is a news program or an entertainment program, the events and topics that are covered often focus on the presumed, or in many cases researched, interests of the prime *consumers* in our society. Currently, the most coveted consumers are young and high-income individuals (Croteau & Hoynes, 2001), a demographic group that is predominantly white.

Modern media outlets are increasingly becoming monopolized in our society (Bagdikian, 1997). In 1996, "America's trade publishers belong[ed] to eight huge media conglomerates" (Miller, 1997, p. 11). The same companies that control the book-publishing businesses also have large holdings in newspapers, magazines, television, cable television, multimedia, and other entertainment industries throughout the world. Because of this concentration of ownership, only the largest companies can afford to advertise on television, and this limits smaller businesses' ability to compete in the market. Therefore, the interests most frequently represented on television are those of big business, both the media itself and the companies who use television for advertisements (Croteau & Hoynes, 2001).

Making use of Larrain's (1983) approach to ideology, crime coverage on television can be shown to give an "inadequate and distorted picture of contradictions" in American society. Crime is considered a safe topic for politicians and big business, because of the way the media disseminates crime information. The media overrepresents the prevalence of certain types of violent crime in the United States on a regular basis, while underemphasizing corporate and white-collar crime and harms to the public that result from corporate negligence (Surette, 1998). Media coverage of crime tends to focus on individual pathology (Meyers, 1997) as the reason for crime, while ignoring endemic social problems that may be the structure supporting crime and other serious social problems (Currie, 1993; Wilson, 1987). Even more problematic, the focus on individual pathology is often combined with racialized depictions of the crime problem.

If crime is depicted as the result of individual pathology, then logical solutions to the crime problem focus on individuals. The most popular political response is incarceration. Solutions that suggest the crime problem is a societal problem caused, in part, by poverty and inequality are ignored, and these endemic conditions continue to worsen even when the economy is flourishing by most official measures (Currie, 1993). "This institutional bias does more than merely protect the corporate system. It robs the public of a chance to understand the real world" (Bagdikian, 1990, p. xvi).

The emphasis on individual pathologies also focuses attention on the characteristics of individual offenders and victims shown on television rather than the social and economic conditions that may foster violence and other crime. In this way, race can become the "coded sub-text" about crime (Entman, 1990). Violent crime is scary to members of all classes and can therefore serve to unite groups in opposition to putative threats. Crime, drugs, and violence are safe issues because they appeal to fear for personal safety that members of all classes hold. Although members of all classes, sexes, and races share these concerns, the unity that they offer is a false one, and our understanding of the crime problem in the United States is in many ways distorted.

While distortions may be great for television ratings, advertising efforts, and political campaigns, they can mask very real problems in the United States. Issues such as racism, sexism, classism, the environment, and other pressing social problems are presented from a very limited perspective by the media. One important issue that has received little attention is the alarming expansion of the prison-industrial complex in the United States.

The prison population in the United States increased 242 percent between 1980 and 1995 (U.S. Department of Justice, 1995b). During this same time period there was an 11 percent decline in violent crime as estimated by the *Uniform Crime Reports* (UCR) (Federal Bureau of Investigation, 1996). The *National Crime Victimization Survey* (NCVS) reports similar findings, with a 4 percent reduction in the violent crime rate in the United States between 1980 and 1992 (U.S. Department of Justice, 1995a).[4] Between 1993 and 1996 the NCVS (U.S. Department of Justice, 1997) recorded a 16 percent reduction in the violent crime rate.[5] Scholars have identified fear of crime as one potential reason why the public keeps demanding punitive responses to criminal behavior, and politicians keep building more prisons to house the expanding prison population (Beckett & Sasson, 2000; Chiricos, Eschholz, & Gertz, 1997; Irwin & Austin, 1997).

A closer examination of the growth in the prison population reveals that the incarceration rate of minorities, especially African Americans, is increasing at a much faster pace than the rate for whites (U.S. Department of Justice, 1995b). Specifically, the rate of incarceration for African American males between 1985 and 1994 increased 40 percent faster than for white males (Crawford, Chiricos, & Kleck, 1998; U.S. Department of Justice, 1995b). Between 1960 and 1992 the percentage of nonwhite inmates in prison increased from 32 percent to 54 percent (U.S. Department of Justice, 1995b). This disparity between races is even greater among women (Crawford, 2000).

This is by no means a new issue. Herbert Blalock (1967), with his seminal power-threat (alternatively called racial-threat) hypothesis, argued that political and economic threats posed by a minority population would be responded to by corrective action or policy that would serve to neutralize or minimize the threat and allow the white majority to maintain power over political and economic institutions. This threat is articulated through ideological systems "which explicitly call the nature of the minority threat to the attention of the dominant group members" (Blalock, 1967, p. 160). Once the minority group is defined as threatening, the majority group mobilizes resources and develops policies that minimize the minority group's ability to share power in society.

In 1992, Liska expanded the racial-threat hypothesis to include social threat. Social threat is not limited to political and economic pressures that impact organizations, but also includes more personal threats to morals, values, and personal safety, often expressed in very simple ideological terms. The political and economical threats posed to white majorities by African Americans have gradually expanded to include the threat of crime (Crawford et al., 1998). Young black males are a frequently referenced symbol of crime in the United States, and for many, their presence triggers a fearful reaction (Barlow, 1998; Entman, 1990; Gilens, 1996). Similarly, Hagan and Palloni (1999) recently explored the myth of a connection between Hispanic immigration and crime, which they argue has resulted in excessively punitive immigration laws. Fear of crime increasingly is seen as a link between racial threat and punitive responses targeted against African Americans and other minorities. Several studies have found television to influence fear of crime (see Eschholz, 1997, for a review of these studies), and one study has shown that the racial composition of offenders on television is a significant predictor of fear of crime for whites (Eschholz, 2002).

Scholars and activists alike have been making claims for decades that media representations of minorities are biased and help to both create and perpetuate racism in modern society (Davis & Gandy, 1999; Entman, 1992; Gilens, 1996; Oliver, 1994). The most basic of these claims is that African Americans are disproportionately shown as offenders on both news and entertainment programs. Alternatively, it may not be the *quantity* of depictions of African American offenders, but rather it may be the *quality* of these depictions (Entman, 1992).

Depictions of African American offenders in the media may solidify the symbolic connection between young African American men and crime in the public consciousness. Several media events in the past fifteen years, including the Willie Horton ads used by Republicans in the presidential campaign in 1988 (Anderson, 1995; Mendelberg, 1997), the crack-cocaine epidemic in the mid-1980s (Brownstein, 1992; Reinarman & Levine, 1989), and the more recent focus on juvenile violence and violent crime (Chiricos, 1995), all depict young African American men as central to the so-called crime problem.

James Q. Wilson argues that

[i]t is not racism that makes whites uneasy about blacks . . . it is fear. Fear of crime, of drugs, of gangs, of violence . . . can produce behavior that is indistinguishable from racism. Fear, like racism, can make an officer seek to intimidate a suspect or use excessive force to subdue him; fear creates tensions that lead to the telling of jokes identical to those told by people motivated by pure racism. (1992)

Others interpret fear and the expressions of fear associated with stereotypes as the *new racism* (Mendelberg, 1997; Sniderman, Piazza, Tetlock & Kendrick, 1991), *symbolic racism* (Sears, 1988), or *modern racism* (Edsall & Edsall, 1991; Entman, 1990, 1992; McConahay, 1986). In other words, racism has not been replaced by fear, but instead fear is a form of racism, and as such is a powerful mechanism of social control. Whereas fear of African Americans is a more subtle form of racism than traditional racism, it manipulates a core value in all of us—the need to feel safe.

Several scholars argue that the emotional force of the symbolic connection between race and crime has been manipulated by politicians to win elections and push through a political agenda that negatively and disproportionately impacts African Americans and other "threatening" minorities (Beckett & Sasson, 2000; Chiricos, 1995; Delgado, 1994; Eschholz, 1997; Hagan & Palloni, 1999). Though these claims are frequently made, little research has actually explored the racial content of the media, one of the most frequently cited institutions for the maintenance and transmission of cultural symbols, and fear of crime.

It is not the point of this chapter to argue that television is the producer of the symbolic connection between African Americans and crime in the public consciousness, however, television may serve to reinforce this connection by either portraying offenders disproportionately as offenders (racial typification of crime) and/or by providing relatively few noncriminal alternative images of African Americans (criminal typification of race).

REVIEW OF LITERATURE

It is well documented that both print media (Davis, 1952; Hubbard, DeFleur, & DeFleur, 1975; Isaacs, 1961) and television—including drama, news, soap operas, and cartoons—all greatly exaggerate the incidence of crime in the United States, particularly violent crime (Chermak, 1995; Gerbner & Gross, 1976; Surette, 1998). Both news and entertainment media consistently convey a more violent and dangerous view of our world than exists in reality. Since most of us lack direct experience with many social problems, including violent crime, television and newspapers serve as primary, albeit vicarious, sources of information about these issues. Exaggerated emphasis on violent crime at the expense of other social problems and issues may produce a distorted image of what is important and how social policy should be developed.

Media representations of crime and race have also been described as distorted. The media is frequently criticized for stereotypically portraying crime as a black phenomenon or, alternatively, that blacks are disproportionately portrayed as criminals. Gomes and Williams (1990, p. 61) represent the racial typification of crime argument in their statement that "African Americans are featured in news stories about crime in numbers that are exceptionally disproportional to the percentage of such crimes they commit." Similarly, Sullivan's (1990, p. 28) statement represents the criminal typification of race argument: "As he [the black male] typically appears in the media, he's either a jewelry-bedecked drug pusher, a misogynous pimp or a vicious thug."

The purpose of this chapter is to assess the previous claims that crime in the media is typified in racial and ethnic terms and that race and ethnicity are typified in criminal terms. The portrayal of Hispanics in the media has rarely been examined (Castro, 2002; Dixon & Linz, 2000; Gilliam, Iyengar, Simon, & Wright, 1996). Because Hispanics are the fastest growing minority in the United States, this study addresses the racial *and* ethnic typification of crime and the criminal typification of race *and* ethnicity.

The majority of studies that have addressed either the racial/ethnic typ-ification of crime and/or the criminal typification of race have focused primarily on television news rather than on crime dramas or reality pro-gramming. Eight of these studies were summarized in a recent study (Chiricos & Eschholz, in press). In studies that looked at the racial typi-fication of all crime, only one study (Dixon & Linz, 2000) found that Af-rican Americans were disproportionately shown as offenders compared with whites, and five other studies found the opposite (Chermak, 1995; Dixon & Linz, 2000; Entman, 1992; Entman & Rojecki, 2000; Klite, Ardwell, & Salzman, 1998). In studies that looked only at *nonviolent* crime (Gilliam et al., 1996; Romer, Jamieson, & DeCoteau, 1998) there is no evidence of black overrepresentation. When studies looked at *violent crime, robbery,* or *felonies* (Dixon & Linz, 2000; Gilliam et al., 1996; Romer et al., 1998; Sheley & Ashkins, 1981), black suspects were disproportionately shown as of-fenders compared with white suspects.

Chiricos and Eschholz conclude that

[w]hen the issue is framed in terms of the totality of news coverage, or in terms of non-violent crime, white suspects are actually shown more often. However, when more serious crime, including violence, is depicted or when suspects are portrayed in the menacing context of physical control by the police, black suspects clearly predominate. (In press)

Additionally, the one news study that examined Hispanics showed that they were underrepresented among television offenders (Gilliam et al., 1996). Studies of fictional crime programs generally find that African Americans are underrepresented as suspects (Potter, Vaughan, Warren, Howley, Land, & Hagemeyer, 1995).

Four studies examined the *criminal typification of race,* or the proportion of offenders compared with other roles, such as victims or police officers in crime stories. These studies all found that blacks are consistently more likely to be shown as offenders than in other roles and that there was no such tendency among white portrayals (Chermak, 1995; Dixon & Linz, 2000; Klite et al., 1998; Romer et al., 1998). Chiricos and Eschholz (in press) found that both blacks and Hispanics were more likely to be shown as offenders than in other roles. A study by Oliver (1994) found similar re-sults for reality-based police programs: African Americans and Hispanics were much more likely to be shown as offenders than police officers.

PRESENT STUDY

Methodology

This study was specifically designed to test the following hypotheses:

Hypothesis 1A: African Americans and Hispanics are overrepresented as offend-ers on crime-related television programming;

Hypothesis 1B: African Americans and Hispanics are underrepresented as victims on crime-related television programming; and

Hypothesis 2: In comparison with whites, a larger proportion of African American and Hispanic characters are shown as criminals than as victims.

Fourteen coders were trained to participate in a content analysis of the television programs. Training consisted of (1) an introduction to the survey instrument, including a definition of crime (violent, property, and white-collar crimes) and offenders; (2) watching sample programs together and discussing the coding scheme; and (3) watching sample programs on their own and collectively discussing the results at a later date. Training was conducted during the three weeks prior to the beginning of the actual content analysis. For the actual content analysis, all coders conducted their work independently.

The content analysis examined twenty-six evening broadcast television programs over an eight-week period in 1996. The programs included in the study were selected on two criteria. The first was that the program have a crime theme (programs that focus on an aspect of the criminal justice system, such as *Cops* or *NYPD Blue*, focusing on policing, or *Law and Order* or *Courthouse*, focusing on the courts) or consistently (defined as almost daily) deal with issues related to crime and justice such as news or news magazine programs.[6] The second criterion was that the program be popular. Nielsen ratings were used to determine the programs with a crime theme that were viewed most frequently in the southern capital city examined in this study. Over 90 percent of the programs that had a crime theme and were shown between the hours of 5:00 P.M. and midnight were included in this study (see appendix 4.1 for a complete listing).

A total of 245 episodes of the twenty-six programs—approximately eight episodes per program—were analyzed. Programs that aired only once a week were coded for the entire eight weeks. Programs that came on nightly, such as the evening news, were coded three times a week. The days in which the nightly programs were coded were selected so that each day of the week was viewed an equal number of times during the eight-week period. This means that no one day is overrepresented in the sample. Each program was coded by at least three coders.

The focal point of the content analysis for this survey is a series of items assessing the number and individual characteristics of offenders in each of the crime stories. Coders recorded the race/ethnicity (when identifiable) of every offender shown or mentioned on each of the stories. The operationalization of race/ethnicity was based on observable characteristics and/or specific mention of race by one of the participants in the television program. Race was initially coded as black (African Americans were not separated from other black individuals because this degree of specification was impossible based on television presentations), white, Hispanic, Asian,

Native American, and other. Only whites, African Americans, and Hispanics were analyzed given the small samples of Asians and Native Americans. Approximately 12 percent of the television stories coded for the content analysis were randomly selected to test the inter-rater reliability, which ranged from $a = 0.88$ for the number of Hispanic offenders to $a = 0.97$ for the number of black offenders in a particular program.

Findings

Hypothesis 1A predicts that blacks and Hispanics will be overrepresented as offenders on television compared with actual arrest data. Although no official data is available for Hispanics, Table 4.1 does not appear to support this hypothesis. Whereas 31 percent of those arrested in 1996 were black, only 27 percent of the offenders shown on television were black. When looking at different television genres, the pattern is the same for four of the six types of programs. Local news and national news programming overrepresent blacks as offenders (39 percent and 41 percent, respectively) compared with national arrest data.

Mixed results were obtained for Hypothesis 1B. In terms of victims, NCVS numbers are almost exactly the same as the total television victimization for blacks (16 percent and 15 percent, respectively). Table 4.2 shows these numbers vary significantly based on the program genre. Local news (27 percent) and crime drama (21 percent) overrepresent blacks as victims; however, news magazines (11 percent), reality police programming (8 percent), and sleaze (0 percent) underrepresent blacks as victims. Tables 4.1 and 4.2 collectively display mixed support for the contention that minor-

Table 4.1
Percentage of Black, Hispanic, and White Offenders on Television and in the Uniform Crime Reports in 1996

		Total	Local	National	News	Reality	Crime	
	UCR	TV	News	News	Mag	Police	Drama	Sleaze
% Black	31%	27%	39%	41%	10%	24%	22%	20%
% Hispanic[1]		13%	4%	20%	8%	21%	9%	2%
% White	67%	60%	57%	39%	81%	55%	68%	79%

[1]Arrest data are reported for black and white. Both categories include an undetermined number of Hispanics.
$N = 660$ total television offenders.

Table 4.2
Percentage of Black, Hispanic, and White Victims on Television and in the
National Crime Victimization Survey in 1996

	NCVS	Total TV	Local News	National News	News Mag	Reality Police	Crime Drama	Sleaze
% Black	16%	15%	27%	15%	11%	8%	21%	0%
% Hispanic[1]		14%	17%	18%	11%	21%	6%	5%
% White	81%	71%	56%	67%	78%	71%	73%	95%

[1]National Crime Victimization Survey data are reported for black and white. Both
categories include an undetermined number of Hispanics.
$N = 628$ total television victims.

ities are disproportionately portrayed as criminals or the racial typification of crime argument. This finding is quite surprising because a survey
of television watchers in 1996 found that 75 percent of the respondents
thought that there were more black offenders on television than white
offenders.[7]

Another explanation for viewers' perceptions of television offenders
and victims may be that television uses crime to construct race. One way
to examine this possibility is to look at the ratio of offenders to victims
within racial categories. Table 4.3 clearly shows that crime is used to typify
race on television. In almost every program genre (with the exception of
news magazines) the ratio of offenders to victims are higher for blacks
than for whites. In the national news, reality police programs, and sleaze,
the ratio for blacks is at least four times higher than the ratio for their
white counterparts. This is quite a distortion given the reality that most
crime occurs between members of the same race (Maguire & Pastore,
1999). Hispanics, moreover, have higher offender-to-victim ratios than
whites in the national news, reality police programs, and crime dramas.

CONCLUSION

Television is a frequently referenced repository of ideology in our culture that contributes to the shaping of social problems and solutions. The
media has often been accused of presenting a one-dimensional picture of
the crime problem in the United States that focuses on both violent crime
and black offenders (Davis & Gandy, 1999; Edsall & Edsall, 1991; Entman,
1990; Oliver, 1994). Despite these claims, few studies have examined racial

Table 4.3
Ratio of Offenders to Victims within Racial Categories on Television

	Black	Hispanic	White
Total TV	1.80	.92	.84
Local News	2.20	.39	1.59
National News	2.29	.94	.49
News Magazine	.67	.53	.71
Reality Police	4.34	1.44	1.09
Crime Drama	1.05	1.46	.91
Sleaze	460[1]	.25	.70

[1]Not an exact ratio because the number of black victims was zero.
$N = 660$ total television offenders.
$N = 628$ total television victims.

threat in media presentations in terms of the racial typification of crime and the criminal typification of race, and the studies that exist focus on either news programming or reality police programming. This chapter examined both of these issues for six different program types in an attempt to begin to decode the ideological messages about race contained in modern television network programming.

Much like past studies examining the racial typification of crime, the data on total television crime programs indicate that neither blacks nor Hispanics are overrepresented among television offenders compared with national arrest data. The finding that blacks are not overrepresented in television news relative to whites for all crimes combined is consistent with results previously reported by Chermak (1995), Entman (1992), Entman and Rojecki (2000), and Klite and colleagues (1998). The finding that blacks are not overrepresented relative to whites in television coverage of violent crime departs from previous results reported for Los Angeles (Gilliam et al., 1996) and Philadelphia (Romer et al., 1998) in the early 1990s and for New Orleans (Sheley & Ashkins, 1981) in the late 1970s.

The results for individual television genres show that blacks were slightly overrepresented as offenders on local and national news, but were in fact underrepresented as offenders in news magazine, crime drama, and sleaze programs. The victim data displays a similar pattern. Total television crime programming and NCVS data mirror each other for the black population. Once again, individual television genres vary significantly. Black victims are underrepresented compared with NCVS data in news magazine, reality police, and sleaze programs, while they are over-represented in the local news. This data provides only limited support for the proposition that the media consistently use race to typify crime.

Looking at the data in terms of the criminal typification of race produces much more definitive results. Blacks are consistently shown more frequently in menacing offender roles than in the sympathetic role of victim. The opposite is true for whites. Hispanics are shown more similarly to whites than blacks in this respect. On the whole, blacks are more than two times as likely as whites to be shown as offenders than as victims, and in the national news, reality police, and sleaze programs the offender-to-victim ratio for blacks is at least four times higher than the ratio for their white counterparts. These findings for blacks are consistent with past studies of television news (Chermak, 1995; Chiricos & Eschholz, in press; Dixon & Linz, 2000; Klite et al., 1998; Romer et al., 1998) and reality police programming (Oliver, 1994). The Hispanic findings are not as definitive as the one other study including Hispanics (Chiricos & Eschholz, in press), but this may be a result of the past study's focus on local Orlando news.

Generally speaking, in terms of race and crime the problem with television crime programming is not that offenders are disproportionately black and/or Hispanic, it is that blacks, and Hispanics to a lesser extent, are disproportionately shown as offenders. Images of blacks are clearly skewed in a direction that supports the stereotype of the black offender. Current depictions of minorities on television reinforce notions of racial threat, where minorities are considered dangerous and a threat to morals and values. A greater diversity of television roles for minorities, including more positive and sympathetic portrayals of blacks and Hispanics, might go a long way in countering the current stereotype of the young black male offender.

NOTES

1. I recognize that the use of *Hispanic* as an identifying term is problematic, not least because it conflates many diverse people who may prefer to identify themselves by their country of origin. Ethnic identity, in the full sociological sense of individuals with such diverse origins as Mexico, Cuba, Colombia, Puerto Rico, etc., is most certainly obscured by the more generic reference to Hispanic. Despite these problems, I use the term *Hispanic* in the remainder of this chapter to refer to individuals with Spanish heritage.

2. Though there are important ethnic and cultural differences among those who might be identified as black, these distinctions were not measured because of the difficulty of doing so in a content analysis.

3. Although Gouldner (1976) argues that there is both positive and negative ideology, Larrain (1983) insists that only negative ideology exists, and his definition of ideology is a reflection of this belief.

4. Methodological changes in collecting victimization data in 1993 make comparisons between earlier years unreliable.

5. It should be noted that both measures of crime (UCR and NCVS) have continued to decline to the present, but I focus on 1996 because this is when the television data were collected.

6. The study included both street crime and white-collar crime in its definition of crime. The reason for this inclusion was that corporate or white-collar crime often results in loss of property and physical harm, which may cause people to fear crime generally.

7. This survey was conducted as part of the same research project. In 1996 in the greater Tallahassee area 1,460 individuals were interviewed using random-digit dialing.

REFERENCES

Anderson, D.C. (1995). *Crime and the politics of hysteria.* New York: Random House.

Bagdikian, B. (1990). *The media monopoly.* Boston: Beacon.

Bagdikian, B. (1997). *The media monopoly* (2nd ed.). Boston: Beacon.

Barak, G. (1996). Mass-mediated regimes of truth: Race, gender, and class in crime "news" thematics. In M. Schwartz & D. Milovanovic (Eds.), *Race, gender, and class in criminology: The intersection* (pp. 105–123). New York: Garland.

Barlow, M. H. (1998). Race and the problem of crime in *Time* and *Newsweek* cover stories, 1946 to 1995. *Social Justice, 25,* 149–183.

Beckett, K., & Sasson, T. (2000). *The politics of injustice.* Thousand Oaks, CA: Pine Forge.

Blalock, H. M., Jr. (1967). *Toward a theory of minority group relations.* New York: John Wiley.

Brownstein, H. (1992). The media construction of random drug violence. *Social Justice, 18,* 85–103.

Castro, D. O. (2002). "Hot blood and easy virtue": Mass media and the making of racist Latino/a stereotypes. In C. R. Mann & M. S. Zatz (Eds.), *Images of color, images of crime* (pp. 82–91). Los Angeles, CA: Roxbury.

Chermak, S. M. (1995). *Victims in the news.* Boulder, CO: Westview Press.

Chiricos, T. (1995). Moral panic as ideology: Drugs, violence, race and punishment in America. In M. Lynch & E. Britt Patterson (Eds.), *Race and criminal justice: A further look* (pp. 19–48). New York: Harrow & Heston.

Chiricos, T., & Eschholz, S. (in press). The racial and ethnic typification of crime and the criminal typification of race and ethnicity in local television news. *Journal of Research in Crime & Delinquency.*

Chiricos, T., Eschholz, S., & Gertz, M. (1997). Crime, news and fear of crime: Toward an identification of audience effects. *Social Problems,* *44,* 342–357.

Crawford, C. (2000). Gender, race, and habitual offender sentencing. *Criminology, 38,* 263–280.

Crawford, C., Chiricos, T., & Kleck, G. (1998). Defendant's race and sentencing as an habitual offender. *Criminology, 36,* 481–512.

Croteau, D., & Hoynes, W. (2001). *The business of the media.* Thousand Oaks, CA: Pine Forge.

Currie, E. (1993). *Reckoning: Drugs, the cities, and the American future.* New York: Hill & Wang.

Davis, F. J. (1952). Crime news in Colorado newspapers. *American Journal of Sociology, 27,* 325–330.

Davis, J., & Gandy, O. (1999). Racial identity and media orientation: Exploring the nature of constraint. *Journal of Black Studies, 29,* 367–397.

Delgado, R. (1994). Rodrigo's eighth chronicle: Black crime, white fears—on the social construction of threat. *Virginia Law Review, 80,* 503–548.

Dixon, T. L., & Linz, D. (2000). Overrepresentation and underrepresentation of African-Americans and Latinos as lawbreakers on television news. *Journal of Communication, 50,* 131–155.

Drummond, W. J. (1990). About face: Blacks and the news media. *The American Enterprise, 1,* 23–29.

Edsall, T. B., & Edsall, M. D. (1991, May). Race. *The Atlantic Monthly,* pp. 53–86.

Entman, R. M. (1990). Modern racism and the images of blacks in local television news. *Critical Studies in Mass Communications, 7,* 332–345.

Entman, R. M. (1992). Blacks in the news: Television, modern racism, and cultural change. *Journalism Quarterly, 69,* 341–361.

Entman, R. M., & Rojecki, A. (2000). *The black image in the white mind.* Chicago: University of Chicago Press.

Eschholz, S. (1997). The media and fear of crime: A survey of the research. *Journal of Law & Public Policy, 9,* 37–59.

Eschholz, S. (2002). Racial composition of television offenders and viewers' fear of crime. *Critical Criminology, 11,* 41–60.

Federal Bureau of Investigation. (1996). *Crime in the United States—1995.* Washington, DC: U.S. Government Printing Office.

Gerbner, G., & Gross, L. (1976). Living with television: The violence profile. *Journal of Communication, 26,* 173–199.

Gilens, M. (1996). "Race coding" and white opposition to welfare. *American Political Science Review, 90,* 593–604.

Gilliam, F. D., Jr., Iyengar, S., Simon, A., & Wright, O. (1996). Crime in black and white: The violent, scary world of local news. *Press/Politics, 1,* 6–23.

Gitlin, T. (1980). *The whole world is watching: Mass media in the making and unmaking of the new left.* Berkeley, CA: University of California Press.

Gitlin, T. (1983). *Inside prime time.* New York: Pantheon.

Gitlin, T. (1986). Introduction: Looking through the screen. In T. Gitlin (Ed.), *Watching television: A pantheon guide to popular culture* (pp. 3–8). New York: Pantheon.

Gomes, R. C., & Williams, L. F. (1990). Race and crime: The role of the media in perpetuating racism and classism in America. *The Urban League Review, 14,* 57–69.

Gouldner, A. (1976). *The dialectic of ideology and technology: The origins, grammar, and future of ideology.* New York: Oxford University Press.

Gramsci, A. (1971). *Selections from the prison notebooks.* New York: International Publishers.

Hagan, J., & Palloni, A. (1999). Sociological criminology and the mythology of Hispanic immigration and crime. *Social Problems, 46,* 617–632.

Heath, L., & Gilbreth, K. (1996). Mass media and fear of crime. *American Behavioral Scientist, 39,* 379–386.

Hubbard, J., DeFleur, M., & DeFleur, L. (1975). Mass media influences on public perceptions of social problems. *Social Problems, 23,* 22–34.

Irwin, J., & Austin, J. (1997). *Its about time: America's imprisonment binge.* Belmont, CA: Wadsworth.

Isaacs, N. (1961). The crime of crime reporting. *Crime & Delinquency, 7,* 312–320.

Klite, P., Ardwell, R. A., & Salzman, J. (1998). Local TV news: Getting away with murder. *Press/Politics, 2,* 102–112.

Krajicek, D. (1998). *Scooped! Media miss real story while chasing sex, sleaze, and celebrities.* New York: Columbia University Press.

Larrain, J. (1983). *Marxism and ideology.* London: MacMillan.

Liska, A. (Ed.). (1992). *Social threat and social control.* Albany, NY: State University of New York Press.

Maguire, K., & Pastore, A. (1999). *Sourcebook of criminal justice statistics—1998.* Washington, DC: U.S. Government Printing Office.

Manning, P. (1996). Dramaturgy, politics and the axial media event. *The Sociological Quarterly, 37,* 261–278.

Marcuse, H. (1964). *One-dimensional man.* Boston: Beacon.

Marin, G., & Marin, B. V. (1991). *Research with Hispanic populations.* Newbury Park, CA: Sage.

McConahay, J. B. (1986). Modern racism, ambivalence, and the modern racism scale. In J. F. Dovidia & S. L. Gaertner (Eds.), *Prejudice, discrimination, and racism* (pp. 91–126). Orlando, FL: Academic.

Mendelberg, T. (1997). Executing Hortons: Racial crime in the 1988 presidential campaign. *Public Opinion Quarterly, 61,* 134–157.

Meyers, M. (1997). *News coverage of violence against women.* Newbury Park, CA: Sage.

Miller, M. C. (1997, March 17). The crushing power of big publishing. *The Nation*, pp. 11–18.

Oliver, M. B. (1994). Portrayals of crime, race, and aggression in "reality-based" police shows: A content analysis. *Journal of Broadcasting & Electronic Media, 38*, 179–192.

Potter, W. J., Vaughan, M., Warren, R., Howley, K., Land A., & Hagemeyer, J. (1995). How real is the portrayal of aggression in television entertainment programming? *Journal of Electronic Broadcasting & Electronic Media, 39*, 496–516.

Reinarman, C., & Levine, H. (1989). Crack in context: Politics and media in the making of a drug scare. *Contemporary Drug Problems, 16*, 535–577.

Romer, D., Jamieson, K. H., & DeCoteau, N. J. (1998). The treatment of persons of color in local television news. *Communications Research, 25*, 286–305.

Sears, D. (1988). Symbolic racism. In P. Katz & D. Taylor (Eds.), *Eliminating racism* (pp. 53–84). New York: Plenum.

Sheley, J. F., & Ashkins, C. D. (1981). Crime, crime news and crime views. *Public Opinion Quarterly, 45*, 492–506.

Skogan, W. G. (1995). Crime and the racial fears of white Americans. *Annals of the American Academy of Political and Social Science, 539*, 59–71.

Sniderman, P., Piazza, T., Tetlock, P., & Kendrick, A. (1991). The new racism. *American Journal of Political Science, 35*, 423–447.

Stossel, S. (1997, May). The man who counts the killings. *The Atlantic*, pp. 86–104.

Sullivan, L. (1990). Quoted in Drummond, William J., About face: Blacks and the news media. *The American Enterprise, 1*, 23–29.

Surette, R. (1998). *Media, crime, and criminal justice: Images and realities* (2nd ed.). Belmont, CA: Wadsworth.

U.S. Bureau of the Census. (1997). *Statistical Abstract of the United States*. Washington, DC: Author.

U.S. Department of Justice. (1995a). *Criminal Victimization 1993*. Washington, DC: Bureau of Justice Statistics.

U.S. Department of Justice. (1995b). *Prisoners in 1994*. Washington, DC: Bureau of Justice Statistics.

U.S. Department of Justice. (1997). *Criminal Victimization, 1996*. Washington, DC: Bureau of Justice Statistics.

Van Dijk, T. A. (1991). *Racism and the press*. London: Routledge.

Wilson, J. Q. (1992, May 6). To prevent riots, reduce black crime. *Wall St. Journal*, p. A16.

Wilson, W. J. (1987). *The truly disadvantaged: The inner city, the underclass and public policy*. Chicago: University of Chicago Press.

APPENDIX 4.1

Television Programs by Genre

Local News

5:00 News on 7
5:30 News on 9
6:00 News on 7
6:00 News on 9
11:00 News on 7
11:00 News on 9

National News

ABC Evening News
CBS Evening News

News Magazines

Dateline
48 Hours
Primetime Live
60 Minutes
20/20

Crime Live

America's Most Wanted
Cops
Highway Patrol

Crime Drama

Courthouse
JAG
Homicide
Law and Order
Murder One
NYPD Blue
NY Undercover
Walker: Texas Ranger

Sleaze

Hard Copy
Inside Edition

PART II

Criminal Justice Responses to Crime and African Americans

A common practice in law enforcement involves the use of criminal profiles in which demographic data are employed to identify those individuals most likely to be involved in criminal activities. This practice becomes controversial when it is used by the police to disproportionately stop and detain people of color. A national study of drivers stopped by the police in 1999 found that black drivers over 24 years of age were more likely than their white counterparts to be stopped by the police. Whereas 11.2 percent of the black drivers were stopped by the police, 8.9 percent of the white drivers were subjected to police stops. And among all non-arrested motorists nationally, blacks (6.8 percent) were more likely than whites (3.5 percent) to be searched (Schmitt, Langan, & Durose, 2002, pp. 3, 13). Moreover, this practice (known as DWB, or driving while black/brown) appears to go beyond traffic stops. According to a recent report from the Office of the Attorney General of New York State, during a 15-month period in which the New York City Police Department (NYPD) was monitored, blacks, who represent 25.6 percent of the population, accounted for 62.7 percent of all persons stopped and frisked by the NYPD's Street Crime Unit (Civil Rights Bureau, 1999, p. 109).

Racial profiling has been harshly criticized by various civil rights and minority groups that contend that it promotes racial harassment and leads to the overrepresentation of people of color in official crime statistics. In California, the California Conference of NAACP Branches, the American Civil Liberties Union of Northern California, the California League of United Latin American Citizens, racial-profiling victims, and taxpayers jointly filed a lawsuit in 2001 against Governor Davis of California for eliminating key racial-profiling data collection requirements in that state's Budget Act of 2001 ("Civil rights groups sue," 2001).

The first two chapters in part 2 examine this controversy using a critical criminology perspective. In "Picasso as a Criminologist: The Abstract Art of Racial Profiling" (chapter 5), Michael J. Lynch and Amie M. Schuck argue that inappropriate data are used in the construction of criminal profiles, resulting in distorted criminal profiles that overemphasize the involvement of people of color in crime. The authors conclude that the practice of racial profiling is unacceptable on both moral and ethical grounds. In " 'Driving While Black': Corollary Phenomena and Collateral Consequences" (chapter 6), Katheryn Russell assesses racial profiling through the extended use of anecdotal narratives. Her analysis reveals the potential negative consequences of this practice on both people of color and the larger society.

Not all criminal justice responses focus on minority perpetrators. The passage of the Hate Crime Statistics Act (HCSA) in 1990 resulted in the creation of a new crime label, *hate crime*. The HCSA authorized the federal government to begin collecting data on hate crimes based on race, ethnicity, religion, and sexual orientation. This legislation was largely the culmination of a political alliance involving African American, Japanese American, Jewish, and gay and lesbian groups (Best, 1999). In 1994 the HCSA list was expanded to include crimes based on disability. In chapter 7 Bryan Byers and colleagues look at the hate crime literature and note that African American victims have been curiously underrepresented in the scholarship. They explore several plausible explanations for the relative absence of research on African American victims.

The remaining chapters in part 2 examine various facets of criminal processing. Marvin D. Free, Jr., offers an overview of the empirical research on race and presentencing decisions in chapter 8. Although the literature is sometimes equivocal regarding the impact of race on judicial processing, Free identifies several presentencing decisions that appear to be influenced by the race of the defendant or victim.

Reacting to an apparent increase in violence among youth, legislators in virtually all jurisdictions have lowered the age at which juveniles can be waived to criminal court to be tried as adults. In chapter 9 Becky Tatum looks at the use of waivers in juvenile court. She reviews race, ethnic, and class inequities underlying the origins of the juvenile court and the effects of public perceptions, juvenile justice and political decision making, and discriminatory transfer procedures and laws on the prosecution of minority youths, especially African Americans, as adults. Tatum also discusses the collateral consequences of juvenile transfer policies on minority youths and minority communities.

Finally, in chapter 10 David V. Baker analyzes the effect of race on the most extreme form of punishment in the United States—capital punishment. Currently 38 states, the federal government, and the United States military have capital punishment statutes in force. Only Alaska, Hawaii, North Dakota, Minnesota, Iowa, Wisconsin, Michigan, West Virginia, Vermont, Massachusetts, Maine, Rhode Island, and the District of Columbia do not have provisions for the death sentence (Bohm & Haley, 2002, p. 329). Baker concludes that race influences death penalty decision making in ways that typically favor white defendants and particularly white victims.

REFERENCES

Best, J. (1999). *Random violence: How we talk about new crimes and new victims.* Berkeley, CA: University of California Press.

Bohm, R., & Haley, K. (2002). *Introduction to criminal justice* (3rd ed.). New York: Glencoe/McGraw-Hill.

Civil Rights Bureau. (1999, December). *The New York City Police Department's "stop and frisk" practices: A report to the people of the state of New York from the Office of the Attorney General.* New York: Attorney General of the State of New York. Retrieved January 8, 2002, from http://www.oag.state.ny.us/press/reports/stop_frisk/stop_frisk.html.

Civil rights groups sue Governor Davis for eliminating key racial profiling data collection provisions from state's budget. (2001, November 1). ACLU press release. Retrieved January 8, 2002, from http://www.aclu.org/news/2001/n110101f.html.

Schmitt, E., Langan, P., & Durose, M. (2002). *Characteristics of drivers stopped by police, 1999.* Washington, DC: Bureau of Justice Statistics.

CHAPTER 5

Picasso as a Criminologist: The Abstract Art of Racial Profiling

Michael J. Lynch and Amie M. Schuck

INTRODUCTION

Pablo Picasso was a renowned twentieth century abstract artist recognized for his abstract human portraits. The subjects that comprise his portraits were based on factual observations of real humans. For example, his abstracts could have two eyes, a nose, ears, a mouth, and hair, or all the individual elements that comprise a human face when organized appropriately. For Picasso, however, the two eyes might be placed on one side of the face, the ears grossly uneven, the mouth enlarged and wildly tilted, and the nose elongated and placed to one side of the head. When we observe the painting, the image looks human because it contains all the elements of the human face. At the same time, the painting's resemblance to humans is far enough removed from reality as to be unreal or to be an almost grotesque representation of reality.

It is our contention that current practices of racial profiling are similar to one of Picasso's portraits: both are unrealistic abstractions based on real observations and data. To be sure, racial profiles are often constructed from real observations and data about crimes and criminals. The statistical methods used to build criminal profiles, however, are often misleading and inappropriate. Furthermore, the choice of data sources may also be improper. And sometimes these errors are combined. To the casual observer, nothing appears amiss. Even if inappropriate methods or improper data are employed, the casual or untrained observer sees a more simple fact: statistical models for building profiles were applied to data and appeared to yield a useful outcome predicting the race of an offender. But appearance and reality can be two different things.

It is our contention that the typical statistical technique used to generate racial profiles of criminals creates invalid or biased outcomes and presents an inadequate picture of the reality of crime and race. The error that is made is quite common, and we will explain how and why this error leads to the wrong conclusion.

The consequences of racial profiling are widespread, and we will also discuss some of these issues. For now, it is appropriate to return to our opening statement: racial profiles are similar to the abstract art produced by Picasso. As abstractions racial profiles distort reality while at the same time they are based on reality. In sum, racial profiles present an exaggerated picture of African Americans' contribution to crime.

In this chapter, we discuss the issues surrounding racial profiling. The chapter begins with a brief discussion of the definition of racial profiling. This section is followed by a discussion of the data used in the constructions of racially based profiles and frequent fallacies made regarding the contribution of racial and ethnic minorities to crime when using these data. In that section, we will argue and illustrate why the real profile of a criminal should be a white offender. To provide evidence supporting our contention we employ data from the *National Crime Victimization Survey* (NCVS) to illustrate the real relationship between race and crime. We conclude with an argument against racial profiling that questions the efficacy of profiling as a law enforcement strategy and as an approach to solving crimes that is contradictory to American principles of law and justice.

RACIAL PROFILING: EXAMPLES AND DEFINITIONS

In May of 1992, Robert Wilkins, an African American Harvard Law School graduate and chief of the special litigation unit in the public defenders office in Washington, D.C. was stopped, detained, and searched by the Maryland Police Department for no apparent reason. Wilkins and his family were returning home from his grandfather's funeral in a rented Cadillac when a white state trooper stopped them on Interstate 68 in western Maryland. Wilkins' 29-year-old cousin was driving. The state trooper asked for consent to search the car. Wilkins cited the 1985 Supreme Court decision in *United States v. Sharpe,* which states that an officer needs "reasonable articulate suspicion" that the citizen is involved in illegal activity before he or she can search a vehicle. The trooper told Wilkins that they had a problem with rental cars and drugs on the highway, and this was common procedure. After refusing to consent to the search, the family was forced to stand on the side of the road in the pouring rain while drug-sniffing dogs were called in to help detect illegal contraband. In the end, no drugs were found and Wilkins' cousin was issued a $105 traffic citation (for details see Meeks, 2000).

Wilkins, represented by the American Civil Liberties Union (ACLU), filed a lawsuit and received a settlement from the state of Maryland in 1995. In the course of the lawsuit, a complicated study was conducted of drivers on I-68 and I-95. Several important findings emerged from the study. First, compared with white drivers, black drivers were disproportionately subjected to police stops and searches. Though blacks made up only 17 percent of the drivers on the two interstate highways, they were between 70 and 75 percent of the people stopped and searched by the Maryland State Police. Second, black drivers were no more likely than white drivers to violate traffic laws. Though nearly all (93 percent) drivers were violating some traffic law, black drivers were no more likely to speed and violate traffic laws than white drivers. And third, when cars were stopped and searched, drugs were found at the same percentages among black and white drivers. That is, if the police stopped and searched one hundred white drivers and one hundred black drivers, they would find drugs the same number of times for both white and black drivers.

This study is important because it illustrates how differences in offending by race were generated by police behavior. Researchers found that Maryland State Police were searching seven hundred black drivers for every one hundred white drivers. Even though the proportion of black and white drivers who were smuggling drugs was nearly equivalent, the arrest statistics made it appear that there were more blacks carrying contraband because seven times as many blacks were stopped. To complicate matters further, the police were using arrest statistics to justify additional scrutiny of black drivers (Meeks, 2000). The results of the additional stops and searches of black drivers justified the actions the police were already taking. However, the police would have come to the reverse conclusion had they stopped more white than black drivers. In the end, this study reveals how police behavior, as reflected in arrest data, can generate invalid conclusions concerning racial profiling of criminals.

Wilkins' case is important because it brought national attention to the issue of racial profiling. The practice of racial profiling certainly existed prior to the early 1990s; however, the Wilkins' case generated national awareness about the subject and set in motion a series of public outcries about unfair treatment of minorities by law enforcement officials. The Wilkins' case, along with other lawsuits and subsequent national media attention, has brought the practice of racial profiling to the forefront of public discussion and debate.

Defining Racial Profiling

Despite the fact that there is no single, universally accepted definition of *racial profiling*, the term is most frequently applied to the law enforcement practice of targeting individuals for heightened scrutiny based on their race, ethnicity, or national origin. It is a practice by which racial minorities, particularly African Americans, are disproportionately singled out and subjected to stops and searches. Mimicking the well-known acronym for drunk driving (DWI), racial profiling has been called DWB (driving while black or driving while brown). However, this law enforcement practice extends far beyond driving and includes activities such as riding the train, flying, and even walking (Meeks, 2000).

Racial profiling developed from the more general police practice of criminal profiling. Criminal profiling is a law enforcement effort to identify demographic characteristics and behavioral patterns of offenders based on characteristics of previous offenders who have committed similar offenses. By comparing specific individuals to developed profiles, criminal profiling is a way for the police to predict who *may* be involved in criminal activity. It is important to note that we are talking about cases where there is no direct evidence that the individual has been involved in a crime; but rather that the individual simply possesses characteristics that are statistically associated with crime. These statistical associations, in turn, form the bases for increased police scrutiny.

The Problem with Profiling

It also bears mention that criminal profiling is not an exact science. Researchers have studied the attributes of criminals for more than a century, producing few useful mechanisms for identifying potential or future criminals. Despite the vast amount of research, our own experiences with this literature suggest that even very good criminal behavior-prediction models are wrong (four out of five times) more often than right.

When race, ethnicity, or national origin are used as criteria in developing a profile, criminal profiling can become racial profiling. Racial profiling treats racial and ethnic minorities as criminal suspects based on the assumption that doing so will increase the likelihood of catching criminals. Racial profiling is based upon an assumption about human behavior: namely, that the color of one's skin is a valid indicator for one's propensity to commit crime. This type of criminal profiling (racial) combined with the highly discretionary nature of police work, often creates situations where racial and ethnic minorities are singled out and subjected to surveillance for no reason other than the color of their skin.

Examples and Evidence of Racial Profiling

Several well-known examples of this practice exist. Using racial profiles, Massachusetts police detained baseball announcer and Hall of Fame baseball player Joe Morgan as a potential drug smuggler. After witnessing the unequal treatment of blacks by police, Diop Kamau (formerly Don Jackson), a California police officer, began his own undercover investigation of racial bias in policing. In 1989, Kamau and a friend took an NBC camera crew with them to collect independent verification of their claim that police single out and use excessive force against minorities unnecessarily. The NBC crew filmed Kamau as the police stopped and questioned him for an alleged traffic violation. Kamau, knowing his rights, asked officers to identify the charge against him. They refused. Kamau then refused to produce identification, noting that unless he was being charged he was not required to produce ID. One officer then threw Kamau up against a store window to frisk him, and took his head and smashed it through the plate glass window (to learn more about Kamau, visit his Web site, http://www.policeabuse.org/director.html).

There is an abundance of personal anecdotes and stories that document the practice of racial profiling. Some observers, including many law enforcement officials, dismiss these accounts as isolated experiences of overly sensitive or discontent minorities. However, in recent years, research has emerged that appears to confirm the notion that racial and ethnic minorities are being singled out for heightened law enforcement scrutiny and harassment.

For example, a series of comprehensive research studies conducted in Maryland, New Jersey, and North Carolina have all supported the existence of racial profiling (Verniero & Zoubek, 1999; Zingraff, Mason, Smith, Tomaskovic-Devey, Warren, McMurray, & Fenlon, 2000). Additionally, more recent research suggests that racial profiling may be more than just a localized problem involving a few law enforcement agencies. A national study of police–citizen contacts by the Bureau of Justice Statistics (BJS) suggests that racial profiling may be a widespread practice requiring national attention (Langan, Greenfeld, Smith, Durose, & Levin, 2001). Based on statistical evidence, it is clear that racial profiling exists and that racial and ethnic minorities are disproportionately subjected to police harassment. Overall, the research suggests that law enforcement officials are more likely to target minority drivers for stops and searches, even though they are no more likely to speed and violate traffic laws than white drivers. Yet, despite the fact that minority drivers are stopped and searched more often than white drivers, police officers are more likely to find evidence of criminal activity for white drivers. The 1999 BJS study found that that only 8 percent of searches of black drivers and their vehicles resulted in the discovery of criminal evidence versus 17 percent of searches involving white drivers.

Racial profiling is based on the premise that minorities commit most crimes. This notion is factually untrue. Though we will ultimately reject racial profiling on legal and philosophical grounds, we begin our discussion by assuming that racial profiling can be accomplished. Before we can examine how racial profiles are and should be created, we present a brief discussion of various sources of data that can be used for the purpose of generating racial profiles. This discussion reveals that certain sources of data are better starting points than others for generating racial profiles.

THE DATA: AN ABSTRACTION OF REALITY

Data on Crime and Criminals

There are two broad kinds of data on crime and criminals that also contain measures of race criminologists can use to construct racial profiles: official and unofficial data. Official data are produced by criminal justice agencies and contain information produced at a particular stage of criminal justice processing. For example, official data can be produced by individual police departments and aggregated into national arrest data (the *Uniform Crime Reports* or UCR). Or, these data may be generated by individual state courts (prosecution, conviction, and sentencing data) or by correctional systems (probation, parole, jail, imprisonment, or alternative punishment data). The validity of each of these various sources of data as accurate measures of crime are threatened by a similar problem: most crime is unknown to criminal justice agencies, and it is possible that the portion of crime and criminals to which criminal justice agencies react (arrest, prosecute, convict, and sentence) represents a biased sample. Criminal justice data can only tell us about the race of suspects who are caught, prosecuted, convicted, and sentenced, or those people officially designated as criminals by formal response mechanisms. The problem is that criminal justice decision making, such as the decision to arrest or the decision to prosecute and charge, may be influenced by the race of the defendant (LaFree 1986; Lynch & Patterson, 1991, 1996). These practices create biased samples that overestimate minority participation in crime.

The effect of criminal justice processing on the racial composition of the population of criminals being processed can be easily demonstrated by examining official criminal justice data from 1999. Let us take a succinct look at four different points in the criminal justice system where we know about the race of offenders. Using victimization data, we know that there were 37 black offenders for every 100 white offenders. At the first processing stage, arrest, the number of black offenders per 100 white offenders increased to 71—nearly twice the number of victimizations. Skipping to convictions, the number of black offenders per 100 white offenders increased to 87. By the time we reach imprisonment, the number of black offenders (103) has exceeded the number of white offenders (100). From victimization to imprisonment, there is a 178 percent increase in the number of blacks processed in the criminal justice system. This is useful information because it shows that estimates of how much crime is committed by blacks and whites will depend on the data we use. White offenders are more likely to be filtered out of criminal justice processes than black offenders, increasing black representation among criminal populations at later stages of criminal justice processing. Furthermore, these data illustrate that criminal justice data on racial proportions substantially overstate the participation of blacks in crime.

In sum, two limitations—the large number of unmeasured crimes and the possible impact of defendant's race on decision-making outcomes—restrict the usefulness of criminal justice data for purposes of generating racial profiles. The data reviewed above also make it clear that unofficial data is more useful for understanding the relationship between race and crime.

Unofficial data are designed to measure the full extent of crime and make special efforts to include people who are excluded from official data (people who commit crimes and are not discovered by police). Because unofficial data include information on crimes and criminals not known to criminal justice agencies, unofficial data are a more valid measure of criminals' attributes. Typically, unofficial data are generated through random survey methods, meaning that an individual's race does not affect the decision to include or exclude that person from a study.

Various sources of unofficial data exist. In the next section we briefly discuss the *National Crime Victimization Survey* (NCVS), the largest national source of unofficial data on crime. After describing these data we will use the NCVS to generate a racial profile of criminals.

The National Crime Victimization Survey

What the NCVS Tells Us about Race and Crime

The NCVS surveys people about many kinds of criminal victimization. Most of the time victims and offenders do not come face-to-face, and we cannot use the NCVS to investigate the race of all kinds of criminal offenders. The NCVS does, however, contain information about the race of offenders for three interpersonal crimes of violence where victims and offenders must confront one another: (1) rape/sexual assault, (2) robbery, and (3) assault. We will focus on victim reports of offender race for these three crimes. We include only crimes where there is a single offender because single-offender victimizations comprise the majority (95 percent) of victimizations reported for these three offenses and because some multiple victimizations include offenders of different races, making the counting of these offenses problematic.

Table 5.1 contains some of the basic information we need to construct a racial profile of criminals from NCVS data. Employing these data, criminologists often derive a *standardized crime rate* or victimization rate. We will tell you why this is *not* the correct approach below. For now, let us follow this logic and see what happens.

Table 5.1
1999 National Crime Victimization Data for Rape, Robbery, and Assaults Involving Single Offenders

| | Victim's Race | | | |
| | Black | | White | |
	Number	%	Number	%
Reported Victimizations	867,150	100.0	4,760,930	100.0
Black Offenders	693,720	80.0	657,008	13.8
White Offenders	91,050	10.5	3,546,893	74.5

Note: Percentages do not add to 100 percent because groups other than white or black were omitted.
Source: U.S. Department of Justice (2001).

Calculating Rates of Offending by Race from Victimization Data

In this section we will discuss two means of calculating rate of offending by race. We will also explain why one yields an appropriate outcome, while the other—which turns out to be the method most often used to generate racial profiles—yields the wrong results.

The Standardized Crime Rate or Population-Standardization Approach

Standardized rates of offending are employed so that certain kinds of comparisons can be made about crime across groups and areas. Standardizing by population size allows us to see how much crime there would be *if* different groups in society all had the same base population, which in this case is set to 100,000 people. When we compare population standardized rates of offending by race, we are mathematically calculating the number of offenders there would be for a population of 100,000 blacks and 100,000 whites.

To make this calculation, we need two pieces of information: the number of offenders from each race and the size of the population for each race. From Table 5.1 we know that there are 3,637,943 white offenders (91,050 + 3,546,893) and 1,350,728 black offenders (693,720 + 657,008). Since these data represent the nation as a whole, we need to know the size of the white (211.5 million) and black (34.6 million) population for the United States. For these data, the white rate of offending per 100,000 is 1,720 (3,637,943/211,500,000 × 100,000), whereas the black rate of offending per 100,000 is 3,904. From these data we would conclude that blacks commit 2.27 (3,904/1,720) times more crime than whites. Others who have used these data for the purposes of racial profiling have come up with even higher estimates (Taylor & Whitney, 2002; for criticisms see Lynch, 2002). But this leads to an erroneous conclusion because it assumes that society is made up of an equal population of blacks and whites— 100,000 in each group. Let us consider the racial breakdown in the real world. The United States population is not made up of an even number of blacks and whites. Rather, the U.S. population is approximately 75 percent white and 12 percent black. This means that if we want to derive an accurate racial profile, we cannot use the ordinary crime-standardization technique just reviewed. Rather, we must use an approach that adjusts for the percentage of the population that makes up each racial group. We illustrate this technique below.

The Adjusted Population Size Approach

First, to facilitate our understanding, let us assume we have a population of 100,000 people. We can assume any size population, but the figure 100,000 will provide the easiest example. Of these 100,000 people we will let 75,000 be white (75 percent) and 12,000 (12 percent) be black to reflect the racial composition of the United States population. Now we need to determine how many white and black offenders there will be in this population. This is easily done because we have already calculated the rate of offending per 100,000 for each racial group earlier. We can now multiply the crime rate per 100,000 by a population adjustment, which reflects the percentage of the population made up of each racial group. For whites, we take the 1,720 offenders/100,000 and multiple by 0.75 (because 75 percent of the population of 100,000 is white). Doing so, we find that there are 1,290 white offenders. For blacks we take the 3,904 offenders/100,000 and multiply by 0.12 (because 12 percent of the population is black). When we make this calculation, we discover that there will be 469 black offenders in our population of 100,000. When we compare the number of black and white offenders in a population that is adjusted to reflect the national racial composition, we find that there are nearly 2.8 times as many white offenders as there are black offenders in a group of 100,000 people of mixed races.

In effect, the population-standardization approach and the adjusted population size approach generate opposite conclusions with respect to the issue of race and crime. To be sure, rates of crime are higher within black populations than they are within white populations. We learn this from using the population-standardization approach. Using the adjusted population approach, however, we learn that whites commit more of the overall crime than blacks. In fact, whites commit almost 2.8 times more of the crimes we measured than do blacks. Because blacks and whites do not exist in equal proportions in the real world, the population-adjusted approach is the preferred method for determining which racial group makes a greater contribution to crime. When we use this method to generate a criminal profile, our profile is an offender who is more likely to be white than black. In other words, when we do the math needed to create a profile in a correct fashion, we find that police should be stopping and frisking white people.

We did not need to use quite as elaborate an example as this to illustrate our point. In fact, one can clearly tell that most offenders are white simply by looking at the data in Table 5.1. Nonetheless, we went through this exercise to illustrate that most people who generate racial profiles do so using the incorrect method (standardized population size or the rate per 100,000 approach).

One final observation on racial profiling from NCVS data should be mentioned. A criminal's race can be accurately predicted by knowing the race of the victim. In cases involving white victims, the offender is white 75 percent of the time (about 3.5 million times out of 4.76 million offenses). When the victim is black, the offender is black about 80 percent of the time (693,720 times out of 867,150 offenses). Crime is largely an intraracial phenomenon, involving an offender and victim of the same race. The *easiest* way to generate a racial profile, then, is from the race of the victim.

In sum, data can sometimes be used in the wrong way and generate outcomes that are misleading or untrue. Like Picasso's art, current practices of racial profiling have used real observations and data to produce unrealistic abstractions of the relationship between race and crime. The current practices of using biased data and the population-standardization approach have created an exaggerated picture of African Americans' contribution to crime. We reject these practices and argue that the population-adjusted size approach based on victimization data creates a more accurate picture of the relationship between race and crime—one where the profile of a criminal is a white offender.

CATEGORIZATION: THE MYTH OF IDENTIFICATION

Another important issue regarding the efficacy of racial profiling is the ability to accurately identify an individual's racial or ethnic origin. What does it mean to look black? What does it mean to look Hispanic, Asian, or Pacific Islander? Racial profiling is based on the idea that criminal justice professionals can accurately identify the race, ethnicity, or national origin of individuals. Racial and ethnic minorities constitute a substantial and growing segment of the United States population, and the United States is becoming more and more multicultural. According to 2000 U.S.

Census figures there are over six million self-identified multiracial individuals.

It is one thing to identify yourself as belonging to a particular race because you know your own heritage, and quite another for someone to look at you and place you in a racial group because of your physical appearance. Furthermore, in an era where an increasing number of people are identifying themselves as multiracial, why should others perform a cursory physical inspection and assign you to the one racial group to which they think you ought to belong? Think of some well-known people such as golfer Tiger Woods, actress Halle Berry, singer Paula Abdul, or basketball player, Shane Battier. Each has a mixed racial heritage. Do you think they should be assigned a particular race? And why would doing so be important?

These are imposing issues. But there is an even larger issue looming in the background. That issue involves the assumption that people from different races behave differently. Some people blame these behavior differences on culture. But, there is *no* single black culture in America, anymore than there is a single white culture. Like whites, blacks have different ethnic backgrounds—further evidence that there is no single black American culture. More disturbing are those who believe that the differences in white and black behavior are genetic. Scientific evidence collected under the Human Genome Project (the government makes these data available to the public at http://www.ornl.gov/hgmis) has proven this claim false. On average, there is, for example, more genetic variation within white or black populations than there is across white and black populations. The idea that race predicts behavior is based on highly suspect and unfounded assumptions (Hannaford, 1996; Montague, 1964a, 1964b; Shipman, 1994; for intelligence–genetic links see: Flynn, 1999; Tittle & Rotolo, 2000; for discussions relevant to criminology see: Cullen, Gendreau, Jarjoura, & Wright, 1997; Free, 1996; Lynch, 1998, 2000). It is worth noting that race is a social rather than a scientific concept (Hannaford, 1996) and that the racial group to which a person is identified as belonging can vary depending upon the country in which one lives (Szymanski & Goertzel, 1979).

LEGAL CONSIDERATIONS: FIGHTING RACIAL PROFILING

The American Civil Liberties Union has taken up the battle to stop racial profiling. The organization has engaged in several activities to increase awareness of the problem and to reduce its practice. The ACLU has commissioned various empirical studies, organized a national Web-based reporting system, engaged in numerous media campaigns about the issue of racial profiling, and educated individuals about their rights when stopped by police. Moreover, and probably most important, the organization has filed several lawsuits on behalf of citizens challenging the law enforcement practice of racial profiling. Over a dozen racial profiling lawsuits have been brought in such states as California, Florida, Illinois, Ohio, Oklahoma, Maryland, Montana, New Jersey, Rhode Island, Ohio, Oklahoma, Pennsylvania, and Texas (Meeks, 2000).

In the course of settling many of these lawsuits, law enforcement officials have been required to collect information on the race and ethnicity of individuals stopped, questioned, and searched by the police. This data collection effort has been vital in uncovering the police practice of racial profiling. However, this data collection effort may have an even greater importance in the future. Publicly available information on police stops may be potential mechanisms for holding police accountable for their behavior. If it is possible to readily identify the racial characteristics of those stopped and the reasons for the stops, it will be more difficult for these police practices to be justified and remedial action can be forthcoming.

Understanding the importance of data collection in this area, some states—notably, Connecticut, North Carolina, Kansas, Massachusetts, Kansas, Missouri, Rhode Island, Tennessee, and Washington—legislatively mandated that law enforcement officials collect race and ethnicity information on individuals stopped by the police. In addition, several hundred other police departments have voluntarily agreed to collect this important information (Meeks, 2000; Ramirez, McDevitt, & Farrell, 2000). Certainly, the data collection efforts will encounter many problems and are not a panacea for solving the problem of racial profiling. It is, nevertheless, an important first step in understanding and controlling the problem of differential policing based upon race.

CONSEQUENCES: INDIVIDUAL AND SOCIETY

Racial profiling has very real and profound consequences for both individuals and society. It is both symptomatic and symbolic of larger race relation problems in the United States. America has a long history of differential treatment of racial and ethnic minorities. "The development of social and economic inequalities based on race and ethnicity has been a central theme—and a central dilemma—of the history of the United States, shaped over many generations by the European conquest of indigenous people and by massive waves of both coerced and uncoerced immigration from all over the world" (Pedraza & Rumbaut, 1996, p. xvi). These historic inequalities have often resulted in the persecution of innocent people based on the color of their skin or their cultural heritage. These practices go far beyond the criminal justice system and include many spheres of social life, such as school, employment, housing, and health care.

Individual Consequences

Several reports, books, and newspaper articles have cited numerous accounts of disparate treatment toward minorities by law enforcement officials. Kenneth Meeks' (2000) *Driving While Black* and David A. Harris' (2002) *Profiles in Injustice* portray some of the most powerful personal anecdotes and stories of victims of racial profiling and police harassment. (See also Cornel West's book, *Race Matters*, 1993. In the introduction, Professor West describes how police in Princeton, New Jersey, treated him for driving too slowly while trying to find his new residence in a white New Jersey suburb.)

At the individual level, experiencing racial profiling can be painful and stressful. Recipients can feel mistreated, disrespected, and angry, and such treatment can often contribute to preventing the achievement of personal and professional goals. The frequency with which any individual encounters racial profiling has important implications for his or her psychological functioning and self-esteem.

In addition to immediate psychological effects, racial profiling can have other more long-term consequences. Continued interaction with law enforcement officials may create situations where relatively minor offenses build up a criminal record that haunts an individual and that may result in lost educational and employment opportunities. Racial profiling makes this more likely to happen to racial and ethnic minorities than to whites.

Societal Consequences

Racial profiling also has very profound consequences for society. The widespread practice of racial profiling has a corrosive effect that deeply undermines the legitimacy—and thus, effectiveness—of the criminal justice system. The practice, as well as the perception, that law enforcement officials treat minorities differently fuels the belief that police are biased and unfair. These beliefs often deter people from cooperating with law enforcement officials and cause individuals of all races and ethnicities to doubt the testimony of police.

There exists a divide between the communities served and the police who serve them. Police scrutiny and harassment of minorities have painfully alienated the members of these communities and created a cloud of suspicion over the police who are sworn to protect them. Today, law enforcement officials are looking to the public for partnerships to engage in collaborative problem solving. Trust is a vital component to the success of these types of community policing outreach initiatives. If these police–public partnerships are going to be successful, law enforcement officials need to gain the trust and respect of minority community members.

SUMMARY AND CONCLUSIONS: FINAL THOUGHTS

The focus of this chapter was on issues of racial profiling. We argued against this practice and demonstrated that racial profiling—the assumption that blacks are the crime problem in America—is not valid when data on crime are analyzed appropriately. In short, we asserted that racial profiling is morally and ethnically wrong. It is unconscionable to treat a group of individuals as criminal suspects simply because of the color of their skin. Under the Constitution all Americans are guaranteed equal protection under the law. However, the practice of racial profiling undermines this fundamental core value of American life.

Even though racial profiling undoubtedly captures some who are guilty, it comes at an unacceptably high individual and social cost. The practice alienates individuals. The practice additionally undermines the legitimacy and effectiveness of the criminal justice system.

We must also realize that the practice of racial profiling is a self-filling prophecy. Because police look for contraband primarily among racial and ethnic minorities, they find a disproportionate number of minorities with contraband. As previously noted, the reverse picture of crime would emerge if police targeted whites rather than blacks.

The costs of racial profiling include violating two important principles that Americans hold dear: individual liberty and the assumption of innocence. These two key principles of a free and democratic society are threatened on a daily basis by the practice of racial profiling.

Racial profiling is based on a supposition of guilt rather than innocence. This supposition is based on other assumptions concerning behavior and the color of one's skin that have nothing to do with the probability of an individual becoming criminal. Using this approach one must further assume that it is possible to predict criminal behavior knowing only an individual's race, yet criminologists know that much more complicated models used to predict criminal behavior fail more often than they succeed. Because there is no reliable means of predicting who will commit a crime, relying on race as a criminal predictor is not only unreliable, it is offensive.

In sum, the practice of racial profiling is offensive from a constitutional and legal standpoint, tends to employ inappropriate methods to derive evidence, and yields inaccurate results. Racial profiling is also predicated on the assumption that race and behavior are linked, albeit there is no evidence supporting this contention. For these reasons we object to the practice of racial profiling.

CASE CITED

United States v. Sharpe, 470 U.S. 675 (1985)

REFERENCES

Cullen, F., Gendreau, P., Jarjoura, G., & Wright, J. (1997). Crime and the bell curve. *Crime & Delinquency, 43*, 387–411.

Flynn, J. (1999). The discovery of IQ gains over time. *American Psychologist, 54*, 5–20.

Free, M. D., Jr. (1996). *African Americans and the criminal justice system.* New York: Garland.

Hannaford, I. (1996). *Race: The history of an idea in the West.* Washington, DC: Woodrow Wilson Press.

Harris, D. (2002). *Profiles in injustice.* New York: New Press.

LaFree, G. (1986). *Rape and criminal justice.* Belmont, CA: Wadsworth.

Langan, P., Greenfeld, L., Smith, S., Durose, M., & Levin, D. (2001). *Contacts between police and the public. Findings from the 1999 National Survey.* Washington, DC: Bureau of Justice Statistics.

Lynch, M. J. (1998). Review essay: An historical and "scientific" examination of the social construction of race. *Social Pathology, 4*, 125–133.

Lynch, M. J. (2000). J. Phillippe Rushton on crime: An examination and critique of the explanation of crime in "Race, evolution and behavior." *Social Pathology, 6*, 228–244.

Lynch, M. J. (2002). Misleading "evidence" and the misguided attempt to generate racial profiles of criminals: Correcting fallacies and calculations concerning race and crime in Taylor and Whitney's "Analysis of racial profiling." *Mankind Quarterly, 43*, 313–330.

Lynch, M. J., & Patterson, E. B. (Eds). (1991). *Race and criminal justice.* Albany, NY: Harrow & Heston.

Lynch, M. J., & Patterson, E. B. (Eds). (1996). *Justice with prejudice.* Albany, NY: Harrow & Heston.

Meeks, K. (2000). *Driving while black.* New York: Broadway Books.

Montague, A. (1964a). *The concept of race.* New York: MacMillan.

Montague, A. (1964b). *Man's most dangerous myth: The fallacy of race.* Cleveland: World Publishers.

Pedraza, S., & Rumbaut, R. (1996). *Origins and destinies: Immigration, race, and ethnicity in America.* Belmont, CA: Wadsworth.

Ramirez, D., McDevitt, J., & Farrell, A. (2000). *A resource guide on racial profiling data collection systems. Promising practices and lessons learned.* Washington, DC: Department of Justice.

Shipman, P. (1994). *The evolution of racism: Human differences and the use and abuse of science.* New York: Simon & Schuster.

Szymanski, A., & Goertzel, T. (1979). *Sociology, class consciousness, and contradiction.* New York: Van Nostrand.

Taylor, J., & Whitney, G. (2002). Racial profiling: Is there an empirical basis? *Mankind Quarterly, 42*, 285–312.

Tittle, C., & Rotolo, T. (2000). IQ and stratification: An empirical evaluation of Herrnstein and Murray's social change argument. *Social Forces, 79*, 1–28.

U.S. Department of Justice. (2001). *Criminal victimization in the United States, 1999: Statistical tables.* Washington, DC: Author.

Verniero, P., & Zoubek, P. (1999). *Interim report of the state police review team regarding allegations of racial profiling.* Trenton, NJ: Attorney General, State of New Jersey.

West, C. (1993). *Race matters.* Boston: Beacon Press.

Zingraff, M., Mason, H., Smith, W., Tomaskovic-Devey, D., Warren, P., McMurray, H., & Fenlon, C. (2000, November 1). *Evaluating North Carolina State Highway Patrol data: Citations, warnings, and searches in 1998.* Report submitted to the North Carolina Department of Crime Control & Public Safety and the North Carolina State Highway Patrol. Raleigh, NC: North Carolina Center for Crime & Justice Research at North Carolina State University; Durham, NC: Center for Criminal Justice Research & International Initiatives at North Carolina Central University.

CHAPTER 6

"Driving While Black": Corollary Phenomena and Collateral Consequences

Katheryn K. Russell

INTRODUCTION: STATEMENT OF THE PROBLEM

In the public arena, issues of race continue to command center stage.[1] The ongoing debates and discussions have raised new questions, while not necessarily answering the old ones. Specifically, the recent dialogues have focused on the role that Blackness plays in today's society. Some assign Blackness a primary role, others believe it is secondary. Still others dismiss it as tertiary. These varied positions, ranging from "race has nothing to do with this" to "race has everything to do with this," have in some ways canceled out any meaningful discussion of racial issues. Each of the racial camps has been allowed to claim victory without giving any ground. The result: racial homeostasis.

This failure of movement is particularly troubling given that in the legal arena, Blackness itself faces increasing criminal penalty—both actual and perceived. One of the clearest examples is the phenomenon of "Driving While Black" ("DWB"). This expression has been used to describe a wide range of race-based suspicion of Black and Brown motorists.[2]

Once an offense known and discussed almost exclusively among African Americans, DWB has risen from relative obscurity. Several factors are

Originally appeared on pages 717–731 in volume 40 (3) of the *Boston College Law Review* in 1999. Reprinted by permission.

The author thanks Professors Bernadette W. Hartfield and Ellen Podgor for the invitation to participate in this symposium.

responsible for this. First, the United States Supreme Court decided *Whren v. United States*, involving a Fourth Amendment challenge to possible racial profiling in routine traffic stops.[3] The *Whren* Court held that earlier Supreme Court decisions "foreclose any argument that the constitutional reasonableness of traffic stops depends on the actual motivations of the individual officers involved."[4] The *Whren* decision thus made clear that, in the Court's eyes, traffic stops motivated by the racial prejudices of individual officers do not violate the Fourth Amendment's search and seizure guarantees, at least when there are other reasons for the stop.[5]

Second, during the same time period the Court issued this decision, there have been several high-profile incidents involving allegations of racial profiling. The case of Robert Wilkins, a Black attorney, is among the most notable.[6] Wilkins was traveling with family members, returning home from a funeral. Their car was stopped by a Maryland State Police officer and detained along a Maryland interstate road. The officer told the driver (Mr. Wilkins' cousin) he had been speeding and then requested consent to search the vehicle. After consent was refused, the officers forced the occupants to wait until a narcotics dog was summoned to sniff the vehicle for drugs. No drugs were found and, almost one hour after they had been pulled over, the Wilkins family was allowed to continue on their journey. Following the incident, Wilkins filed a federal lawsuit, alleging constitutional and civil rights violations resulting from racial profiling practices by Maryland State Troopers.[7]

Another case involved a police shooting along the New Jersey Turnpike.[8] Four young men, three Black and one Hispanic, were traveling south on their way to a basketball camp. New Jersey state troopers stopped the van due to excessive speed. The police said that as they approached the vehicle from the rear it moved into reverse. The troopers responded with several rounds of gunfire, striking the van and its occupants 11 times.[9]

Third, in response to the Supreme Court's rollbacks and the escalating number of well-publicized race-based traffic stops, Congressman John Conyers introduced the Traffic Stops Statistics Act.[10] The 1997 bill did not make it through Congress. In April of 1999, however, Conyers introduced an updated version of the earlier legislation.[11] The newer version has several additions, including a requirement that police collect data on gender and record whether the immigrant status of occupants was questioned. The earlier bill was successful in placing a spotlight on the problem of racially motivated traffic stops. The American Civil Liberties Union, for example, initiated a national campaign which highlighted DWB. It ran notices in national publications, including the *New York Times* and *Emerge* magazine.[12] The ad copy read, "Let me ask you something . . . Should 'Driving While Black' be a crime?" It also encouraged support for the Conyers bill.[13]

Finally, journalists have given increasing airtime to DWB.[14] As the number of DWB stories has increased, so has the number of DWB stories involving Black celebrities.[15] In turn, this media coverage prompted the call for stepped-up measures to address DWB.

The prevalence of DWB is unknown. Determining its breath, however, is particularly important as a sociological phenomenon, given the role that cars play in American life.[16] This is particularly true for Blacks who have a historically unique relationship with their cars. During the era of Jim Crow, separate and unequal laws and racial discrimination by white business owners meant that Blacks could not secure hotel accommodations or eat in public restaurants.[17] This forced many of those Blacks driving long distances to sleep and eat in their cars.

The fact that the expression DWB has become commonplace is both heartening and depressing. The DWB shorthand indicates that this form of racial profiling has entered the public's vocabulary. Can it be a good sign that a questionable police policy is so firmly entrenched that it earns an acronym? The very fact that DWB has become so widespread that it has an acronym may mean that it has become an acceptable practice—the acronym makes DWB appear routine, normal, and inevitable.

This Article explores DWB and related phenomena. Further, it considers how these problems affect criminal justice processing in particular and social policy in general. The discussion is divided into three parts. The first part considers ways in which Blackness has become a standard indicator of criminality. The second part provides an overview of the 1997 Traffic Stops Statistics Act. The final part evaluates the social fallout of DWB and its collateral consequences.

COROLLARY PHENOMENA: DWB'S KIN

In recent years, there has been mounting evidence that Blackness has become an acceptable risk factor for criminal behavior.[18] In all facets of life, Blacks report being stigmatized and labeled based on their race. As several high-profile cases make clear, this labeling can have wide-ranging—even deadly—consequences. These cases point to the problem of determining what role race plays in interactions with law enforcement. At the same time, however, these examples indicate that in some instances the *perception* that race matters means that race matters. Further, individual cases can be explained, dismissed, and justified. In their aggregate, the stream of anecdotal cases which suggest that Blackness can be equated with criminality has social consequences. A few examples follow.[19]

Walking While Black

Paul Butler, a Black professor in Washington, D.C., describes his experience of being stopped, questioned, and hassled by police, as he returned home by foot one evening.[20] Butler details his ongoing discussion with Metropolitan Police officers, who insisted that he show them identification before being allowed to continue on this way. Butler stood his ground, and the officers left only after a neighbor identified him.

Idling While Black

In December of 1998, Tyisha Miller, a nineteen-year-old Black woman, was shot and killed by Riverside, California, police after they responded to a call.[21] Miller's car had a bad tire late one night, and she stayed with the car, parked at a gas station, while her friend got a ride home and called Miller's family. As her friend left, Miller rolled up the windows, turned up the car's heat and radio, and tipped her seat back. When Miller's cousin and a friend arrived at the gas station to help, the cousin found Miller locked in the car, foaming from the mouth, and unresponsive to shouts and banging on the window. A gun was in Miller's lap.

The friend called 911 to summon police help, reporting they could not wake Miller and that she had a gun in her lap. When the police arrived, Miller's cousin told them that Miller was in medical distress and again mentioned the gun. The police responded by breaking Miller's car window and shooting inside. Miller was struck twelve times in the head and back.

Police initially claimed that Miller shot at them and they simply returned fire. The four officers involved subsequently backed away from their initial story, and the police found no evidence that Miller had fired the gun. One of the more unsettling aspects of the case has been that, for many Blacks, it underscores the paradoxical threat of the police. Some even blame Miller's cousin for her death, claiming "You killed her! You called 911!"[22]

Standing While Black

This is the name Professor David Cole gives to the crime created by the ordinance at issue in *City of Chicago v. Morales*.[23] The controversial Chicago ordinance makes it a crime for gang members, or anyone who associates with them, to stand on a public street with no discernible purpose. It empowers police to stop anyone they "reasonabl[y] believe to be a criminal street gang member loitering in any public place with one or more other persons."[24] The *Morales* Court observed that the vagueness of such an ordinance does not discourage arbitrary or discriminatory enforcement.[25] The ordinance is eerily reminiscent of a Georgia slave code statute which stated, "Any person who sees more than seven men slaves without any white person, in a high road, may whip each slave twenty lashes."[26]

Shopping While Black

In a widely reported 1995 incident, three young Black men, shopping at a suburban Washington, D.C., Eddie Bauer store, reported being harassed and embarrassed.[27] An off-duty police officer, moonlighting as a store security officer, suspected that one of the youths, Alonzo Jackson, had stolen a shirt from the store. The youth, when questioned, told store employees that he had purchased the shirt at that store the previous day. His story was not considered credible and he was told he would have to *remove the shirt he was wearing* before he would be allowed to leave the store. The three youths filed a federal civil rights lawsuit against Eddie Bauer, alleging "consumer racism." After finding that the young men had been falsely imprisoned and defamed and that Eddie Bauer negligently supervised its security guards, the jury awarded $1 million in damages.[28]

... While Black

There are numerous other miscellaneous offenses which fall under the *while Black* umbrella. One example is bus riding while Black. One such incident involved John Gainer, a Black music professor at the University of Oregon. Based on a grainy enlarged photo of a different man suspected in a motel robbery, a mall security guard mistook Gainer for the robbery suspect and called the police. Police boarded the city bus Gainer was leaving on and asked him to exit the bus to answer questions. Soon after Gainer left the bus, however, police discovered the mistake. This was the second time in two years that police pulled Gainer off a city bus to question him about crimes he did not commit. The first time, after a series of mail thefts, a bystander saw Gainer closely scrutinizing mailbox numbers and called the police. Gainer, who is legally blind, told the police he was simply looking for a house to rent.[29]

The above anecdotes exemplify the extent to which society allows Blackness to be equated with criminality. Further, it is noted that there are numerous other ways in which Blackness has been targeted and criminalized, such as legislation enacted explicitly to address what is perceived as Black deviance.[30] Although some might argue that race-based police practices simply reflect crime rates, this view raises as many questions as it answers.[31]

A review of American history indicates that equating Blackness with criminality has long been a profitable enterprise. Professor Frederick Dennis Greene provides an interesting analysis of the parallels between the economics of the U.S. slave trade and today's prison system, as evidenced by the explosion in incarceration and prison construction.[32] In this mushrooming incarceration, Blacks are six times more likely than whites to be held in jail or prison.[33] This incarceration suggests that DWB and other While Black offenses are part of a much larger social problem.[34]

Mountains of anecdotes from the rich, famous, and otherwise, have not resulted in a tangible, productive response to the problem of DWB. In order to move the debate beyond anecdote and personal narrative, it is clear that something more is needed. Enactment of the Traffic Stops Statistics Act has the potential to further transform the debate from an individual, microlevel issue, to a societal, macrolevel concern. The next section details and critiques this legislative response to DWB.

RAY OF LIGHT? THE TRAFFIC STOPS STATISTICS ACT[35]

For almost two years, the proposed Traffic Stops Statistics Act ("the Act"), offered a beacon of hope for altering the racial landscape of routine traffic stops.[36] The 1997 act and its updated version would require record keeping for each traffic stop. An officer who pulled over a motorist would have had to record an array of data for each traffic stop, including the race and age of the person stopped, whether a search was conducted and whether it produced contraband, whether a citation or ticket was issued, and the legal basis for the stop.[37]

Not surprisingly, the proposed legislation and its state-level counterparts[38] have sparked a good bit of controversy and support. Police unions, for instance, have raised two main objections. First, such a law would place an undue burden on an already overworked police force. Second, such legislation would reverse years of police training designed to discourage officers from seeing race. The International Association of Chiefs of Police, the largest organization of police executives, opposes any such legislation.[39] The National Organization of Black Law Enforcement Executives, however, has voiced support for the Conyers legislation.[40]

Aside from objections raised by law enforcement, the bill's wording was problematic and its approach too narrow. First, it did not require any data about the police officer (e.g., age, race). Second, it would not have provided information on the location of traffic stops (e.g., city, state). As a result, the data could not be used to discern possible trends in DWB stops. Furthermore, the collected data were only to be used for research or data collection; the data would not be available for litigation purposes.

The failure to pass either federal or state legislation—or adopt other measures in their place—that would provide a picture of the role of race and traffic stops leaves us where we started. The law's failure to respond proactively to the documented problem of DWB has several consequences. For one, the absence of a way to measure the breadth and scope of the practice forces reliance on anecdotes and lawsuits. As a result, a great deal of what has been learned about racial profiling in traffic stops has been filtered through civil actions, such as Robert Wilkins' case.[41]

The settlement in *Wilkins* revealed the degree to which Maryland State

Troopers target Black motorists.[42] The terms of the settlement mandated the maintenance of computer records for all motorist stops. Along the Interstate 95 corridor, Black motorists, who comprise about 17 percent of motorists, comprised *more than 70 percent* of the people stopped by the Maryland State Troopers between 1995 and 1997.[43] Amazingly, the racial imbalance in traffic stops persisted even after troopers were notified that their stops were being monitored.[44]

The singling out of minority motorists represents an egregious, identifiable harm. There are, however, other, subtler outcomes that may sprout from these practices. The next section considers the possible fallout from society's failure to rein in DWB and DWB-related incidents.

COLLATERAL CONSEQUENCES OF FAILURE TO ACT

This Article has argued that DWB is part of a larger phenomenon that increasingly criminalizes Blackness. There are several potential outcomes from our continued failure to respond to the increased equating of Blackness with criminality. Two recent examples follow.

Legal Circumvention

In *United States v. Leviner*,[45] Federal District Judge Nancy Gertner issued a downward departure in the federal sentencing guidelines.[46] The reasoning behind the downward departure makes this otherwise unremarkable case remarkable. Alexander Leviner had several prior convictions before the subject of the case—being a felon in possession of a handgun. Under the guidelines, Leviner's criminal history classified him as a Category V offender, the second-highest category.[47] After reviewing the record, Judge Gertner made two observations. First, that Leviner was Black. Second, she pointed out that most of his prior convictions were for motor vehicle offenses.[48] These factors led Judge Gertner to conclude that Leviner's priors were likely a result of DWB stops:

Motor vehicle offenses in particular, raise deep concerns about racial disparity. Studies from a number of scholars, and articles in the popular literature have focused on the fact that African American motorists are stopped and prosecuted for traffic stops, more than any other citizens. And if that is so, then it is not unreasonable to believe that African Americans would also be imprisoned at a higher rate for these offenses, as well.[49]

It is unclear whether other judges have taken action similar to Gertner. It is known, however, that in other contexts federal judges have sought relief from harsh, racially disparate laws. The response of some federal judges to the federal crack statute provides one such example. Indeed, more than a few federal judges have balked at the disparity between crack and powder cocaine sentences and at their racially disparate impact.[50] Some judges have resigned in protest,[51] while others have apologized to defendants in advance of sentencing.[52]

Public Policy Fallout

A recent case involving the National Urban League illustrates another negative consequence of failing to address the DWB issue. In the fall of 1998, the Urban League withdrew from the Clinton administration's Buckle Up America campaign.[53] The drive, which would make failure to wear a safety belt a primary traffic offense, would allow police officers to stop and ticket motorists for neglecting to do so. Citing concerns and fears that such a practice would result in increased racial profiling of Blacks, the Urban League withdrew its support.

The Urban League's response, though understandable, is problematic. This is especially true given that young Black and Hispanic motorists are *twice* as likely as their white counterparts to die in crashes due to failure to wear seat belts.[54] Furthermore, the failure to address the problem of seat belt use in Black and Hispanic communities increases the probability of not only higher mortality rates, but also increased auto insurance premiums and hospital costs for crash-related injuries. The Urban League's response indicates that the problem of DWB extends beyond the criminal justice system and impacts support for social policies. This stance has the potential for creating as much harm as it seeks to prevent. The Urban League's position symbolizes the tension between Blacks and the law enforcement community.

Other Responses

In addition to legal circumvention and public policy fallout, the DWB problem undoubtedly has additional ramifications. Moreover, the overarching issue of equating Blackness with deviance has a wide range of social costs. These include racial hoaxes,[55] anti-Black conspiracies,[56] lack of trust between police and Black and Hispanic communities, and a more general racial alienation.[57]

CONCLUSION

This Article provides a brief overview of various ways that Blackness has been criminalized and associated with deviance. The discussion has primarily centered on DWB and the host of legal, social, and empirical questions raised by this recent phenomenon. It is argued that although

DWB is among the most well-known crimes of Blackness, it is hardly the only one of its kind. In fact, the net which criminalizes Blackness has been cast far and wide.

It is, therefore, not surprising that the societal consequences of failing to address DWB and related phenomena, are grave indeed. The association of crime and deviance triggers a predictable cycle of events. First, it increases the probability that Blacks will be targeted for arrest. This in turn increases the probability that Blacks will be convicted and incarcerated for crimes.[58] Following logically, the enhanced likelihood of a felony conviction increases the likelihood of disenfranchisement.[59] Further, a felony conviction increases social marginality in many tangible ways, such as circumscribing employment possibilities (thereby increasing the probably of reoffending).

The impact of this goes far beyond those particular African Americans who have directly experienced racial targeting. As discussed above, it affects Blacks as a group and alters their response to the criminal justice system. As important, however, is the fact that criminalizing Blackness taints the image that every other racial group—whites, American Indians, Asians, and Hispanics—have of Blacks. These images, which have historically materialized into racially skewed criminal justice policy, regenerate the cycle.

NOTES

1. One salient example is President Clinton's 1997 initiative on race. *See* PRESIDENT'S INITIATIVE ON RACE, ONE AMERICA IN THE 21ST CENTURY: THE PRESIDENT'S INITIATIVE ON RACE (1998). Another is the public debate following publication of Richard J. Herrnstein and Charles Murray's book, THE BELL CURVE: INTELLIGENCE AND CLASS STRUCTURE IN AMERICAN LIFE (1994).

2. DWB has also been used to indicate *driving while Brown*—the racial profiling of Hispanic motorists. Blacks and Hispanics, however, are not the only minorities who report being subjected to traffic stops on the basis of race. *See, e.g.*, LESLIE MARMON SILKO, YELLOW WOMAN AND A BEAUTY OF THE SPIRIT: ESSAYS ON NATIVE AMERICAN LIFE TODAY 107–23 (1996) (describing the Immigration and Naturalization Service Border Patrol's detention and harassment of Native American motorists). Racial profiling could be the result of an express police department policy, for example, where police department memoranda identify a particular racial group as part of its drug courier profile. It could also be the result of an informal, implied policy in which race is relied upon to determine whether stops are made. *See infra* notes 8–9 and accompanying text (discussing practices of New Jersey State Troopers). Racial profiling might also be the result of an individual officer's practices, based on stereotypes and prior experiences.

3. 116 S. Ct. 1769, 1772–73 (1996); *see also* Maryland v. Wilson, 117 S. Ct. 882 (1997) (regarding police conduct during routine traffic stops); Ohio v. Robinette, 117 S. Ct. 417 (1996) (same).

Though the U.S. Supreme Court has not expressly used the term *driving while Black*, it has appeared in decisions by lower courts. *See, e.g.,* Washington v. Lambert, 98 F.3d 1181, 1188 (9th Cir. 1996) ("There's a moving violation that many African Americans know as D.W.B.: Driving While Black." [quoting Henry L. Gates, Jr., *Thirteen Ways of Looking at a Black Man,* NEW YORKER, Oct. 23, 1995, at 59]).

4. 116 S. Ct. at 1774.

5. The Court did note, however, that selective enforcement of the law based upon race could be challenged under the Equal Protection Clause. *See id.* For detailed discussion and analyses of the *Whren* decision, *see* Angela J. Davis, *Race, Cops, and Traffic Stops,* 51 U. MIAMI L. REV. 425, 432–38 (1997); David A. Harris, *Car Wars: The Fourth Amendment's Death on the Highway,* 66 GEO. WASH. L. REV. 556 (1998); Carl J. Schifferle, *After* Whren v. United States: *Applying the Equal Protection Clause to Racially Discriminatory Enforcement of the Law,* 2 MICH. L. & POL'Y REV. 159 (1997); David A. Sklansky, *Traffic Stops, Minority Motorists, and the Future of the Fourth Amendment,* 1997 SUP. CT. REV. 271, 277–79 (1998); Craig M. Glantz, Note, *"Could" This Be the End of Fourth Amendment Protections for Motorists?:* Whren v. United States, *116 S. Ct. 1769 (1996),* 87 J. CRIM. L. & CRIMINOLOGY 864 (1997); Jennifer A. Larrabee, Note, *"DWB (Driving While Black)" and Equal Protection: The Realities of an Unconstitutional Police Practice,* 6 J.L. & POL'Y 291 (1997).

6. *See, e.g.,* Melba Newsome, *Power: The Usual Suspects,* VIBE, Sept. 1998, at 109.

7. The eventual settlement of the Wilkins case involved monetary damages and injunctive relief. *See* Davis, *supra* note 5, at 440. As Davis relates:

The Maryland State Police consented to adopt a policy prohibiting the use of race-based drug courier profiles as a law enforcement tool. They further agreed that the policy would direct all Maryland State Police not to use a race-based profile as a cause for stopping, detaining or searching motorists traveling on Maryland roadways.

Id. (citing Settlement Agreement, Wilkins v. Maryland State Police, United States District Court for the District of Maryland, Civil Action No. MJG-93-468). For an interesting analysis of the Wilkins case and discussion of related issues, *see* Davis, *supra* note 5, at 438–42.

8. *See* John Kifner & David M. Herszenhorn, *Racial "Profiling" at Crux of Inquiry Into Shooting by Troopers,* N.Y. TIMES, May 8, 1998, at B1. For an overview and critique of racial profiling on the New Jersey Turnpike, *see* John Lamberth, *Driving While Black; A Statistician Proves that Prejudice Still Rules the Road,* WASH. POST, Aug. 16, 1998, at C1.

9. During the past year, the New Jersey Attorney General's office investigated traffic stops made by 164 New Jersey Troopers. Investigators discovered that some troopers routinely falsified the race of the drivers they stopped. Further, the investigation revealed the practice of *ghosting.* Some troopers may have used this scheme to hide the fact that they were targeting minority drivers for traffic stops. "Two state police supervisors said it was common practice for troopers on the turnpike to jot down the license plate number of white motorists who were not stopped and use them on the reports of blacks who were pulled over." David Kocieniewski, *Trenton Charges 2 Troopers with Faking Drivers' Race,* N.Y. TIMES, Apr. 20, 1999, at A23.

10. *See* H.R. 118, 105th Cong. (1997); *see also* Kevin Merida, *Decriminalizing "Driving While Black,"* EMERGE, Dec.-Jan. 1999, at 26 (noting John Conyers' introduction of the bill and discussing the bill's provisions); *infra* notes 35–44 and accompanying text.

11. *See* Traffic Stops Statistics Study Act of 1999, H.R. 1443, 106th Cong. (1999).

12. *See, e.g.,* EMERGE, Dec.-Jan. 1998, at 31.

13. The notice also includes the ACLU Web site, (http://www.aclu.org/forms/trafficstops.html) and encourages readers to complete a complaint form. *See id.*

14. *See, e.g.,* Timothy Egan, *On Wealthy Island, Being Black Means Being a Police Suspect,* N.Y. TIMES, May 10, 1998, at 12; Michael A. Fletcher, *Driven to Extremes; Black Men Take Steps to Avoid Police Stops,* WASH. POST, Mar. 29, 1996, at A1; Newsome, *supra* note 6; Hart Seely, *Black Males Say Its Normal for Police to Find an Excuse to Stop Their Cars and Hunt for Drugs,* SYRACUSE HERALD AM., Oct. 22, 1995, at A12.

15. A short roll call of names of well-known Black men, who have been subject to DWB, include: Marcus Allen, Le Var Burton, Calvin Butts, Johnnie Cochran, Christopher Darden, Miles Davis, Michael Eric Dyson, Al Joyner, Wynton Marsalis, Joe Morgan, Walter Mosley, Edwin Moses, Will Smith, Wesley Snipes, Blair Underwood, Cornel West, Jamaal Wilkes, Roger Wilkins, and William Julius Wilson. *See, e.g.,* KATHERYN K. RUSSELL, THE COLOR OF CRIME: RACIAL HOAXES, WHITE FEAR, BLACK PROTECTIONISM, POLICE HARASSMENT, AND OTHER MACROAGGRESSIONS 36 (1998). For many Blacks, including the author, stories of DWB are part of family lore. As a child, I heard stories about racially motivated traffic stops. One incident, involving my father's brother, stands out. My uncle, who at the time drove a Lamborghini—a distinctive, rare sports car—was stopped by the police. The officer informed him that there had been a report of a stolen vehicle fitting his car's description. My uncle asked him the make of the stolen vehicle. The officer, apparently not sure what type of car my uncle was driving, could not answer.

16. *See, e.g.,* Harris, *supra* note 5, at 576 ("[N]o activity is common to more Americans than driving or riding in a car.").

17. *See, e.g.,* Katzenbach v. McClung, 379 U.S. 294 (1964); Heart of Atlanta Motel, Inc. v. United States, 379 U.S. 241 (1964).

18. For an interesting discussion of the historical and contemporary link between Blackness and criminality, *see* Tracey Maclin, *Race and the Fourth Amendment,* 51 VAND. L. REV. 333, 333–36 (1998). Professor Maclin observes that "[t]oday, police departments across the nation . . . continue to target blacks in a manner reminiscent of the slave patrols of colonial America." *Id.* at 336; *see also* CHARSHEE C.L. MCINTYRE, CRIMINALIZING A RACE: FREE BLACKS DURING SLAVERY 167–88 (1993).

19. It is noted that while most of the DWB incidents referenced in this Article involve Black males, Black females also report being subject to race-based traffic stops. *See* RUSSELL, *supra* note 15, at 36 (describing Black astronaut Mae Jemison's brush with police); *infra* note 28 (summarizing Lubbock, Texas, incident involving Hampton University basketball coaches, Patricia Bibbs and Vanetta Kelso).

20. *See* Paul Butler, *"Walking While Black": Encounters with the Police on My Street,* LEGAL TIMES, Nov. 10, 1997, at 23.

21. *See* William Booth, *Calif. Police Shooting, Veiled in Gray, Becomes Black-White Issue,* WASH. POST, Jan. 10, 1999, at A3; Don Terry, *Unanswered Questions in a Fatal Police Shooting,* N.Y. TIMES, Jan. 9, 1999, at A8. The U.S. Attorney's office has an-

nounced that it will initiate an inquiry into whether Miller's civil rights were violated. *See U.S. to Investigate Killing of Teenager*, N.Y. TIMES, Jan. 5, 1999, at A13.

22. Terry, *supra* note 21, at A8.

23. *See* David Cole, *"Standing While Black,"* THE NATION, Jan. 4, 1999, at 24. *See generally* CHICAGO, ILL., MUNICIPAL CODE § 8-4-015 (added June 17, 1992), *available* <http://www.chicityclerk.com/legislation/codes/chapter8_4.html >; City of Chicago v. Morales, 687 N.E.2d 53 (Ill. 1997). For a discussion of the ordinance, *see* Cole, *supra*.

24. CHICAGO, ILL., MUNICIPAL CODE § 8-4-015. The ordinance carries up to a $500 fine, six months imprisonment, and 120 hours of community service. *See id.*

25. *See Morales*, 687 N.E.2d at 63.

26. J. Clay Smith, Jr., *Justice and Jurisprudence and the Black Lawyer*, 69 NOTRE DAME L. REV. 1077, 1109 (1994) (quoting Georgia's Act of Dec. 13, 1792).

27. *See, e.g.*, Joann Loviglio, *Eddie Bauer Discrimination Case Goes to Jury in Greenbelt Court*, DAILY REC. (Baltimore), Oct. 8, 1997, at 19.

28. *See, e.g.*, Joann Loviglio, *Civil Rights Not Violated, But Eddie Bauer Told to Pay $1 Million in Shoplifting Case*, LEGAL INTELLIGENCER, Oct. 10, 1997, at 4 (Alonzo Jackson was awarded $850,000 and the other young men awarded $75,000 apiece). There have been other court cases which have alleged consumer racism. *See, e.g.*, Steven A. Holmes, *Large Damage Award to Black Whom Store Suspected of Theft*, N.Y. TIMES, Dec. 11, 1997, at A17 (citing case finding Dillard's department store engaged in systematic discrimination against Black customers, with federal jury awarding plaintiff Paula Hampton $1.56 million). Anecdotal incidents of racial discrimination while shopping abound. *See, e.g.*, PATRICIA J. WILLIAMS, THE ALCHEMY OF RACE AND RIGHTS 44–47 (1991). In a recent case, two Black Hampton University basketball coaches were stopped and detained by police in Lubbock, Texas. The coaches, in town for a game against Texas Tech, were arrested and charged with running a confidence game. It was later determined that the two had been mistakenly suspected. *See* Mark Asher, *Hampton Coach Decries Being "Falsely Accused,"* WASH. POST, Nov. 19, 1998, at E1.

29. *See Black Professor Mistaken for Robbery Suspect—Again*, Associated Press, Dec. 29, 1998; *cf. How About Some Common Sense?*, THE BULLETIN (Bend, Or.), Jan. 6, 1999, at A6 (editorial recounting these repeated mistaken police apprehensions of Gainer but arguing racism was not involved). For more examples of how Blackness has been used as indicia of criminality, *see* DAVID COLE, NO EQUAL JUSTICE: RACE AND CLASS IN THE AMERICAN CRIMINAL JUSTICE SYSTEM 16–62 (1999).

30. *See, e.g.*, DOROTHY ROBERTS, KILLING THE BLACK BODY: RACE, REPRODUCTION, AND THE MEANING OF Liberty 150–201 (1997). Roberts offers an incisive critique of how laws have been used to criminalize Black reproduction. The federal crack statute, which punishes possession of crack one hundred times more severely than powder cocaine, is another example of a law enacted partly due to racial fears. The bill was passed partly in response to the wide-spread fear that inner city crack and its problems would spread to the suburbs. For a detailed discussion of the historical relationship between race and federal drug laws, *see* United States v. Clary, 846 F. Supp. 768 (E.D. Mo. 1994), *rev'd*, 34 F.3d 709 (8th Cir. 1994).

31. The argument is that Blacks are more likely to arouse police suspicion because Blacks are more likely to commit street crime. It is true that Blacks are

disproportionately more likely to engage in street crime. Their rates of criminal involvement, however, do not approximate their encounters with the police. While Blacks are responsible for approximately one-third of all street crime, studies indicate that nearly half report having been watched or stopped by the police when they have done nothing wrong. *See, e.g.,* Sandra Lee Browning et al., *Race and Getting Hassled by the Police,* 17 POLICE STUD. 1, 3, 6 (1994) (finding that about 47 percent of Blacks and 10 percent of whites surveyed report being "personally hassled" by police; 66 percent of Blacks and 12.5 percent of whites report "vicarious hassling" by police [knowing someone who has been hassled by police]).

32. *See* Frederick Dennis Greene, *Immigrants in Chains: Afrophobia in American Legal History—The Harlem Debates Part 3,* 76 OR. L. REV.537, 562–65 (1997). Notably, increases in incarceration and prison construction are occurring despite the fact that since 1980 the total crime rate has generally decreased. *See* SOURCEBOOK OF CRIMINAL JUSTICE STATISTICS—1997, at 261 tbl. 3.111, 285 tbl. 3.120 (Kathleen Maguire & Ann L. Pastore eds., 1998).

33. *See* Fox Butterfield, *Number of Inmates Reaches Record 1.8 Million,* N.Y. TIMES, Mar. 15, 1999, at A12 (Blacks six times more likely than whites to be held in jail and now make up over 40 percent of inmate population).

34. Professor Derrick Bell has argued that racial progress for Blacks is more likely to take place if the relief serves "the best interests of the country." DERRICK BELL, RACE, RACISM, AND AMERICAN LAW (3d ed. 1992). In other words, such progress is more likely if the relief benefits more than just Black people.

35. H.R. 118, 105th Cong. (1997); *see also* H.R. REP. No. 105–435 (1998), *available in* 1998 WL 105467 (discussing a later version of the bill). The version of the bill that passed the House in 1998 was known as the Traffic Stops Statistics Study Act of 1998.

36. Draft notes following the original Conyers bill state:

No American should have to live with the constant fear of an unwarranted pullover. African Americans across the country are familiar with the offense of "DWB," driving while Black. There are virtually no African American males—including Congressmen, actors, athletes and office workers—who have not been stopped at one time or another for an alleged traffic violation, then harassed with questions and searches. They may not receive tickets, but they do receive humiliation and more reason to distrust the justice system. (notes on file with author).

37. *See* H.R. 118.

38. Several states and jurisdictions have taken up this issue. For example, in California, A.B. 1264, a bill introduced by State Representative Kevin Murray, would have required annual record keeping through the year 2003. *See* California Traffic Stops Statistics Act, A.B. 1264, 1997–98 Regular Sess. (Cal. 1997); *see also* Doc Anthony Anderson, III, *They're Guilty of Driving While Being Black or Brown,* SAN DIEGO UNION-TRIBUNE, Dec. 24, 1998, at B7 (discussing origins of the bill). In contrast to the federal bill, A.B. 1264 explicitly mandated recording the *gender* of the person stopped. *See generally* S. COMM. ON PUB. SAFETY, COMMITTEE REP. FOR 1997 CAL. ASSEMBLY BILL NO. 1264, 1997–98 Regular Sess. (Cal. 1998), *available in* Westlaw CCA Database (discussing features of California bill). In 1998, then-governor Pete Wilson vetoed the bill. *See* Anderson, *supra.* In April of 1999, the North Carolina legislature gave final approval to a bill which would mandate data

collection for routine traffic stops. *See The State Requires Study of Highway Patrol Stops; N.C. House Approves "Driving While Black" Bill,* MORNING STAR (Wilmington, N.C.), Apr. 8, 1999, at 3B. Rhode Island has similar legislation pending. *See* Traffic Stops Statistics Act of 1998, S. 98-2434, Jan. Sess. (R.I. 1998). In addition, in at least two cities, San Jose and San Diego, California, law enforcement officials are voluntarily keeping race-based statistics on traffic stops. Julie N. Lynem & Marshall Wilson, *When Police Stop People for "Driving While Black"; Cities Move To Track Who Is Getting Pulled Over,* SAN FRANCISCO CHRONICLE, Apr. 7, 1999, at A1.

39. *See* Kevin Johnson & Gary Fields, *Police Chiefs Resist Race-Related Tallies,* USA TODAY, Apr. 8, 1999, at 7A.

40. *See id.*

41. *See supra* notes 6–7 and accompanying text.

42. *See supra* note 7; *see also* RUSSELL, *supra* note 15, at 40–43; Lamberth, *supra* note 8.

43. *See* RUSSELL, *supra* note 15, at 41–42.

44. This result raises the issue of what the impact of a bill such as the Traffic Stops Statistics Act would be. If the *Wilkins* case is any guide, the institution of a Conyers-like bill would do little to deter racial profiling, at least in the short term.

45. Criminal No. 97-10260-NG, 1998 U.S. Dist. LEXIS 20323 (D. Mass. Dec. 22, 1998).

46. This decision has been widely reported. *See, e.g.,* Fox Butterfield, *Bias Cited in Reducing Sentence of Black Man,* N.Y. TIMES, Dec. 17, 1998, at A22; David Cole, *"Driving While Black": Curbing Race-Based Traffic Stops,* WASH. POST, Dec. 28, 1998, at A25.

47. *See Leviner,* 1998 U.S. Dist. LEXIS 20323, at *25. Category VI is the highest criminal history category under the sentencing guidelines. *See id.* Scores 10–12 are in category V. *See id.* at *25 n.17. Leviner's total score was 11. *See id* at *25.

48. *See id.* at *26–28.

49. *Id.* at *33–34 (citations omitted). Judge Gertner sentenced Leviner to a thirty-month term. *See id.* at *38.

50. *See* RUSSELL, *supra* note 15, at 133 & 188 n.6.

51. *See id.*

52. *See, e.g., Judge Is Forced to Lengthen Sentences for Crack,* N.Y. TIMES, Nov. 27, 1995, at B5 ("[Judge Lyle Strom] who has bucked Federal sentencing guidelines in crack cocaine cases, arguing that they discriminate against blacks, reluctantly obeyed a higher court's instructions last week and used those guidelines to sentence two brothers. But in issuing the sentence [he] . . . apologized and told the brothers he would continue working to soften the guidelines.").

53. *See* Warren Brown, *Urban League Quits Seat Belt Drive; Group Cites Fears of Increased Police Harassment of Minorities,* WASH. POST, Dec. 11, 1998, at A14.

54. *See id.*

55. *See* RUSSELL, *supra* note 15, at 69–93.

56. *See, e.g., id.* at 145–46; Regina Austin, *Beyond Black Demons & White Devils: Anti-Black Conspiracy Theorizing & the Black Public Sphere,* 22 FLA. ST. U. L. REV. 1021 (1995). *See generally* PATRICIA A. TURNER, I HEARD IT THROUGH THE GRAPEVINE: RUMOR IN AFRICAN AMERICAN CULTURE (1993).

57. *See, e.g.,* Vincene Verdun, *The Only Lonely Remedy,* 59 OHIO ST. L.J. 793, 794 (1998) ("I put all [the racial slights] in [my] gunnysack, then and every time since

then, until the sack got full. I threw all the hurt that comes from being black into the gunnysack, and then I moved on. But now, the gunnysack is full and heavy, and I sometimes get really tired of carrying it around. . . . You see, once the sack is full, any new weight that is picked up must be put somewhere else, so *it is stored in the heart, the mind, the kidneys, or somewhere.*" [emphasis added]); *see also* RUSSELL, *supra* note 15, at 138–48.

58. Increasing incarceration of Blacks seems likely despite the fact that crime is on the decline. *See generally* Fox Butterfield, *Inmates Serving More Time, Justice Department Reports,* N.Y. TIMES, Jan. 11, 1999, at A10 (quoting observation of Frank Zimring, director of the Earl Warren Legal Institute at University of California at Berkeley, that "the changes in the American prison population are the result of a shift in policy, rather than any basic change in the nature of criminals or the crime rate"); Butterfield, *supra* note 33 (number of inmates at record high though crime rates have dropped for seven consecutive years; Blacks six times more likely than whites to be held in jail).

59. *See generally* THE SENTENCING PROJECT & HUMAN RIGHTS WATCH, LOSING THE VOTE: THE IMPACT OF FELONY DISENFRANCHISEMENT LAWS IN THE UNITED STATES (1998). This report indicates that 13 percent of Black men (1.4 million) are disenfranchised due to criminal conviction for certain types of crimes. *See id.* at 1. Black men represent more than one-third (36 percent) of all persons ineligible to vote due to a felony conviction. *See id.*

CHAPTER 7

A Critical Examination of Hate Crime Scholarship and the Underrepresentation of African Americans in Victimization Research

Bryan D. Byers, Paul J. Becker, and Kelly J. Opiola

In this chapter we attempt to shed light on the underrepresentation of African Americans as a victimized group within existing hate crime literature. The chapter is divided into several parts. We begin with a discussion of the history and nature of hate crime victimization within American society. We then examine the social construction of the hate crime problem and the literature specific to hate crime, with a particular focus on victimization. Finally, we analyze hate crime literature, focusing on the groups that have been represented in the literature, particularly African Americans. In this chapter we attempt to demonstrate that although African Americans have repeatedly been deemed the most likely target of hate crime, their relative representation in hate crime literature has been limited. In short, even though there has been proliferation of hate crime research and literature, African American victimization has been underrepresented. In the last section we offer some possible reasons for this pattern.

ON THE NATURE AND HISTORY OF HATE CRIME IN AMERICA

Though the term *hate crime* is of recent origin, history is replete with examples, such as the genocide of Native Americans and the lynching of African Americans. The United States has a long history of victimization predicated upon race, religion, ethnicity, sexual orientation, and other categories typically found in hate crime legislation. Several accounts have traced some of this history (see Becker, Jipson, & Katz, 2001; Newton & Newton, 1991). Nevertheless, the term hate crime is fairly new, with the first state hate crime law appearing in 1987 in California (Grattet, Jenness, & Curry, 1998).

One of the growing research areas related to hate crimes explores the creation of hate crime legislation. This research includes microapproaches, such as Becker's (1999) study examining the creation of Ohio's Ethnic Intimidation Law in 1987. Other research has taken a macroapproach to examining hate crime laws across the United States (e.g., Grattet, Jenness, & Curry, 1998; Jenness & Grattet, 2001.) A key point of hate crime legislation involves assigning protected status to certain groups. In other words, for which victims would an offender be eligible for an enhanced criminal penalty? Each state that passes a penalty enhancement hate crime law determines what groups will be protected. Categories such as race, religion, and ethnicity are typically included, whereas attempting to include sexual orientation has sometimes resulted in fierce opposition. Groups may lobby legislators to have their group included as a protected group. Czajkoski (1992) argues that African American groups, in particular, played an instrumental role in the enactment of hate crime legislation.

The research area of greatest concern to us examines the hate crime victimization of various groups. Cacas (1994) discussed the efforts of the National Asian Pacific American Legal Consortium to deal with anti-Asian hate crimes. Byers and Crider (2002) and Byers, Crider, and Biggers (1999) explored hate crimes against the Amish. Another approach has been to examine hate crime victimization among a large segment of the population composed of different groups covered by hate crime legislation. For example, Downey and Stage (1999) examined hate crimes on college campuses. Most victimization research has focused on sexual orientation bias (see, for example, Berrill, 1990; Green, Strolovitch, Wong, & Bailey, 2001; Herek, 1989; Herek & Berrill, 1992; Herek, Cogan, & Gillis, 1999; Tewksbury, Grossi, Suresh, & Helms, 1999).

There is conflicting research as to which group is most likely to be victimized. Torres (1999), for instance, suggests that historical evidence shows African Americans are victimized by hate crimes more than any other group. Torres (1999) refers to the *Uniform Crime Reports* (UCR) data from 1996, which shows that African Americans accounted for 66 percent of victims of racially motivated offenses. This finding is corroborated by Byers and Zeller (1997, 2001) and Perry (2001, p. 29). Others, however, claim hate crimes motivated by sexual orientation bias (anti-gay/lesbian/bisexual) constitute the largest group, given that these offenses frequently go unreported (Herek, 1989; Herek & Berrill, 1992). In one study, Berrill (1990) found that gay men of color—in this case Hispanics and Blacks—were most likely to experience threats and violence. In contrast, data from

Florida indicate that whites experience the highest rate of victimization and that in most cases the offender's race is unknown. These data additionally suggest that the most likely offender–victim relationship is an African American offender and a white victim (Czajkoski, 1992). This investigation notwithstanding, the most consistent national victimization pattern reveals that African Americans have experienced the highest victimization rates since 1991 (Byers & Zeller, 2001).

There is also a research interest in the fear of being a hate crime victim. According to Newport (1999) and a recent Gallup Poll, 13 percent of Americans worry about being the victim of a hate crime. Twenty-eight percent of nonwhites feared becoming a hate crime victim, whereas 11 percent of whites admitted to fearing hate crime victimization. In another study exploring fear of hate crime, Craig (1999) showed a group of white and African American men two different videotaped scenes. One scene involving a bias-motivated assault and the other an assault that was not bias motivated. One of Craig's findings was that African Americans feared becoming the victim of a hate crime more than whites. With a different population, Tewksbury and colleagues (1999) found that 73 percent of their sample of gay men and lesbian women feared becoming a hate crime victim.

The victimization literature also examines the effects of hate crimes on victims. By comparing data on hate crimes reported to the Boston police to national data on all crimes, Levin and McDevitt (1993) found several ways in which crimes motivated by hate differ from non–hate crimes. Among their findings were that hate crimes are "excessively brutal." For example, although seven percent of all crimes are assaults, half of hate crimes are assaults. Among hate crimes that are assaults, nearly 75 percent result in some physical injury compared with 29 percent of assaults not labeled hate crimes. A second finding is that hate crimes are more likely to be committed by strangers to the victim; nationally, 61 percent of violent crimes are committed by strangers compared with 85 percent of hate crimes reported in the Boston study. A third finding shows that hate crimes are more likely to involve more than one offender; nationally 25 percent of violent crimes are committed by multiple offenders compared with 64 percent of hate crimes. Thus, at least one study has found that hate crime victimizations are particularly brutal, tend to be committed by strangers, and are more likely to involve multiple offenders.

Crocker (1993) states that victims of hate crimes feel more victimized because the crime is due to their identity. Crocker also proposes that hate crimes are worse because of the history of racism. In other words, people who commit hate crimes are not worse perpetrators, but the fact that they are able to commit such an acts, given historical realities, is what makes the crimes worse. According to Craig (1999, pp. 138–139), hate crime victims may experience "depression, anxiety, hostility, fear, and posttraumatic stress." Moreover, Barnes and Ephross (1994) determined that victims of hate crimes, regardless of the motivation, share the same experiences.

THE SOCIAL CONSTRUCTION OF HATE CRIMES

To suggest that a social problem is *constructed* means that knowledge has been generated to support its existence. Anecdotal evidence may indicate that a social problem exists, but the aggregate data to support the claim may be scant or nonexistent. The social construction of social problems has been a topic of much concern and research in the social sciences since the original and thought-provoking work of Peter Berger and Thomas Luckmann in *The Social Construction of Reality* (1966). In this landmark work, Berger and Luckmann maintain that since knowledge is socially constructed in society, the sociology of knowledge bears responsibility for ascertaining the process whereby knowledge is constructed or generated by society. An important corollary of this principle is to be a critical consumer of information concerning hate crimes.

Few would claim that hate crime doesn't exist. In fact, one only needs to examine the anecdotal cases of James Byrd in Jasper, Texas, and Matthew Shepard in Laramie, Wyoming, to illustrate that crime can sometimes be motivated by hatred for a group that is taken out on an individual possessing the loathed affiliation. In the Byrd case, the black male victim was given a ride by a group of white supremacists and chained to the rear of a pickup truck. He was dragged until dismembered. The Shepard case, also widely publicized, involved two men taking Mr. Shepard to a remote area, robbing and beating him, and leaving him for dead. Interestingly, even celebrated cases can give us an impression of the seriousness of hate crime and which groups are worthy of attention. Even though both the Byrd and Shepard cases were featured in the national media, only one resulted in subsequent attention by the media in the form of a film, documentary, and a play. This was the Shepard case. Although we unequivocally acknowledge the pain and suffering that were the result of the Shepard case, it seems curious that an equally heinous crime occurred in Jasper, Texas, yet has not received as much attention as the Shepard case. The media have a tremendous amount of power and influence over what society defines as important and worthy of attention, but so do scholars. Scholars occupy an important role in the proliferation and dissemination of knowledge about social events, forces, and movements. Hate crimes are no exception.

Knowledge, or information, about hate crime is disseminated within American society through a number of avenues. As mentioned above, print, radio, and television media play a significant role in creating information for public consumption. An informal examination of media attention given to hate crimes reveals that most stories address what might be termed celebrated cases or those cases that cannot be characterized as mundane. Scholars also play an important role in producing knowledge about hate crimes. Some work is empirical, some legal, and some theoretical. Such work typically comes in the form of scholarly articles and books. Much of the literature appearing in professional journals, however, has come in two forms: articles with a focus on legal questions germane to the hate crime debate and articles that address issues of victimization. More recently, articles have questioned our commonly held assumptions about hate crimes and the process of passing hate crime legislation (Jacobs, 1992, 1993; Jacobs & Henry, 1996; Jacobs & Potter, 1997). A third source of knowledge is also extremely important. Interest groups and interest group politics have been the focus of some scholarly work on hate crime (Herek & Berrill, 1992). Interest groups such as the National Gay and Lesbian Task Force (NGLTF), the Anti-Defamation League (ADL), the Antiviolence Project (AVP), the National Asian Pacific American Legal Consortium, and the Southern Poverty Law Center have played a role in providing information in the form of news releases, legal briefs, data on hate crimes, and Web pages. Some scholars have warned of the potential bias of such sources whereas others have uncritically accepted information from them (Jacobs & Potter, 1998).

From the media, interest groups, and scholarly research, the public consciousness has developed an impression of hate crime and hate crime victimization. The first, and perhaps most controversial, issue in hate crime scholarship is the assumption that the number of hate crimes has grown in the past decade (Levin & McDevitt, 1993). In fact, this has not been confirmed empirically (Byers & Zeller, 1997, 2001; Jacobs & Potter, 1998). The data on hate crimes, as measured by national sources, suggest a relatively stable pattern of hate crimes occurring from year to year, regardless of bias motivation and offense type (Byers & Zeller, 2001; Jacobs & Potter, 1998). Another impression is that gays and lesbians are the most likely victims of hate crimes, which is based on the assumption that UCR data underrepresent gay and lesbian hate crime incidents (Perry, 2001).

In this chapter, however, we wish to argue that though African Americans are the most likely victims of hate crimes, they are underrepresented in the scholarly literature, which focuses mainly on gay and lesbian victims. Based on national UCR data since 1991 (Byers & Zeller, 2001; Jacobs & Potter, 1998), African Americans have consistently been the most victimized group. African Americans make up about 12 percent of the U.S. population, yet racial motivation accounts for more than 50 percent of the hate crime victimizations in the United States. For instance, in 2000, 35.6 percent of hate crime victims were African American, whereas gay and lesbian hate crime consisted of 15.5 percent of all victimizations, and anti-Semitic victimizations accounted for 12.8 percent (Federal Bureau of

Investigation, 2001). According to Perry (2001), the NGLTF/AVP is the only special interest group, of the aforementioned, that consistently claims that between 1992 and 1998 gay and lesbian victims were underrepresented in national statistics. Even if the NGLTF/AVP data are correct, the number of gay and lesbian victims pales in comparison to the proportion of African American victims.

Although African Americans are more victimized by hate crimes than any other group in American society, special interests, the media, and researchers have not brought sufficient attention to their disproportionate level of victimization. Since the onset of the hate crime debate, interest groups have been active in disseminating information about anti-Semitic and anti-gay/lesbian victimization, but have not made a similar effort on behalf of African Americans. Given the amount of recorded hate crime against African Americans as compared with other groups, it is curious that such efforts have not taken place.

Hate crime scholars and special interest groups have been successful purveyors of knowledge about hate crimes. Since both sources are often seen as speaking with authority, society is more likely to accept their claims as true. The result of such authoritative information dissemination has been a collection of perceptions about hate crimes in society. One could be persuaded, then, to think that anti-gay/lesbian, and perhaps anti-Semitic, hate crime is the most common type of bias-motivated offense.

A CRITICAL EXAMINATION OF HATE CRIME LITERATURE: AFRICAN AMERICAN REPRESENTATION

In light of the aforementioned discussion, we pose a question: To what extent are African Americans represented in the scholarly hate crime literature as compared with other groups? Given the extent of African American victimization, which is supported by most sources, one would expect a reasonable representation of scholarly literature addressing the problems and plights of this population. However, if the research agenda has been influenced or set by special interests and like-minded individuals, we would not expect the literature to reflect the most accurate portrayal of actual hate crime. Rather, we would expect the literature to reflect a more skewed interpretation of reality.

To conduct this critical analysis, we collected literature on the topic of hate crime. Others have conducted similar types of analyses on race and crime stories in the media (Rome & Chermak, 1994) and the representation of women of color in criminal justice textbooks (Eigenberg & Baro, 1994). We employed two criteria to determine inclusion/exclusion of the literature for our analysis. First, only articles published in journals that can be classified as scholarly in nature were included (e.g., refereed, academic publications). We purposely excluded scholarly books, given how difficult it would be to summarize such works based on our method. Second, we examined seven different genres of publications (theoretical, legal, empirical, policy, socio-legal, socio-historical, and policy-legal). Though it was sometimes difficult to classify articles in a particular genre, we tried to classify articles based on the author's prominent approach or focus.

With articles selected, we then constructed Table 7.1, which depicts the literature by author, year, type of research, focus, victimized group(s) examined in the piece, and whether or not African Americans, as a victim-

Table 7.1
Hate Crime Literature

Author(s)	Publication Year	Type of Research	Focus of the article or research	Victimized Group(s) Addressed	African American Representation?
Ault, A.	1997	Theoretical	A feminist argument that hate crimes against women based on misogyny should be included in hate crime laws in order to fully capture anti-female victimization that may or may not be anti-lesbian in nature.	Lesbians and women.	No
Bakken, T.	2000	Legal	Author argues that hate crime laws erode liberty and equality while adversely affecting minority group members.	No specific focus.	No
Becker, P.J.	1999	Legal	Ethnic intimidation law with a focus on interest group activity.	No specific focus.	No
Becker, P.J., Byers, B.D., & Jipson, A.	2000	Legal	An examination of the First Amendment debate and internet-based hate speech.	No specific focus.	No
Berk, R.	1990	Empirical	Hate crime victimization and future bias crime research needs.	No specific focus.	No
Berrill, K.T.	1990	Empirical	An examination of NGLTF data on anti-gay hate crime and victimization	Gays and lesbians.	No
Berrill, K.T. & Herek, G.M.	1990a	Empirical	A examination of anti-gay and lesbian hate crime with a focus on basic characteristics and dynamics.	Gays and lesbians	No
Berrill, K.T. & Herek, G.M.	1990b	Empirical	An examination of primary victimization (a hate crime) and possible secondary victimization (job loss) experienced by gay and lesbian hate crime victims.	Gays and lesbians.	No
Boyd, E.A., Berk, R.A., & Hammer, K.M.	1996	Policy	The classification and categorization of bias motivated crimes in two police jurisdictions.	No specific focus.	No
Byers, B.D. & Crider, B.W.	2002	Empirical	Examination of hate crimes against the Amish as applicable to routine activities theory.	Amish.	No

Table 7.1
Hate Crime Literature (continued)

Byers, B.D., Crider, B.W. & Biggers, G.K.	1999	Empirical	Examination of hate crimes against the Amish as applicable to techniques of neutralization.	Amish.	No
Byers, B.D. & Zeller, R.A.	2001	Empirical	Examination of national hate crime statistics as compiled by the UCR, characteristics of victimization by motivation and offense, and trends in victimization from 1991-1998.	No specific focus but African Americans are discussed in reference to hate crime data along with other groups.	Yes
Byers, B. & Zeller, R.A.	1997	Empirical	Examination of national hate crime statistics as compiled by the UCR, characteristics of victimization by motivation and offense, and trends in victimization from 1991-1994.	No specific focus but African Americans are discussed in reference to hate crime data along with other groups.	Yes
Craig, K.M.	1999	Empirical	Study of emotional reactions to hate crime situations by whites and African Americans.	Whites and African Americans.	Yes
Craig, K.M. & Waldo, C.R.	1996	Empirical	Examined perceptions of hate crime victimization and the impact of respondent demographic traits.	African Americans in the context of perceivers (subjects) and scenarios.	Yes
Cramer, E.P.	1999	Legal	Argues that it is constitutionally in violation to exclude protections based on sexual orientation in hate crime laws.	Gays and lesbians.	No
Crocker, L.	1993	Legal	Focuses on the wisdom and constitutionality of hate crime statutes.	No specific focus.	No
Czajkoski, E.	1992	Empirical	Using data from the state of Florida, the author empirically examines the characteristics of hate crime victimizations. He finds that whites were more likely in Florida to be victims of hate crimes.	Whites, Asians, and African Americans.	Yes

ized group, were represented in the piece. We did not collect and analyze this literature with the expectation that all studies should address issues of African American hate crime victimization. Therefore, if an article did not represent African Americans as a victimized group, this should not be taken as an indictment and criticism of the article, research, or author; rather, it is simply an indication of the author's focus.

Table 7.1 features published articles of a scholarly nature that adhere to the criteria outlined above. Seventy-one articles are included in this table

Table 7.1
Hate Crime Literature (continued)

Downey, J.P. & Stage, F.K.	1999	Policy	Focuses on hate crime victimization on the college campus with attention given to myths and realities of such crime.	No specific focus.	No
Dunbar, E.	1999	Legal	An examination of legal defenses that might be used for the commission of hate crimes.	No specific focus.	No
Ehrlich, H.J.	1990	Theoretical	Examines the sources of prejudice and hate with particular attention given to ant-gay and lesbian hate crime victimization experiences.	Gays and lesbians.	No
Ehrlich, H.J.	1989	Empirical	An examination of hate crime in the workplace.	No specific focus.	No
Finn, P.	1988	Legal	An examination of the difficulties in the conceptual definition of hate crime and the practical problems of prosecution.	No specific focus.	No
Franklin, K.	2000	Empirical	A study of survey results examining self-reports of anti-gay activities concluding that the plurality of young adults view anti-gay violence and harassment as socially acceptable.	Gays.	No
Freeman, S.	1992/1993	Legal	Examination of appropriate legal reactions to hate crimes and the unique nature of such offenses for victims.	No specific focus.	No
Garnets, L., Herek, G.M., & Levy, B.	1990	Policy	An examination of the psychosocial consequences of anti-gay/lesbian hate crime.	Gays and lesbians.	No
Gelber, K.	2000	Legal	Examines the issue of gender inclusion in hate crime laws and public policy implications.	Gender.	No
Goldberger, D.	1993	Legal	Focuses on the issue of hate crime laws and infringements on First Amendment assurances.	No specific focus.	No
Grattet, R. & Jenness, V.	2001	Policy	An examination of the progression of how hate crimes are understood and that societal understanding is the result of how the concept has been clarified socially, politically, and legally.	No specific focus.	No

spanning the legal, theoretical, policy, and empirical realms of research. No article was published prior to 1988, indicating that hate crime study is a relatively new field of inquiry. From the contents of Table 7.1, it is apparent that most hate crime scholarship published since 1990 tends to address legal and empirical areas and either focuses on sexual orientation or has no specific focus. The latter means that hate crime scholarship does not typically concentrate on any particular victimized group, but discusses many victimized groups in a general fashion.

Table 7.1
Hate Crime Literature (continued)

Grattet, R., Jenness, V., & Curry, T.R.	1998	Empirical	Analyzes the political environment that was conducive to the proliferation of hate crime laws in the United States.	No specific focus.	No
Green, D.P., Glaser, J. & Rich, A.	1998	Empirical	An examination of possible causal variables for hate crime.	African Americans (in an analysis of lynching)	Yes
Green, D.P., McFalls, L.H., & Smith, J.K.	2001	Empirical*	Examines the difficulty in defining, measuring, and explaining hate crime.	No specific focus.	No
Green, D.P., Strolovitch, D.Z., Wong, J.S., & Bailey, R.W.	2001	Empirical	Examines anti-gay victimization as a function of gay population characteristics and dynamics.	Gays.	No
Haider-Markel, D.P.	1998	Empirical	Examines the extent of hate crime victimization and state legislative efforts to proscribe such behavior.	Several groups via an examination of FBI hate crime statistics.	Yes
Herek, G.M.	1989	Empirical*	An examination of hate crimes and a productive research agenda.	Gays and lesbians.	No
Herek, G.M., Cogan, J.C., & Gillis, J.R.	1999	Empirical	Survey results of a California study of hate crimes based on sexual orientation.	Lesbians, gays, and bisexuals.	No
Herek, G.M., Gillis, J.R., Cogan, J.C., & Glunt, E.K.	1997	Empirical	Results of a street fair survey of victimization based on sexual orientation.	Lesbians, gays, and bisexuals.	No
Iganski, P.	2001	Legal	Examines the perceived need for greater punishments for hate crimes given the interpretation that bias crimes cause greater harm.	No specific focus.	No
Israel, M.	1999	Legal	Legal-theoretical examination of hate crimes and the First Amendment.	No specific focus.	No
Jacobs, J.B.	1993	Legal	A prediction of issues, controversies, and problems of hate crime legislation.	No specific focus.	No

Table 7.2 presents a breakdown of the research from Table 7.1, with a specific examination of scholarly work classification and African American representation. Overall, 68.9 percent of this research does not specifically address issues of African American hate crime victimization. Though the number of articles published in each research genre varies considerably, African Americans are represented in less than 10 percent of the articles in three categories (legal, policy, and policy-legal).

Table 7.3 was constructed to address which groups are examined based

Table 7.1
Hate Crime Literature (continued)

Jacobs, J.B.	1992	Legal	The author provides caveats and identifies issues germane to hate crime legislation and enforcement.	The article addresses African American victimization insofar as hate crime data from NYC are presented showing that most hate crimes are committed against blacks.	Yes
Jacobs, J.B. & Henry, J.S.	1996	Socio-legal	Examines the social construction of hate crime in America and the resulting public assumption of an "epidemic" given special interest group definitional power.	African American victimization is examined in the historical context of lynching.	Yes
Jacobs, J.B. & Potter, K.A.	1997	Socio-legal	Argues that having a special category of "hate crime" can further polarize society and social groups given how difficult this concept is to define, measure, and enforce.	No specific focus.	No
Jenness, V.	1999	Socio-legal	A socio-historical examination of the emergence of hate crime legislation and the inclusion of protected groups.	No specific focus.	No
Jenness, V. & Grattet, R.	1996	Socio-legal	Authors examine social structural and political factors that might influence hate crime legislation passage.	No specific focus.	No
Jolly-Ryan, J.	1999-2000	Legal	An examination of Kentucky's hate crime law designed to advocate for a strengthening of the current law.	No specific focus.	No
Levin, B.	2001	Legal	Examines free expression and the legal environment where hate speech is allowed to flourish.	No specific focus.	No
Levin, B.	1999	Empirical	Examines the difficulties in defining hate crime in jurisprudence.	No specific focus.	No

on the type of research genre. We excluded the more obscure categories (e.g., socio-legal, socio-historical, policy-legal) because these accounted for only seven articles in Table 7.2. One should also note that only 37 articles are examined in Table 7.3, given that the purpose of the table is to present data on the primary victimized group addressed. Thus, unless the article appeared to have a primary victim focus or had no specific victim focus at all, it was excluded from the analysis in this table.

A perusal of Table 7.3 discloses that 54.1 percent of the articles had no specific victimization focus, 35.1 percent addressed victims based on sex-

Table 7.1
Hate Crime Literature (continued)

Levin, B.	1992-1993	Empirical	An examination of hate crime data from local jurisdictions and the need for enabling legislation to combat bias motivated crime.	No specific focus.	No
Maroney, T.	1998	Socio-historical	An examination of the anti-hate movement as an outgrowth of the civil rights movements.	African Americans are examined through historical referents to the civil rights movement.	Yes
Martin, S.E.	1996	Empirical	An examination of bias crime data as collected by two police jurisdictions in New York City and Baltimore County, Maryland.	African Americans insofar as the data indicate that African Americans were often victimized.	Yes
Martin, S.E.	1995	Empirical	An examination of how hate crime reports were handled in one police jurisdiction.	No specific focus.	No
McDevitt, J., Balboni, J., Garcia, L. & Gu, J.	2001	Empirical	Discussion of the victim impact experienced by hate crime victims based on data from the city of Boston, MA.	No specific focus.	No
McPhail, B.A.	2000	Policy-legal	Examines the debate over the need for hate crime legislation and policy and practice considerations for social workers.	No specific focus.	No
Medoff, M.H.	1999	Empirical	An application of rational-choice modeling to hate crime prevalence concluding that hate crimes decrease with increases in the market wage rate, the value of time, age, and law enforcement activity.	No specific focus.	No
Miller, A.J.	2001	Empirical	Examination of the definitional preferences of criminal justice students versus other majors in determining if a case is a hate crime	African Americans are included as a possible victimized group in vignettes.	Yes

ual orientation (gays, lesbians, bisexuals, women), and 10.8 percent dealt with African Americans as a primary group for purposes of analysis. With few exceptions, articles that focused on sexual orientation were a dominant category. This was especially evident in the empirical research, where eight of eleven articles with a primary focus analyzed hate crimes based on sexual orientation. Perhaps it should come as no surprise that hate crime publications of a legal nature were focused on sexual orientation,

Table 7.1
Hate Crime Literature (continued)

Morsch, J.	1992	Legal	A legal examination of the issue of determining motivation in racially motivated hate crimes.	Insofar as racial motivation is examined as a motivating factor in hate crimes.	Yes
Newport, F.	1999	Empirical	Features Gallup Poll results suggesting that nonwhites have a greater concern over the occurrence of hate crime.	African Americans are examined in reference to their higher percentage of fear of hate crime victimization.	Yes
Nolan, J.J. & Akiyama, Y.	1999	Policy	An examination of the organizational and social forces at work that might explain local law enforcement participation in FBI-UCR hate crime data collection efforts.	No specific focus.	No
Oliver, W.	2001	Theoretical	An examination of cultural racism and its impact on anti-African American crime and mistreatment.	African Americans.	Yes
Perry, B.	2000	Theoretical	Examination of the more intricate nature of ethnoviolence given that hate crimes do not always consist of clear "black" and "white" victim/offender identities.	African American-Asian Americans, Jewish American-African American, and gay men in communities of color.	Yes
Petrosino, C.	1999	Socio-historical	An attempt to shed light on the current state of hate crimes by examining the history of hate against groups within the United States.	Several groups are examined and African Americans are discussed.	Yes
Phillips, S. & Grattet, R.	2000	Empirical	Examines how the concept of hate crime has gone from an ambiguous concept to a more refined legal concept.	No specific focus.	No

since the inclusion of gays and lesbians in hate crime law has been an extremely controversial issue. What is conspicuously absent from the literature is a focus on anti-Semitic victimization. Jewish victims in 2000 accounted for approximately 12.8 percent of all hate crime victims in the United States. During the same year, hate crimes based on sexual orientation (gay, lesbian, bisexual) accounted for about 15.5 percent (Federal Bureau of Investigation, 2001). Thus, whereas there has been ample re-

Table 7.1
Hate Crime Literature (continued)

Redish, M.H.	1992	Legal	An examination of the free speech-hate crime law debate and the tensions which exist as a result of competing interests.	No specific focus.	No
Robinson, P.H.	1993	Legal	Examines the problem of examining motive in hate crimes and how such an examination is not consistent with the traditional focus of criminal law and liability.	No specific focus.	No
Schauer, F.	1992	Legal	An examination of messages, motives and hate crime sentencing enhancements.	No specific focus.	No
Scott, J.	1999	Policy	The author examines the rhetoric link with hate crime and suggests that unchecked rhetoric can lead to hate crimes.	Hate crimes against abortionists.	No
Sloan, L.M., King, L., & Sheppard, S.	1998	Empirical	In a survey of state-level individuals responsible for crime data, the authors reveal that states with mandatory hate crime reporting have higher compliance rates and few states include law enforcement training concerning the inclusion of sexual orientation bias in hate crime data.	Gays and lesbians.	No
Soule, S.A. & Earl, J.	2001	Empirical	An examination of factors affecting state adoption of hate crime laws that concludes that neighboring state laws tend not to influence hate crime enactments in nearby states.	No specific focus.	No
Torres, S.	1999	Empirical	A specific examination of African American hate crime victimization.	African Americans	Yes
Weinstein, J.	1992	Legal	Examines the constitutionality of hate crime laws.	No specific focus.	No

*Though the article addresses empirical issues in hate crime research, the piece also discusses some of the research issues one might confront and suggestions for future study.

search on sexual orientation bias crime, Jews, a group with nearly the same amount of victimization, have been practically ignored by researchers.

DISCUSSION AND CONCLUSION

This analysis reveals that special interest groups and the popular press influence the research agenda of scholars. Though we cannot definitely conclude that knowledge about hate crimes has been created from such influences, we can reasonably suggest that hate crime scholarship follows a pattern that reflects such an impact. Our examination of the hate crime

Table 7.2
Research Classification of Scholarly Works on Hate Crimes by African American Representation

Classification

African American Representation	Theoretical	Legal	Empirical	Policy	Socio-Legal	Socio-Historical	Policy-Legal	Total
Yes	50.0% (2)	9.5% (2)	33.3% (11)	0.0% (0)	25.0% (1)	100.0% (2)	0.0% (0)	31.1%
No	50.0 (2)	90.5 (19)	66.6 (22)	100.0 (6)	75.0 (3)	0.0 (0)	100.0 (1)	68.9
Total	100.0% (4)	100.0% (21)	99.9% (33)	100.0% (6)	100.0% (4)	100.0% (2)	100.0% (1)	100.0% (71)

Table 7.3
Research Classification of Scholarly Works on Hate Crimes by Victimized Group Addressed

Research Classification

Primary Victimized Group Addressed	Theoretical	Legal	Empirical	Policy	Total
African Americans	33.3% (1)	0.0% (0)	10.7% (3)	0.0% (0)	10.8% (4)
Sexual Orientation	66.6 (2)	50.0 (2)	28.6 (8)	50.0 (1)	35.1 (13)
No Specific Focus	0.0 (0)	50.0 (2)	60.7 (17)	50.0 (1)	54.1% (20)
Total	99.9% (3)	100.0% (4)	100.0% (28)	100.0% (2)	100.0% (37)

literature shows that more than two-thirds of the literature specifically addresses hate crime in reference to sexual orientation, but only about 11 percent focuses directly on African Americans. It is also noteworthy that 54 percent of the hate crime literature examined did not have a primary focus, but examined multiple groups or more general themes. For legal and empirical research—two prominent areas of hate crime scholarship—we tend to see the same general pattern. Moreover, when examining the question of the presence or absence of African American victim representation in empirical, scholarly hate crime publications, the margin of unrepresented to represented is 2 to 1.

What might we conclude, then, about this pattern? First, the low level of African American victim focus in hate crime scholarship seems to be out of balance given the group's frequency of victimization based on national data. While not all research by scholars concludes that African Americans are the most frequently victimized group, many more sources confirm this pattern. Thus, there may be an issue of research equity when addressing certain types of victims over others. Second, we might theorize as to the reason for the underrepresentation of African Americans in scholarly literature. One possibility is that African American hate crime victimization might be taken for granted. All U.S. state laws that proscribe hate crime include African Americans as a protected group (i.e., bias crime based on race), yet only about half include sexual orientation, which includes gays, lesbians, transgendered people, and bisexuals, as a protected class. Given that fewer hate crime laws protect those based on sexual orientation than race, this could be part of the reason for the dominance of sexual orientation bias crime victimization within the hate crime literature. Thus, research on sexual orientation bias crime might be considered action or advocacy research. This point is supported, in part, by the fact that many studies examining anti-gay/lesbian bias crimes use advocacy group data (Herek & Berrill, 1992). Another possibility for the underrepresentation of African Americans in hate crime scholarship is the possibility that black victims are devalued by the American criminal justice system. When a group is devalued, its worth as a victim category is also devalued. This phenomenon has occurred in murder cases where murders with black victims are much less likely to be tried as capital cases than those with white victims (Bohm, 1999). Consequently, the underrepresentation of black victim hate crimes in the research may be, in part, a function of the criminal justice system taking for granted African American victimization, the devaluation of black victims by the criminal justice system, or both.

Third, advocacy groups have played a key role in American society by keeping the focus on hate crime victimization in the public's consciousness (Jacobs & Henry, 1996; Jacobs & Potter, 1998). Two of the most influential of these groups are the NGLTF and the ADL, with the latter providing model hate crime legislation since 1981. Although the efforts of such groups are admirable, one must ask if such advocacy has influenced the research agenda for hate crime scholarship. Jacobs and Potter (1998) and Jacobs and Henry (1996) have made the argument that such advocacy has been influential in creating a sense that hate crimes are an urgent problem in American society and that the proliferation of hate crime legislation is therefore justified. Even though we cannot definitely assert that advocacy has created a proliferation of dominant hate crime scholarship, it stands to reason that such an influence might exist. This leads us to our fourth point.

If advocacy groups, such as the NGLTF and the ADL, have had an influence on the social construction of knowledge about hate crimes in the form of scholarship, then we might expect that research on sexual orientation victimization and anti-Semitic hate crime would be prominent. However, as we discussed earlier, this is only the case for research on bias crime based on sexual orientation. This is puzzling insofar as one might expect both groups to be represented in the hate crime research at similar levels.

As previously stated, we are not attempting to minimize the seriousness or unique aspects of hate crimes motivated by sexual orientation. However, researchers need to excise caution so that their work is not influenced or guided by interest groups and the media. We must recognize the seriousness of all hate crimes and examine the experiences of all hate crime victims. Although the majority of research on victimization has focused on sexual orientation hate crimes, scholars can use this wealth of information for comparative analyses. For example, research can be conducted comparing the experiences of African American hate crime victims to gay and lesbian victims. We would expect that there are unique aspects of being a hate crime victim depending on group affiliation or membership. For African Americans, the legacy of slavery and racism may require special consideration. Research beyond hate crime motivated by sexual orientation may also tell us more about the offenders.

In conclusion, this literature review suggests that African American victimization is underrepresented in hate crime scholarship and is in need of greater attention by scholars in this field. Until researchers explore all aspects of hate crime victimization for all hate crimes, the impact of hate crime on the individual and society cannot be fully appreciated and understood.

REFERENCES

Ault, A. (1997). When it happens to men, it's "hate" and "a crime": Hate crime policies in the contexts of gay politics, movement organizations, and feminist concerns. *Journal of Poverty, 1,* 49–63.

Bakken, T. (2000). Liberty and equality through freedom of expression: The human rights questions behind "hate crime" laws. *International Journal of Human Rights, 4,* 1–12.

Barnes, A., & Ephross, P. (1994). The impact of hate violence on victims: Emotional and behavioral responses to attacks. *Social Work, 39,* 247–251.

Becker, P. (1999). The creation of Ohio's ethnic intimidation law: Triggering events, media campaigns, and interest group activity. *American Journal of Criminal Justice, 23,* 247–263.

Becker, P., Byers, B., & Jipson, A. (2000). The contentious American debate: The First Amendment and Internet-based hate speech. *International Review of Law, Computers & Technology, 14,* 33–41.

Becker, P., Jipson, A., & Katz, R. (2001). A timeline of the racialist movement in the United States: A teaching tool. *Journal of Criminal Justice Education, 12,* 427–453.

Berger, P., & Luckmann, T. (1966). *The social construction of reality: A treatise in the sociology of knowledge.* Garden City, NY: Doubleday.

Berk, R. (1990). Thinking about hate-motivated crimes. *Journal of Interpersonal Violence, 5,* 334–349.

Berrill, K. (1990). Anti-gay violence and victimization in the United States: An overview. *Journal of Interpersonal Violence, 5,* 274–294.

Berrill, K., & Herek, G. (1990a). Violence against lesbians and gay men. *Journal of Interpersonal Violence, 5,* 269–273.

Berrill, K., & Herek, G. (1990b). Primary and secondary victimization in anti-gay hate crimes: Official response and public policy. *Journal of Interpersonal Violence, 5,* 401–413.

Bohm, R. (1999). *Deathquest: An introduction to the theory and practice of capital punishment in the United States.* Cincinnati, OH: Anderson.

Boyd, E., Berk, R., & Hammer, K. (1996). Motivated by hatred or prejudice: Categorization of hate-motivated crimes in two police divisions. *Law & Society Review, 30,* 819–848.

Byers, B., & Crider, B. (2002). Hate crimes against the Amish: A qualitative analysis of bias motivation using routine activities theory. *Deviant Behavior, 23,* 115–148.

Byers, B., Crider, B., & Biggers, G. (1999). Bias crime motivation: A study of hate crime and offender neutralization techniques used against the Amish. *Journal of Contemporary Criminal Justice, 15,* 78–96.

Byers, B., & Zeller, R. (1997). An examination of official hate crime offenses and bias motivation statistics for 1991–1994. *Journal of Crime & Justice, 20,* 91–106.

Byers, B., & Zeller, R. (2001). Official hate crime statistics: An examination of the epidemic hypothesis. *Journal of Crime & Justice, 24,* 73–99.

Cacas, S. (1994). Asians under attack. *Human Rights, 21,* 34–35.

Craig, K. (1999). Retaliation, fear, or rage: An investigation of African

American and white reactions to racist hate crimes. *Journal of Interpersonal Violence, 14*, 138–151.

Craig, K., & Waldo, C. (1996). So, what's a hate crime anyway? Young adults' perceptions of hate crimes, victims, and perpetrators. *Law & Human Behavior, 20*, 113–129.

Cramer, E. (1999). Hate crime laws and sexual orientation. *Journal of Sociology & Social Welfare, 26*, 5–24.

Crocker, L. (1993). Hate crime statutes: just? constitutional? wise? *Annual Survey of American Law, 1992/1993*, 485–506.

Czajkoski, E. (1992). Criminalizing hate: An empirical assessment. *Federal Probation, 56*, 36–40.

Downey, J., & Stage, F. (1999). Hate crimes and violence on college and university campuses. *Journal of College Student Development, 40*, 3–9.

Dunbar, E. (1999). Defending the indefensible: A critique and analysis of psycholegal defense arguments of hate crime perpetrators. *Journal of Contemporary Criminal Justice, 15*, 64–77.

Ehrlich, H. (1989). Studying workplace ethnoviolence. *International Journal of Group Tensions, 19*, 69–80.

Ehrlich, H. (1990). The ecology of anti-gay violence. *Journal of Interpersonal Violence, 5*, 359–365.

Eigenberg, H., & Baro, A. (1994). Invisibility and marginalization of women of color. In J. Hendricks & B. Byers (Eds.), *Multicultural perspectives in criminal justice and criminology* (pp. 291–322). Springfield, IL: Charles C. Thomas.

Federal Bureau of Investigation. (2001). *Hate crime statistics*. Retrieved February 3, 2002, from http://www.fbi.gov/ucr/cius_00/hate00.pdf.

Finn, P. 1988. Bias crime: Difficult to define, difficult to prosecute. *Criminal Justice, 3*, 19–48.

Franklin, K. (2000). Antigay behaviors among young adults: Prevalence, patterns, and motivators in a noncriminal population. *Journal of Interpersonal Violence, 15*, 339–362.

Freeman, S. (1993). Hate crime laws: Punishment which fits the crime. *Annual Survey of American Law, 1992/1993*, 581–585.

Garnets, L., Herek, G., & Levy, B. (1990). Violence and victimization of lesbians and gay men: Mental health consequences. *Journal of Interpersonal Violence, 5*, 366–383.

Gelber, K. (2000). Hate crimes: Public policy implications of the inclusion of gender. *Australian Journal of Political Science, 35*, 275–289.

Goldberger, D. (1993). Hate crime laws and their impact on the First Amendment. *Annual Survey of American Law, 1992/1993*, 569–580.

Grattet, R., & Jenness, V. (2001). The birth and maturation of hate crime policy in the United States. *American Behavioral Scientist, 45*, 668–696.

Grattet, R., Jenness, V., & Curry, T. (1998). The homogenization and differentiation of hate crime law in the United States, 1978 to 1995: Innovation and diffusion in the criminalization of bigotry. *American Sociological Review, 63*, 286–307.

Green, D., Glaser, J., & Rich, A. (1998). From lynching to gay bashing: The elusive connection between economic conditions and hate crime. *Journal of Personality & Social Psychology, 75*, 82–92.

Green, D., McFalls, L., & Smith, J. (2001). Hate crime: An emergent research agenda. *Annual Review of Sociology, 27*, 479–504.

Green, D., Strolovitch, D., Wong, J., & Bailey, R. (2001). Measuring gay populations and antigay hate crime. *Social Science Quarterly, 82*, 281–296.

Haider-Markel, D. (1998). The politics of social regulatory policy: State and federal hate crime policy and implementation effort. *Political Research Quarterly, 51*, 69–88.

Herek, G. (1989). Hate crimes against lesbians and gay men: Issues for research and policy. *American Psychologist, 44*, 948–955.

Herek, G., & Berrill, K. (Eds.). (1992). *Hate crimes: Confronting violence against lesbians and gay men.* Newbury Park, CA: Sage.

Herek, G., Cogan, J., & Gillis, J. (1999). Psychological sequelae of hate-crime victimization among lesbian, gay, and bisexual adults. *Journal of Counseling & Clinical Psychology, 67*, 945–951.

Herek, G., Gillis, J., Cogan, J., & Glunt, E. (1997). Hate crime victimization among lesbian, gay, and bisexual adults: Prevalence, psychological correlates, and methodological issues. *Journal of Interpersonal Violence, 12*, 195–215.

Iganski, P. (2001). Hate crimes hurt more. *American Behavioral Scientist, 45*, 626–638.

Israel, M. (1999). Hate speech and the First Amendment. *Journal of Contemporary Criminal Justice, 15*, 97–110.

Jacobs, J. (1992). Rethinking the war against hate crimes: A New York City perspective. *Criminal Justice Ethics, 11*, 55–60.

Jacobs, J. (1993). Implementing hate crime legislation: Symbolism and crime control. *Annual Survey of American Law, 1992/1993*, 541–553.

Jacobs, J., & Henry, J. (1996). The social construction of a hate crime epidemic. *Journal of Criminal Law & Criminology, 86*, 366–391.

Jacobs, J., & Potter, K. (1997). Hate crimes: A critical perspective. *Crime & Justice, 22*, 1–50.

Jacobs, J., & Potter, K. (1998). *Hate crimes: Criminal law and identity politics.* New York: Oxford University Press.

Jenness, V. (1999). Managing difference and making legislation: Social movements and the racialization, sexualization, and gendering of federal hate crime law in the U.S., 1985–1998. *Social Problems, 46*, 548–571.

Jenness, V., & Grattet, R. (1996). The criminalization of hate: A comparison

of structural and polity influences on the passage of bias-crime legislation in the United States. *Sociological Perspectives, 39,* 129–154.

Jenness, V., & Grattet, R. (2001). *Making hate a crime: From social movement
to law enforcement.* New York: Russell Sage Foundation.

Jolly-Ryan, J. (1999/2000). Strengthening hate crime laws in Kentucky. *Kentucky Law Journal, 88,* 63–86.

Levin, B. (1992/1993). Bias crime: A theoretical and practical overview.
Stanford Law & Policy Review, 4, 165–181.

Levin, B. (1999). Hate crimes: Worse by definition. *Journal of Contemporary
Criminal Justice, 15,* 6–21.

Levin, B. (2001). Extremism and the Constitution: How America's legal
evolution affects the response to extremism. *American Behavioral Scientist, 45,* 714–755.

Levin, J., & McDevitt, J. (1993). *Hate crimes: The rising tide of bigotry and
bloodshed.* New York: Plenum Press.

Maroney, T. (1998). The struggle against hate crime: Movement at the
crossroads. *New York University Law Review, 73,* 564–620.

Martin, S. (1995). "Cross-burning is not just an arson": Police social
construction of hate crimes in Baltimore County. *Criminology, 33,*
303–326.

Martin, S. (1996). Investigating hate crimes: Case characteristics and law
enforcement responses. *Justice Quarterly, 13,* 455–480.

McDevitt, J., Balboni, J., Garcia, L., & Gu, J. (2001). Consequences for victims: A comparison of bias- and non-bias-motivated assaults. *American Behavioral Scientist, 45,* 697–713.

McPhail, B. (2000). Hating hate: Policy implications of hate crime legislation. *Social Service Review, 74,* 635–653.

Medoff, M. (1999). Allocation of time and hateful behavior: A theoretical
and positive analysis of hate and hate crimes. *American Journal of
Economics & Sociology, 58,* 959–973.

Miller, A. (2001). Student perceptions of hate crimes. *American Journal of
Criminal Justice, 25,* 293–305.

Morsch, J. (1992). The problem of motive in hate crimes: The argument
against presumptions of racial motivation. *Journal of Criminal Law
& Criminology, 82,* 659–670.

Newport, F. (1999, February 23). One in four nonwhites worried about
hate crimes. *Gallup Poll Monthly,* 27–29.

Newton, M., & Newton, J. (1991). *Racial and religious violence in America:
A chronology.* New York: Garland.

Nolan, J., & Akiyama, Y. (1999). An analysis of factors that affect law
enforcement participation in hate crime reporting. *Journal of Contemporary Criminal Justice, 15,* 111–127.

Oliver, W. (2001). Cultural racism and structural violence: Implications for

African Americans. *Journal of Human Behavior in the Social Environment, 4*, 1–26.

Perry, B. (2000). Beyond black and white: Ethnoviolence between oppressed groups. *Sociology of Crime, Law, & Deviance, 2*, 301–323.

Perry, B. (2001). *In the name of hate: Understanding hate crime.* New York: Routledge.

Petrosino, C. (1999). Connecting the past to the future: Hate crime in America. *Journal of Contemporary Criminal Justice, 15*, 22–47.

Phillips, S., & Grattet, R. (2000). Judicial rhetoric, meaning-making, and the institutionalization of hate crime law. *Law & Society Review, 34*, 567–606.

Redish, M. (1992). Freedom of thought as freedom of expression: Hate crime sentencing enhancement and First Amendment theory. *Criminal Justice Ethics, 11*, 29–42.

Robinson, P. (1993). Hate crimes: Crimes of motive, character, or group terror? *Annual Survey of American Law, 1992/1993*, 605–616.

Rome, D., & Chermak, S. (1994). Race in crime stories. In J. Hendricks & B. Byers (Eds.), *Multicultural perspectives in criminal justice and criminology* (pp. 185–210). Springfield, IL: Charles Thomas.

Schauer, F. (1992). Messages, motives, and hate crimes. *Criminal Justice Ethics, 11*, 52–54.

Scott, J. (1999). From hate rhetoric to hate crime: A link acknowledged too late. *The Humanist, 59*, 8–14.

Sloan, L., King, L., & Sheppard, S. (1998). Hate crimes motivated by sexual orientation: Police reporting and training. *Journal of Gay & Lesbian Social Services, 8*, 25–39.

Soule, S., & Earl, J. (2001). The enactment of state-level hate crime law in the United States: Intrastate and interstate factors. *Sociological Perspectives, 44*, 281–305.

Tewksbury, R., Grossi, E., Suresh, G., & Helms, J. (1999). Hate crimes against gay men and lesbian women: A routine activity approach for predicting victimization risk. *Humanity & Society, 23*, 125–142.

Torres, S. (1999). Hate crimes against African Americans: The extent of the problem. *Journal of Contemporary Criminal Justice, 15*, 48–63.

Weinstein, J. (1992). First Amendment challenges to hate crime legislation: Where's the speech? *Criminal Justice Ethics, 11*, 6–20.

CHAPTER 8

Race and Presentencing Decisions: The Cost of Being African American

Marvin D. Free, Jr.

INTRODUCTION

In 1944 Gunnar Myrdal wrote *An American Dilemma*, a critique of black–white relations in the United States. Almost sixty years later African Americans remain a marginalized group. African Americans, for example, are considerably more likely than whites to be impoverished. In 1999 almost one-fourth of all African Americans lived in poverty, a rate that is approximately three times greater than that of non-Hispanic whites (Dalaker & Proctor, 2000). Perhaps nowhere, though, is African American marginality more apparent than in their overrepresentation in the criminal justice system, where African Americans account for 46 percent of all inmates with sentences of more than one year in state or federal jurisdictions (Beck, 2000). Additionally, adult African American males are almost 7 times more likely than their white counterparts to be held in a correctional facility, whereas adult African American females are almost 6.5 times more likely than adult white females to be incarcerated (Pastore & Maguire, 2000). African Americans further comprised 43 percent of the death row population in state and federal prisons at year-end 1998 (Snell, 1999).

Given the overrepresentation of African Americans in criminal justice statistics, a question regarding the impact of race in the criminal justice system inevitably arises. Whereas the U.S. Supreme Court maintains that aggregate racial disparities do not constitute prima facie evidence of racial discrimination in specific cases,[1] researchers continue to debate the issue of racial discrimination in sentencing (for reviews see Free, 1996, chapter 4; Hagan, 1974; Kempf & Austin, 1986; Kleck, 1981; Weitzer, 1996). Empirical research generally suggests that racial disparities are more prevalent during the earlier in/out stage than during the later punishment stage (e.g., Chiricos & Crawford, 1995; Eterno, 1993; Free, 1996, chapter 4; Kramer & Steffensmeir, 1993; Spohn, 2000). However, racial disparities are not confined to the sentencing stage. As Spohn, Gruhl, and Welch (1987) note, even when

there may be little or no racial discrimination in convicting and sentencing, a significant amount of racial bias could exist at . . . less formal and visible pre- and post-trial stages. Being less formal, these stages may not require decision makers to follow equally strict procedures. Being less visible, they are by definition less subject to scrutiny by outsiders. Thus, there is greater potential for discrimination at the pre- and post-trial stages than at the convicting and sentencing stages. (p. 176)

Directly and indirectly prosecutors influence case outcomes. Prosecutors affect case outcomes indirectly through their recommendations regarding bail amount. Because high bail makes it more difficult for a defendant to post bail, and because a defendant who is unsuccessful in making bail is more likely to be found guilty (Patterson & Lynch, 1991), the bail amount decision can affect case outcome. Moreover, prosecutorial recommendations regarding pretrial detention are important since pretrial detention increases the probability of conviction (Ares, Rankin, & Sturz, 1963; Farrell & Swigert, 1986; Foote, 1959) and incarceration (Ares et al., 1963; Bernstein, Cardascia, & Ross, 1979; Chiricos & Bales, 1991; Holmes & Daudistel, 1984; Humphrey & Fogarty, 1987; Nagel, Cardascia, & Ross, 1982; Rankin, 1964; Spohn & Holleran, 2000; Unnever, 1982). Additionally, length of pretrial detention is positively related to sentence length (Landes, 1974) and severity of the final conviction charge (Bishop & Frazier, 1984).

Prosecutors are directly responsible for determining whether charges will be brought against offenders, what the specific charges will be, and if plea bargains will be proffered. The immense power of the prosecutorial position also extends to jurisdictions with grand juries, where prosecutors are commonly in charge of choosing the witnesses to be called, questioning the witnesses, interpreting the law, and making recommendations to the grand jury regarding cases. Furthermore, neither the accused nor the legal representative of the accused may be in attendance, and information about the proceedings is denied to the accused and his/her legal counsel as well as the general public (Davis, 1998).

In jurisdictions with capital statutes, prosecutors additionally determine the applicability of the death penalty, an area of considerable import. As Pokorak (1998) observes:

The broad scope of capital statutes and the recent increase in both the number and the type of capital crimes have expanded, by necessity, the prosecutors' discretion. Of the many death-eligible defendants, only a relatively small number actually will go to trial, and even fewer will face a capital penalty trial. Yet, in most cases, there are no clear policies, procedures, or other objective criteria that govern the exercise of prosecutorial discretion. (p. 1813)

Recent legislation has also enhanced prosecutorial power. Seventeen states and the federal system had sentencing guidelines in place by 1996 (Bureau of Justice Assistance, 1998). Sentencing guidelines expand the relative power of prosecutors vis-à-vis judges and juries since the specific charge (a prosecutorial decision) interacts with prior record (partially a function of earlier prosecutorial discretion) to determine the range of punishment. Whether defendants qualify for mandatory minimum sentences stipulated by so-called three-strikes statutes also depends upon the specific charges brought by prosecutors. All states, moreover, have some form of mandatory sentencing provisions that further empower prosecutors, since their charges determine the applicability of these provisions. Clearly, prosecutorial influence on case outcome today surpasses that of the past.

Given the significance of early decision making on case outcomes, this chapter reviews and evaluates presentencing research. After examining the role of race on bail and pretrial release, the chapter analyzes the impact of race on prosecute/dismiss decisions. The chapter concludes with an investigation of racial differences in recommendations for the death penalty in capital-eligible homicide cases involving whites and African Americans. Support for a discrimination hypothesis that African Americans receive harsher treatment by the criminal justice system than their white counterparts is assessed throughout the chapter.

Two databases—Ebsco Host and the Criminal Justice Periodical Index— were used. To maximize the presence of multivariate statistical techniques, studies prior to the 1970s were excluded. To complement the database searches, bibliographies from every study were examined for other possibly relevant empirical investigations. Again, research before 1970 was eliminated. Collectively, these procedures yielded a total of sixty-five usable studies that form the foundation of this review and evaluation (see Table 8.1).

BAIL AND PRETRIAL RELEASE DECISIONS

Twenty-five studies appearing in Table 8.1 analyzed the impact of race on bail and/or pretrial release decisions. Studies using more recent data were more likely than those using older data to reflect racial disparities. Whereas all three studies using data from the 1990s found racial disparities, 62.5 percent of the investigations using 1980s data and 58.3 percent of the investigations using 1970s data reported racial disparities. Limiting

Table 8.1
Empirical Studies of Race and Presentencing Since 1970

Source	Areas Covered	Support for the Discrimination Hypothesis
Adams & Cutshall (1987)	P/D (d)	Yes
Albonetti (1986)	P/D (d)	No
Albonetti (1987)	P/D (d)	No
Albonetti (1989)	B/PR	No
Albonetti et al. (1989)	B/PR	Yes
Ayres & Waldfogel (1994)	B/PR	Yes
Baldus et al. (1983)	DP (v)	Yes
Baldus et al. (1990)	DP (d, v)	DP (d): Mixed DP (v): Yes
Barnes & Kingsnorth (1996)	P/D (d)	No
Baumer et al. (2000)	P/D (d, v)	P/D (d): Mixed P/D (v): No
Bernstein et al. (1977)	P/D (d)	No
Bernstein et al. (1979)	P/D (d)	Yes
Bienen et al. (1988)	DP (d, v)	DP (d): No DP (v): Yes
Bock & Frazier (1977)	B/PR	No
Bowers (1983)	DP (v)	Yes
Bowers & Pierce (1980)	DP (v)	Yes
Bynum (1982)	B/PR	Yes
Chiricos & Bales (1991)	B/PR	Yes
Crew (1991)	B/PR	Yes
Curran (1983)	P/D (d)	Yes
Ewing & Houston (1991)	B/PR	Yes
Farnworth & Horan (1980)	B/PR	Yes
Feeley (1979)	B/PR	Yes
Foley & Powell (1982)	P/D (d, v)	P/D (d): No P/D (v): No
Frazier et al. (1980)	B/PR	No
Ghali & Chesney-Lind (1986)	P/D (d)	No
Holmes et al. (1987)	B/PR	No
Holmes et al. (1996)	B/PR	No
Jacoby & Paternoster (1982)	DP (v)	Yes
Juszkiewicz (1993)	B/PR, P/D (d)	B/PR: Yes P/D (d): No
Keil & Vito (1989)	DP (v)	Yes
Keil & Vito (1990)	DP (v)	Yes
Keil & Vito (1995)	DP (v)	Yes

Table 8.1
Empirical Studies of Race and Presentencing Since 1970 (continued)

Source	Areas Covered	Support for the Discrimination Hypothesis
Kingsnorth et al. (1998)	P/D (v)	No
Kruttschnitt (1984)	B/PR	Yes
LaFree (1980)	P/D (v)	No
Lizotte (1978)	B/PR	Yes
Mann (1984)	B/PR, P/D (d)	B/PR: No P/D (d): No
Murphy (1984)	DP (v)	Yes
Myers (1982)	P/D (d)	Mixed
Myers & Hagan (1979)	P/D (d, v)	P/D (d): No P/D (v): Yes
Nagel (1983)	B/PR	Yes
Nagel & Weitzman (1979)	B/PR	Yes
Nagel et al. (1982)	B/PR, P/D (d)	B/PR: Yes P/D (d): Yes
Nakell & Hardy (1987)	P/D (d, v) , DP (d, v)	P/D (d): No P/D (v): No DP (d): Mixed DP (v): No
Pallesen (1991)	B/PR	Yes
Paternoster (1983)	DP (v)	Yes
Paternoster (1984)	DP (v)	Yes
Paternoster & Kazyaka (1988)	DP (d, v)	DP (d): No DP (v): Yes
Patterson & Lynch (1991)	B/PR	Yes
Petee (1994)	B/PR	Yes
Radelet (1981)	DP (d, v)	DP (d): No DP (v): Yes
Rauma (1984)	P/D (v)	No
Rohrlich & Tulsky (1996)	P/D (d, v), DP (v)	P/D (d): No P/D (v): Yes DP (v): Yes
Schmitt (1991)	P/D (d)	Mixed
Sorensen & Wallace (1995)	DP (d, v)	DP (d): No DP (v): Yes
Sorensen & Wallace (1999)	DP (v)	Yes
Spears & Spohn (1997)	P/D (d, v)	P/D (d): No P/D (v): No
Spohn & Spears (1996)	P/D (v)	No
Spohn et al. (1987)	P/D (d)	No
Steury & Frank (1990)	B/PR	No
Stryker et al. (1983)	B/PR	No
U.S. GAO (1990)	DP (d, v)	DP (d): Yes DP (v): Yes
Vito & Keil (1988)	DP (v)	Yes
Welch et al. (1984)	P/D (d)	No

B/PR = bail/pretrial release; P/D (d) = prosecute/dismiss (defendant race); P/D (v) = prosecute/dismiss (victim race); DP (d) = death penalty (defendant race); DP (v) = death penalty (victim race).

the analysis to investigations that controlled for prior record, offense type, and at least one other legal variable, revealed that 62.5 percent of the studies reported racial disparities. A geographical assessment of the studies disclosed racial disparities in both southern and non-southern jurisdictions.

Race and Bail Decisions

When the review focused on investigations of bail amount, strong support for the racial discrimination hypothesis emerged. Only two studies (Frazier, Bock, & Henretta, 1980; Steury & Frank, 1990) failed to support a discrimination hypothesis. Conversely, six studies (Ayres & Waldfogel, 1994; Ewing & Houston, 1991; Farnworth & Horan, 1980; Kruttschnitt, 1984; Nagel, 1983; Patterson & Lynch, 1991) disclosed racial disparities even when controls for legal variables were present. Nor was the racial disparity limited to African American males. In research conducted in New Haven, Connecticut, Ayres and Waldfogel (1994) observed that both African American males and females were charged higher bail than their white counterparts despite controls for risk of flight. Additionally, Patterson and Lynch's (1991) investigation of felonies involving non-narcotics in Florida disclosed that whereas white females were more likely than white males to receive low bail (i.e., bail that is below guideline), there were no gender differences in bail bond amounts for nonwhites. This finding is significant because nonwhites overall were less likely than their white counterparts to receive low bail.

In contrast, findings regarding bail severity were mixed. There was, nevertheless, some evidence of the differential treatment of African Americans. Feeley's (1979) analysis of over 1,600 cases (primarily misdemeanors) in New Haven, Connecticut, for example, revealed that African Americans were more likely than whites to be required to put up cash or surety bonds before their release from detention. Similarly, an investigation of over five thousand felonies and misdemeanors in New York City disclosed that white defendants were more likely than minority defendants (African Americans and Hispanics) to receive cash alternative options for release (Nagel, 1983). Likewise, Albonetti, Hauser, Hagan, & Nagel (1989) reported that race interacted with several extralegal variables in federal courts in ways that favored white defendants. They noted that bail severity (from least [release on recognizance] to most restrictive [denied bail]) was greater for African American males with prior felony records than for similarly situated whites. They further observed that higher social class (as measured by education and income), while being related to less restrictive bail for both white and African American males, had a stronger beneficial impact on bail severity for white males.

Race and Pretrial Release

Interpretation of the data on pretrial release is hindered by the need to differentiate between court *decisions* and the *consequences* of those decisions (see Steury and Frank, 1990). Because the literature infrequently distinguishes between the two, care must be exercised when attributing race to pretrial confinement and release decisions. With that caveat in mind, let us now examine the research.

Although four investigations (Frazier et al., 1980; Holmes, Daudistel, & Farrell, 1987; Holmes, Hosch, Daudistel, Perez, & Graves, 1996; Stryker, Nagel, & Hagan, 1983) found no evidence of a race/pretrial release relationship, Steury and Frank's (1990) examination of the Milwaukee County, Wisconsin, criminal justice system exemplifies the difficulty associated with ferreting out the contributions of various extralegal variables. They reported that while offender race was unrelated to pretrial release terms, offender race was an important determinant of pretrial freedom. Of those required to post cash bond, whites were almost twice as likely as nonwhites to receive their freedom during the pretrial period. One might therefore surmise that the racial disparity in pretrial freedom was attributable to racial differences in poverty. Yet, this may be a fallacious interpretation of the data. An investigation of pretrial release in Palm Beach, Florida, by Pallesen (1991), for instance, demonstrated that poverty differentially affected whites and African Americans. Indigent white criminal defendants were almost twice as likely as indigent African American defendants to be granted supervised release from jail while awaiting trial. Furthermore, the private company that supervised pretrial release was more likely to accept indigent whites than indigent African Americans (61.1 percent versus 46.2 percent, respectively).

DECISIONS TO PROSECUTE VERSUS DISMISS

Both defendant race and victim race may influence decisions regarding prosecution versus dismissal. Because each of these variables may independently affect prosecutorial decision making, each is examined separately in this chapter. Let us commence with an analysis of the impact of defendant race on these decisions.

Defendant Race and Prosecute/Dismiss Decisions

Two-thirds of the twenty-one studies in Table 8.1 that examined defendant race and prosecute/dismiss decisions lacked evidence supportive of the discrimination hypothesis. Moreover, geographic region (south/nonsouth) had no effect on these decisions. Yet, a broad-stroke approach to prosecute/dismiss decisions leaves latent some potentially important differences in the treatment of African Americans and whites by the criminal justice system. Two investigations of federal court, for instance, demonstrated the impact of offense seriousness on differential processing. Myers (1982) reported that whites charged with misdemeanors were more likely than similarly situated African Americans to have their cases dismissed, albeit the reverse was true for felonies. Similarly, Adams and Cutshall (1987) observed that misdemeanant African American shoplifters were less likely than their white counterparts to have their charges dismissed. They further noted that racial disparity was greater when shoplifting was the only offense than when multiple charges were involved. Taken together, these studies suggest that African American defendants in federal court may be treated more harshly than white defendants when their offenses are misdemeanors.

One may also question whether the assumption that no racial differences in dismiss/prosecute decisions always supports a nondiscrimination argument. Petersilia (1983), for example, suggests that California police are more likely to arrest African Americans on scant evidence than similarly situated whites.[2] Thus, if an investigator were to discover that African Americans and whites in California were equally likely to have their cases dismissed, the investigator might incorrectly conclude that no racial bias existed if controls for evidentiary strength were missing.

Drug offenses represent an area where the potential for inflated arrests of persons of color is great. As Barnes and Kingsnorth (1996) acknowledged in their investigation of drug arrests in Sacramento County, California:

The highly political nature of the war on drugs, with its attendant pressures on law enforcement to produce a high number of arrests, leads law enforcement to favor strategies most likely to produce those results. Thus, minorities, and African Americans in particular, are more at risk of arrest because of the more public nature of the drug market in which they are involved. In streets, parks, and known crack houses, sweeps, sting operations, and proactive enforcement strategies generally produce immediate organizational rewards in the form of large numbers of easy arrests. Because these enforcement strategies often subordinate quality to quantity, many such arrests offer insufficient evidence for a prosecutor to sustain the burden of proof. Thus, a greater proportion of African American and Latino drug cases are rejected and dismissed by the prosecutors. (p. 52)

Despite the possible influence of evidentiary strength on prosecute/ dismiss decisions, only one-third of the studies examining defendant race included this measure. Even though inclusion of evidentiary strength lowered the probability of finding racial differences in the studies reviewed here,[3] it would be imprudent to dismiss race as a non-factor in prosecutorial decisions given the small number of investigations containing this variable.

Whether racial differences are detected may additionally depend on the processing stage. The importance of the processing stage is manifested in an examination of almost two thousand random murder cases throughout the United States by Baumer, Messner, & Felson (2000). Although decisions to reject cases during initial screening were unaffected by defendant race, cases with nonwhite defendants were more likely than those with white defendants to be carried forward during postindictment screening.

Victim race may also be a factor in prosecute/dismiss decisions. Because the protections afforded by the American legal system have been largely reserved for white victims, offenses against African Americans have frequently resulted in less severe sanctions against the perpetrators of such acts. The devaluation of black lives is particularly evident historically in sexual assault, where the criminal justice system differentiated between white and black victims. Exemplary is the Georgia Penal Code of 1816, which provided for a death sentence for a black man (free or slave) convicted of rape (or attempted rape) of a *white* woman, but a fine for a white man convicted of the same offense involving a *black* woman (Wriggens, 1995).

Sexual assault is not the only area in which African American victims receive less protection under the law than their white counterparts. Cases involving white murder victims are more likely than those with black victims to terminate in a death sentence. Since the reinstatement of the death penalty in 1976, only 13 percent of all capital cases have involved black victims, yet about half of all murder victims are nonwhite (Death Penalty Information Center, 2001).

An absence of racial disparity between white and African American defendants in prosecute/dismiss decisions may therefore be a product of victim choice. African Americans, being more likely than whites to target other African Americans for their crimes, decrease their probability of being prosecuted. Whites, by contrast, enhance their chances for prosecution because their victims are typically other whites. To explore this possibility we now turn our attention to victim race.

Victim Race and Prosecute/Dismiss Decisions

Eight of the ten investigations examining victim race or offender/victim racial composition and prosecute/dismiss decisions supported a nondiscrimination argument (see Table 8.1). Evidentiary strength, moreover, did not affect these findings.[4] Jurisdiction location (south/non-south) was also unrelated to prosecute/dismiss decisions.

These observations notwithstanding, several caveats are in order. First, Spohn and Spears' (1996) finding that sexual assault charges were more likely to be dismissed in black-on-white cases than black-on-black or white-on-white cases may be attributable to racial prejudice on the part of police and prosecutors who view interracial incidents differently than intraracial incidents.

Police and prosecutors may regard black-on-white sexual assaults as inherently more serious than intraracial sexual assaults; consequently they may be more willing to take a chance with a reluctant victim or a victim whose behavior at the time of the incident was questionable. The police may be willing to make an arrest and the prosecutor may be willing to charge, despite questions about the procedures used to obtain physical evidence or about the validity of the defendant's confession. If this is true, then cases involving black offenders and white victims will be more likely than other types of cases to "fall apart" before or during trial (Spohn & Spears, 1996, pp. 672, 674).

Second, failure to detect racial differences in prosecute/dismiss decisions does not preclude racial disparities elsewhere. LaFree (1980), for example, observed that African Americans who sexually assaulted white women were more likely than other offender/victim combinations to have felony charges brought against them. Furthermore, this finding persisted despite controls for prior criminal record of the offender, victim prosecution preference, availability of an eyewitness, use of a weapon, and offense seriousness.

Third, offense seriousness may affect the findings. Research focusing on the most serious offenses may be examining areas in which prosecutors have the least amount of discretion to independently determine whether to prosecute or dismiss a case.

Finally, it may be premature to discount the role of region in prosecute/ dismiss decisions because only Foley and Powell (1982) and Nakell and Hardy (1987) analyzed southern jurisdictions, and both focused on homicide, which, because of its gravity, may minimize prosecutorial discretion.

DECISIONS TO SEEK THE DEATH PENALTY IN CAPITAL-ELIGIBLE CASES

Thirty-eight states plus the federal government and the military provide for capital punishment under certain circumstances. Of the numerous murder cases that potentially qualify for capital punishment, only a fraction culminate in a death sentence. In 1996 state courts convicted 11,430 individuals of murder (Brown & Langan, 1999, table 2), but only 295 death-sentenced individuals were admitted to state prisons that year (Maguire & Pastore, 1999, table 6.85). Because prosecutors have considerable discretion in deciding whether to seek the death sentence in capital-eligible cases, and given the overrepresentation of African Americans on death row (see Snell, 1999, table 7), a question emerges regarding the role of race in prosecutorial decisions to try cases as capital offenses. Let us now examine the literature beginning with those investigations that have analyzed the impact of defendant race on this decision.

Defendant Race and Death Penalty Charging

Table 8.1 offers mixed support for the discrimination hypothesis. An examination of two data sets from Georgia by Baldus, Woodworth, & Pulaski (1990), for instance, found no defendant-race effect in the Procedural Reform Study data set. However, after holding constant all factors in the file (including statutory aggravating and mitigating factors) in the larger Charging and Sentencing Study data set, prosecutors were more likely to seek the death penalty in homicides involving African American defendants.

Nakell and Hardy's (1987) investigation of homicide cases in North Carolina hints at the complexity of this relationship. The researchers found that whether defendant race was related to a first-degree murder indictment was dependent in part on the courtroom actor. Whereas defendant race was not related to a first-degree murder indictment when a grand jury and a prosecutor shared in the decision, defendant race was related to a first-degree murder indictment when the actor was a prosecutor or a trial judge. Prosecutors were ten times more likely to request the death penalty for nonwhite defendants with no aggravating circumstances and a high level of culpability than for a similarly situated white defendant. Similarly, trial judges were more likely to submit to the jury as first-degree murder those cases involving nonwhite defendants with no prior record and zero to one aggravating circumstances.

Further evidence that the influence of defendant race on the decision to seek the death penalty is contextual is revealed in a study of homicides in South Carolina (Paternoster & Kazyaka, 1988). When urban and rural jurisdictions were analyzed separately, urban prosecutors were more likely to seek the death penalty when defendants were white, whereas rural prosecutors were more likely to seek the death penalty when defendants were African American. The latter finding, nonetheless, failed to attain statistical significance.

Radelet (1981) conducted an investigation of death penalty charging in Florida. Although he concluded that defendant race was unrelated to the likelihood of a first-degree murder indictment for nonprimary homicides (those in which the perpetrator and victim are not acquainted), an absence of background data on the homicides precluded an examination of possible interaction effects.

Two investigations of death penalty charging were from non-southern jurisdictions. Bienen, Weiner, Denno, Allison, & Mills' (1988) analysis of capital punishment in New Jersey revealed that homicides involving white defendants were more likely than those involving African American or Hispanic defendants to be death-certified. In contrast, Sorensen and Wallace's (1995) investigation of capital punishment in Missouri disclosed no relationship between defendant race and death penalty charging when the level of aggravation was high. Ergo, when murder was particularly egregious, defendant race did not affect prosecutorial decisions regarding the death penalty. However, in low- to mid-range levels of aggravation, white defendants were more likely than African American defendants to proceed to penalty trial. Collectively, these non-southern jurisdictions tend to refute the notion that African American defendants are more likely than white defendants to be prosecuted under capital statutes.

Nonetheless, some support for the discrimination hypothesis can be gleaned from an extensive review of empirical research conducted by the U.S. General Accounting Office (GAO) in 1990. The GAO examined twenty-three different data sets from twenty-eight empirical studies of death penalty sentencing since the *Furman* (1972) decision. That review noted that "more than half of the studies found that race of defendant influenced the likelihood of being charged with a capital crime or receiving the death penalty" (p. 6), and over three-fourths of those reporting racial differences found that African American defendants were treated more harshly than white defendants. These findings, nevertheless, must be qualified since the GAO study did not differentiate between presentencing (e.g., charging defendants with capital crimes) and sentencing (e.g., finding defendants guilty of capital crimes) in its results.

Victim Race and Death Penalty Charging

Studies of victim race and the decision to seek the death penalty are also enumerated in Table 8.1. The table displays strong support for a discrimination argument that murders involving white victims are more likely than those involving African American victims to evoke a death penalty response from prosecutors. Only Nakell and Hardy (1987) failed to corroborate the discrimination hypothesis of the twenty investigations reported in the table. According to the GAO (1990), victim race was associated with the decision to charge the defendant with capital murder or receive the death penalty in 82 percent of the reviewed studies, and "[t]his finding was remarkably consistent across data sets, states, data collection methods, and analytic techniques" (p. 5).

The impact of victim race on death penalty charging was strongest in those cases having relatively few aggravating factors (Baldus, Pulaski, & Woodworth, 1983; Baldus et al., 1990; Paternoster & Kazyaka, 1988; Sorensen & Wallace, 1995). As Baldus and colleagues (1990) observed in their analysis of data from the Procedural Reform Study in Georgia:

[T]he data indicate that, for both the pre- and post-*Furman* periods, the race-of-victim effects were particularly strong in the midrange of cases when prosecutors and juries have the greatest room for the exercise of discretion. In this zone of cases, the race of victim appears to determine the outcome of *more than one-third of the cases* [italics added]. (p. 185)

In addition, the proclivity to seek the death penalty in white victim cases increased when the offender was African American (Bowers, 1983; Bowers & Pierce, 1980; Jacoby & Paternoster, 1982; Keil & Vito, 1989, 1990, 1995; Murphy, 1984; Paternoster, 1984; Sorensen & Wallace, 1995, 1999; Vito & Keil, 1988). According to Bowers (1983): "That a black has killed a white is virtually as strong a predictor of a first degree indictment as any of the legally relevant factors except felony circumstance, i.e., the commission of a separate felony in the course of the homicide" (p. 1074).

The differential importance attached to African Americans and whites by the legal system is further evidenced in white-on-black homicides. Bienen and colleagues (1988) found that homicide cases in which the offender was white and the victim was African American were the least likely to be death-certified in New Jersey. Similar findings were reported in Florida (Bowers, 1983; Bowers & Pierce, 1980), Kentucky (Keil & Vito, 1989, 1990), and Ohio (Bowers & Pierce, 1980).

SUMMARY AND CONCLUSION

Research on bail and pretrial release revealed that more recent data were more likely than older data to display racial disparities. These disparities, moreover, persisted even when introducing controls for legal variables. Over 60 percent of the investigations that controlled for prior record, offense type, and at least one additional legal variable reported racial differences. Furthermore, racial disparities were not confined to southern jurisdictions. Support for the discrimination hypothesis was most evident in investigations of bail amounts where African Americans were typically charged more for their pretrial freedom than their white counterparts.

The impact of race on bail severity and pretrial release, however, was less obvious. Complicating the issue of pretrial freedom is the possibility that a defendant may be granted pretrial release but be unable to meet the conditions for release (due to other pending charges, probation violations, etc.). Additionally, the factors that make the offender ineligible for release are themselves susceptible to manipulation by the criminal justice system.

Although most examinations of prosecute/dismiss decisions failed to detect significant racial differences once legal variables were introduced, some studies suggested that the impact of race was conditional (e.g., African American defendants in federal court were treated more harshly than their white counterparts in misdemeanor cases, but not in felony cases). Because racial discrimination may exist even in the absence of racial differences if discriminatory treatment of African American offenders preceded that stage, findings of no racial differences are subject to misinterpretation. Collaterally, if police overcharge or arrest African Americans on insufficient or questionable evidence, the higher dismissal rates for African Americans may represent attempts by prosecutors to eliminate those cases with low probabilities of conviction rather than the preferential handling of African Americans.

Prosecutorial discretion in capital charging evidenced the most consistent racial disparity. Even though there was scattered evidence that defendant race affects death penalty requests, results from southern and non-southern jurisdictions alike disclosed the greater value attached to white victims by the legal system. Research uniformly demonstrated that prosecutors were more likely to charge defendants with capital offenses when their victims were white, irrespective of legal controls. Furthermore, studies showed that the offender/victim racial dyad influenced the likelihood of a capital trial. Cases in which the defendant was African American and the victim was white frequently had the greatest probably of being classified as capital eligible. Finally, some research suggested that the impact of victim race on capital charging was strongest in the least-serious homicides (i.e., those with few aggravating circumstances).

In conclusion, the literature provides a measure of support for the discrimination hypothesis in many areas of presentencing. Yet, much research is flawed in that it fails to include a measure of evidentiary strength, the absence of which may conceal racial differences in criminal processing. Moreover, with the exception of studies of homicide and possibly sexual assault, the impact of victim race has been largely ignored, despite evidence that victim race may be a better predictor of presentencing decisions than defendant race. Thus, race may affect presentence decision making in ways not fully explored in the literature.

NOTES

1. For a prima facie case of racial discrimination to be established "there must be relatively substantial evidence that others similarly situated have not been prosecuted" (Applegate, 1982, p.74). However, what constitutes "substantial evidence" has been narrowly defined since *McCleskey v. Kemp* (1987). Evidence presented to the Supreme Court in *McCleskey* showed that African Americans who killed whites in Georgia were twenty-two times more likely to receive death sentences than African Americans who killed other African Americans. Despite overwhelming statistical evidence of racial disparity in the administration of the death penalty, the Court concluded that *aggregate* statistical evidence may not be used to prove discrimination in a particular case.

2. Petersilia (1983) is not the only researcher to report questionable police charging practices. Miller (1996) observed overcharging of African Americans by police in Duval County, Florida (Jacksonville). He found that approximately 80

percent of the aggravated assault charges were later downgraded to simple assault or to a misdemeanor due to insufficient evidence.

3. Studies of defendant race and prosecute/dismiss decisions that included a measure of evidentiary strength were: Adams and Cutshall (1987), Albonetti (1986, 1987), Myers (1982), Myers and Hagan (1979), Nakell and Hardy (1987), and Spears and Spohn (1997). Support for the discrimination hypothesis was found only in Adams and Cutshall (1987) and Myers (1982), although the latter investigation provided only mixed support.

4. Seven investigations controlled for the impact of evidence on prosecute/dismiss decisions: Kingsnorth, Lopez, Wentworth, and Cummings (1998), LaFree (1980), Myers and Hagan (1979), Nakell and Hardy (1987), Rauma (1984), Spears and Spohn (1997), and Spohn and Spears (1996). Only Myers and Hagan's (1979) analysis of felonies was supportive of the discrimination hypothesis.

CASES CITED

Furman v. Georgia, 408 U.S. 238 (1972)
McCleskey v. Kemp, 481 U.S. 279 (1987)

REFERENCES

Adams, K., & Cutshall, C. (1987). Refusing to prosecute minor offenses: The relative influence of legal and extralegal factors. *Justice Quarterly, 4,* 595–609.

Albonetti, C. (1986). Criminality, prosecutorial screening, and uncertainty: Toward a theory of discretionary decision making in felony case processings. *Criminology, 24,* 623–644.

Albonetti, C. (1987). Prosecutorial discretion: The effects of uncertainty. *Law & Society Review, 21,* 291–313.

Albonetti, C. (1989). Bail and judicial discretion in the District of Columbia. *Sociology & Social Research, 74,* 40–47.

Albonetti, C., Hauser, R., Hagan, J., & Nagel, I. (1989). Criminal justice decision making as a stratification process: The role of race and stratification resources in pretrial release. *Journal of Quantitative Criminology, 5,* 57–82.

Applegate, A. (1982). Prosecutorial discretion and discrimination in the decision to charge. *Temple Law Quarterly, 55,* 35–88.

Ares, C., Rankin, A., & Sturz, H. (1963). The Manhattan Bail Project: An interim report on the use of pre-trial parole. *New York University Law Review, 38,* 67–95.

Ayres, I., & Waldfogel, J. (1994). A market test for race discrimination in bail setting. *Stanford Law Review, 46,* 987–1047.

Baldus, D., Pulaski, C., & Woodworth, G. (1983). Comparative review of death sentences: An empirical study of the Georgia experience. *Journal of Criminal Law & Criminology 74,* 661–753.

Baldus, D., Woodworth, G., & Pulaski, C. (1990). *Equal justice and the death penalty: A legal and empirical analysis.* Boston: Northeastern University Press.

Barnes, C., & Kingsnorth, R. (1996). Race, drug, and criminal sentencing: Hidden effects of the criminal law. *Journal of Criminal Justice, 24,* 39–55.

Baumer, E., Messner, S., & Felson, R. (2000). The role of victim characteristics in the disposition of murder cases. *Justice Quarterly, 17,* 281–307.

Beck, A. (2000). *Prisoners in 1999.* Washington, DC: Bureau of Justice Statistics.

Bernstein, I., Cardascia, J., & Ross, C. (1979). Defendant's sex and criminal court decisions. In R. Alvarez, K. Lutterman, and associates (Eds.), *Discrimination in organizations: Using social indicators to manage social change* (pp. 329–354). San Francisco: Jossey-Bass.

Bernstein, I., Kelly, W., & Doyle, P. (1977). Societal reaction to deviants: The case of criminal defendants. *American Sociological Review, 42,* 743–755.

Bienen, L., Weiner, N., Denno, D., Allison, P., & Mills, D. (1988). The reimposition of capital punishment in New Jersey: The role of prosecutorial discretion. *Rutgers Law Review, 41,* 27–361.

Bishop, D., & Frazier, C. (1984). The effects of gender on charge reduction. *The Sociological Quarterly, 25,* 385–396.

Bock, E., & Frazier, C. (1977). Official standards versus actual criteria in bond dispositions. *Journal of Criminal Justice, 5,* 321–328.

Bowers, W. (1983). The pervasiveness of arbitrariness and discrimination under post-*Furman* capital statutes. *Journal of Criminal Law & Criminology, 74,* 1067–1100.

Bowers, W., & Pierce, G. (1980). Arbitrariness and discrimination under post-*Furman* capital statutes. *Crime & Delinquency, 26,* 563–635.

Brown, J., & Langan, P. (1999). *Felony sentences in the United States, 1996.* Washington, DC: Bureau of Justice Statistics.

Bureau of Justice Assistance. (1998). *1996 National survey of state sentencing structures.* Washington, DC: Author.

Bynum, T. (1982). Release on recognizance: Substantive or superficial reform? *Criminology, 20,* 67–82.

Chiricos, T., & Bales, W. (1991). Unemployment and punishment: An empirical assessment. *Criminology, 29,* 701–724.

Chiricos, T., & Crawford, C. (1995). Race and imprisonment: A contextual assessment of the evidence. In D. F. Hawkins (Ed.), *Ethnicity, race, and crime: Perspectives across time and place* (pp. 281–309). Albany, New York: State University of New York Press.

Crew, B. (1991). Race differences in felony charging and sentencing: Toward an integration of decision-making and negotiation models. *Journal of Crime & Justice, 14*, 99–122.

Curran, D. (1983). Judicial discretion and defendant's sex. *Criminology, 21*, 41–58.

Dalaker, J., & Proctor, B. (2000). *Poverty in the United States: 1999.* Washington, DC: U.S. Government Printing Office.

Davis, A. (1998). Prosecution and race: The power and privilege of discretion. *Fordham Law Review, 67*, 13–67.

Death Penalty Information Center. (2001). Race and defendants executed since 1976. Retrieved March 30, 2001, from http://www.death penaltyinfo.org/dpicrace.html.

Eterno, J. (1993, March). *Ethnicity and sentencing: A study of the effect of ethnicity on sentencing of female prostitutes in New York City.* Paper presented at the annual meeting of the Academy of Criminal Justice Sciences, Kansas City, MO.

Ewing, J., & Houston, B. (1991, June 18). Inequalities in bail persist 10 years after reforms. *Hartford Courant,* pp. A1, A6.

Farnworth, M., & Horan, P. (1980). Separate justice: An analysis of race differences in court processes. *Social Science Research, 9*, 381–399.

Farrell, R., & Swigert, V. (1986). Adjudication in homicide: An interpretive analysis of the effects of defendant and victim social characteristics. *Journal of Research in Crime & Delinquency, 23*, 349–369.

Feeley, M. (1979). *The process is the punishment: Handling cases in a lower criminal court.* New York: Russell Sage Foundation.

Foley, L., & Powell, R. (1982). The discretion of prosecutors, judges, and juries in capital cases. *Criminal Justice Review, 7*, 16–22.

Foote, C. (1959). The bail system and equal justice. *Federal Probation, 23*, 43–48.

Frazier, C., Bock, E., & Henretta, J. (1980). Pretrial release and bail decisions: The effects of legal, community, and personal variables. *Criminology, 18*, 162–181.

Free, M., Jr. (1996). *African Americans and the Criminal Justice System.* New York: Garland.

Ghali, M., & Chesney-Lind, M. (1986). Gender bias and the criminal justice system: An empirical investigation. *Sociology & Social Research, 70*, 164–171.

Hagan, J. (1974). Extra-legal attributes and criminal sentencing: An assessment of a sociological viewpoint. *Law & Society Review, 8*, 357–383.

Holmes, M., & Daudistel, H. (1984). Ethnicity and justice in the southwest: The sentencing of Anglo, black, and Mexican origin defendants. *Social Science Quarterly, 65*, 265–277.

Holmes, M., Daudistel, H., & Farrell, R. (1987). Determinants of charge reductions and final dispositions in cases of burglary and robbery. *Journal of Research in Crime & Delinquency, 24*, 233–254.

Holmes, M., Hosch, H., Daudistel, H., Perez, D., & Graves, J. (1996). Ethnicity, legal resources, and felony dispositions in two southwestern jurisdictions. *Justice Quarterly, 13*, 11–30.

Humphrey, J., & Fogarty, T. (1987). Race and plea bargained outcomes: A research note. *Social Forces, 66*, 176–182.

Jacoby, J., & Paternoster, R. (1982). Sentencing disparity and jury packing: Further challenges to the death penalty. *Journal of Criminal Law & Criminology, 73*, 379–387.

Juszkiewicz, J. (1993, March). *More evidence of racial and ethnic disparity in criminal justice outcomes: Is it more evidence of racial and ethnic bias?* Paper presented at the annual meeting of the Academy of Criminal Justice Sciences, Kansas City, MO.

Keil, T., & Vito, G. (1989). Race, homicide severity, and application of the death penalty: A consideration of the Barnett scale. *Criminology, 27*, 511–535.

Keil, T., & Vito, G. (1990). Race and the death penalty in Kentucky murder trials: An analysis of post-*Gregg* outcomes. *Justice Quarterly, 7*, 189–207.

Keil, T., & Vito, G. (1995). Race and the death penalty in Kentucky murder trials: 1976–1991. *American Journal of Criminal Justice, 20*, 17–36.

Kempf, K., & Austin, R. (1986). Older and more recent evidence on racial discrimination in sentencing. *Journal of Quantitative Criminology, 2*, 29–48.

Kingsnorth, R., Lopez, J., Wentworth, J., & Cummings, D. (1998). Adult sexual assault: The role of racial/ethnic composition in prosecution and sentencing. *Journal of Criminal Justice, 26*, 359–371.

Kleck, G. (1981). Racial discrimination in criminal sentencing: A critical evaluation of the evidence with additional evidence on the death penalty. *American Sociological Review, 46*, 783–805.

Kramer, J., & Steffensmeir, D. (1993). Race and imprisonment decisions. *The Sociological Quarterly, 34*, 357–376.

Kruttschnitt, C. (1984). Sex and criminal court dispositions: The unresolved controversy. *Journal of Research in Crime & Delinquency, 21*, 213–232.

LaFree, G. (1980). The effect of sexual stratification by race on official reactions to rape. *American Sociological Review, 45*, 842–854.

Landes, W. (1974). Legality and reality: Some evidence on criminal procedure. *Journal of Legal Studies, 3*, 287–337.

Lizotte, A. (1978). Extra-legal factors in Chicago's criminal courts: Testing the conflict model of criminal justice. *Social Problems, 25*, 564–580.

Maguire, K., & Pastore, A. (1999). *Sourcebook of criminal justice statistics— 1998*. Washington, DC: Bureau of Justice Statistics.

Mann, C. (1984). Race and sentencing of female felons: A field study. *International Study of Women's Studies, 7*, 160–172.

Miller, J. (1996). *Search and destroy: African-American males in the criminal justice system.* New York: Cambridge University Press.

Murphy, E. (1984). Application of the death penalty in Cook County. *Illinois Bar Journal, 93*, 90–95.

Myers, M. (1982). Common law in action: The prosecution of felonies and misdemeanors. *Sociological Inquiry, 52*, 1–15.

Myers, M., & Hagan, J. (1979). Private and public trouble: Prosecutors and the allocation of court resources. *Social Problems, 26*, 439–451.

Myrdal, G. (1944). *An American dilemma: The Negro problem and modern democracy.* New York: Harper.

Nagel, I. (1983). The legal/extra-legal controversy: Judicial decisions in pretrial release. *Law & Society Review, 17*, 481–515.

Nagel, I., Cardascia, J., & Ross, C. (1982). Sex differences in the processing of criminal defendants. In D. K. Weisberg (Ed.), *Women and the law: A social historical perspective* (Vol. 1) (pp. 259–282). Cambridge, MA: Schenkman.

Nagel, S., & Weitzman, L. (1979). Women as litigants. In F. Adler and R. Simon (Eds.), *The criminology of deviant women* (pp. 264–272). Boston: Houghton Mifflin.

Nakell, B., & Hardy, K. (1987). *The arbitrariness of the death penalty.* Philadelphia: Temple University Press.

Pallesen, T. (1991, June 3). Bias accused in supervised jail releases: Whites freed more often among suspects who can't afford bail. *Palm Beach Post*, p. A1.

Pastore, A., & Maguire, K. (2000). *Sourcebook of criminal justice statistics 1999.* Washington, DC: U.S. Government Printing Office.

Paternoster, R. (1983). Race of victim and location of crime: The decision to seek the death penalty in South Carolina. *Journal of Criminal Law & Criminology, 74*, 754–785.

Paternoster, R. (1984). Prosecutorial discretion in requesting the death penalty: A case of victim-based racial discrimination. *Law & Society Review, 18*, 437–478.

Paternoster, R., & Kazyaka, A. (1988). The administration of the death penalty in South Carolina: Experiences over the first few years. *South Carolina Law Review, 39*, 245–411.

Patterson, E., & Lynch, M. (1991). Bias in formalized bail procedures. In M. Lynch & E. Patterson (Eds.), *Race and criminal justice* (pp. 36–53). Albany, NY: Harrow & Heston.

Petee, T. (1994). Recommended for release on recognizance: Factors affecting pretrial release recommendations. *The Journal of Social Psychology, 134*, 375–382.

Petersilia, J. (1983). *Racial disparities in the criminal justice system.* Santa Monica, CA: Rand.

Pokorak, J. (1998). Probing the capital prosecutor's perspective: Race of the discretionary actors. *Cornell Law Review, 83,* 1811–1820.

Radelet, M. (1981). Racial characteristics and the imposition of the death penalty. *American Sociological Review, 46,* 918–927.

Rankin, A. (1964). The effect of pretrial detention. *New York University Law Review, 39,* 641–655.

Rauma, D. (1984). Going for the gold: Prosecutorial decision making in cases of wife assault. *Social Science Research, 13,* 321–351.

Rohrlich, T., & Tulsky, F. (1996, December 3). Not all L.A. murder cases are equal. *Los Angeles Times,* pp. A1, A14–A15.

Schmitt, C. (1991, December 8). Plea bargaining favors whites as blacks, Hispanics pay price. *San Jose Mercury News,* p. 1A.

Snell, T. (1999). *Capital punishment 1998.* Washington, DC: Bureau of Justice Statistics.

Sorensen, J., & Wallace, D. (1995). Capital punishment in Missouri: Examining the issue of race. *Behavioral Sciences & the Law, 13,* 61–80.

Sorensen, J., & Wallace, D. (1999). Prosecutorial discretion in seeking death: An analysis of racial disparity in the pretrial stages of case processing in a midwestern county. *Justice Quarterly, 16,* 559–578.

Spears, J., & Spohn, C. (1997). The effect of evidence factors and victim characteristics on prosecutors' charging decisions in sexual assault cases. *Justice Quarterly, 14,* 501–524.

Spohn, C. (2000). Thirty years of sentencing reform: The quest for a racially-neutral sentencing process. In *NIJ Criminal Justice 2000* (Vol. 3). Washington, DC: U.S. Department of Justice.

Spohn, C., Gruhl, J., & Welch, S. (1987). The impact of the ethnicity and gender of defendants on the decision to reject or dismiss felony charges. *Criminology, 25,* 175–191.

Spohn, C., & Holleran, D. (2000). The imprisonment penalty paid by young, unemployed black and Hispanic male offenders. *Criminology, 38,* 281–306.

Spohn, C., & Spears, J. (1996). The effect of offender and victim characteristics on sexual assault case processing decisions. *Justice Quarterly, 13,* 649–679.

Steury, E., & Frank, N. (1990). Gender bias and pretrial release: More pieces of the puzzle. *Journal of Criminal Justice, 18,* 417–432.

Stryker, R., Nagel, I., & Hagan, J. (1983). Methodological issues in court research: Pretrial release decisions for federal defendants. *Sociological Methods & Research, 11,* 469–500.

U.S. General Accounting Office. (1990). *Death penalty sentencing: Research indicates pattern of racial disparities.* Washington, DC: Author.

Unnever, J. (1982). Direct and organizational discrimination in the sentencing of drug offenders. *Social Problems, 30,* 212–225.

Vito, G., & Keil, T. (1988). Capital sentencing in Kentucky: An analysis of the factors influencing decision making in the post-*Gregg* period. *Journal of Criminal Law & Criminology, 79,* 483–503.

Weitzer, R. (1996). Racial discrimination in the criminal justice system: Findings and problems in the literature. *Journal of Criminal Justice, 24,* 309–322.

Welch, S., Gruhl, J., & Spohn, C. (1984). Dismissal, conviction, and incarceration of Hispanic defendants: A comparison with Anglos and blacks. *Social Science Quarterly, 65,* 257–263.

Wriggens, J. (1995). Rape, racism, and the law. In P. Searles and R. Berger (Eds.), *Rape and Society* (pp. 215–222). Boulder, CO: Westview.

CHAPTER 9

Trying Juveniles as Adults: A Case of Racial and Ethnic Bias?

Becky Tatum

INTRODUCTION

Juvenile justice policies have become increasingly punitive over the last two decades. Symbolizing a tough, no-nonsense approach to serious juvenile crime, these policies abandon the traditional principles of the juvenile justice system and adopt punishment, accountability, and public safety as primary goals. The general argument is that to protect the public, serious juvenile offenders must be held accountable for their behavior and receive punishment that is equivalent to their criminal acts (Feld, 1999, 2000; Jackson & Pabon, 2000; Redding, 2000; Zimring, 1998). These policies further suggest that the juvenile justice system is ill equipped to handle serious juvenile offenders and that there are no important psychological differences between juveniles and adults to consider in determining criminal responsibility (Feld, 1999; Jackson & Pabon, 2000; Steinberg, 2000; Zimring, 1998).

Juvenile transfer reforms clearly reflect this shift in the perception and treatment of juvenile offenders. Despite declines in both violent and property juvenile crime rates, virtually all states have revised and/or adopted policies to increase the prosecution of juveniles as adults. For example, in March 2000, California passed the Gang Violence and Youth Crime Prevention Act (Proposition 21) requiring juveniles 14 and older to be tried as adults for specific violent crimes and giving prosecutors the option of transferring certain types of juvenile cases (e.g., gang involvement) to adult court without judicial review (Dorfman & Schiraldi, 2001; Gonzales, 2000; Weick & Angulo, 2000). At the federal level, both Houses of Con-

gress have passed legislation in which juveniles 14 years and older arrested for violent crimes can be charged and sentenced as adults (Randall,
1999; Weick & Angulo, 2000).[1] Juvenile transfer reforms have increased
the number of delinquency cases transferred to adult court, with approximately 200,000 American youths being prosecuted as adults each year
(American Bar Association, 2001).[2]

As with other aspects of the juvenile justice system, the impact of juvenile transfer policies is not borne equitably by all juveniles. Minority
youths are far more likely to be transferred to adult court, convicted in
these courts, and incarcerated in adult prison facilities than white youths
(Bortner, Zatz, & Hawkins, 2000; Feld, 1999; Weick & Angulo, 2000; Zimring, 1998). African American youths experience the most disparate treatment. The number of African American youths transferred to adult court
between 1985 and 1994, for example, increased almost 100 percent; currently, they represent approximately 50 percent of all transferred cases and
58 percent of all juveniles behind bars in adult facilities (Love, 2000; Weick
& Angulo, 2000).

The disparate effects of juvenile transfer and other juvenile justice policies on minority youths often are linked to the paucity of minority justice
officials and lawmakers in the United States. Minority representation
plays a critical role in both the administration of justice and the way the
nation is governed. Minority justice officials and lawmakers have been
instrumental in raising issues important to minority communities, addressing disparities in the application of laws, and recommending strategies to address minority crime (Kiely, 2002; Washington, 1994). A specific
example of the role of minority justice officials in the administration of
juvenile justice is the Juvenile and Family Court Judges' Leadership Council, a national network of African American and family court judges whose
goals are to reduce the number of poor and minority youths who come
into contact with criminal and juvenile justice authorities and to ensure
that youths in the system receive fair and individualized treatment (Black
Community Crusade for Children, 2002). Minority judges, prosecutors,
and lawmakers, however, account for less than 3 percent of the professionals in their respective professions (Kiely, 2002; Kopp, 2001; Washington, 1994). This greatly reduces their ability to have an impact in their
workplaces and in minority communities. Minority justice officials and
lawmakers, however, have sponsored and supported punitive juvenile
justice policies, a factor that underscores the importance of class in the
association between minority representation and the equitable treatment
of minority individuals (Brown, 2002; Fishman, 2002). Underclass minorities sometimes are considered to be the *other*—that is, unlike well-
educated, hardworking, and conventionally oriented minorities and thus
deserving of punitive treatment by the legal system (Fishman, 2002).

This chapter examines the differential effects of juvenile transfer provisions and laws on minority youths, especially African Americans. The chapter begins with a brief overview of the three methods of transferring juveniles to adult criminal court. This discussion is followed by arguments of racial and ethnic disparity regarding the origins of the juvenile court and the role of public perceptions and juvenile justice and political decision making in the development and differential application of juvenile transfer provisions and laws. Research identifying discriminatory transfer procedures and laws is also reviewed. Next, the chapter examines collateral consequences of juvenile transfer policies as a crime control strategy and what this means for African American and other minority youths and minority communities. The chapter ends with a discussion of recommendations and methods for addressing racial and ethnic disparity in the transfer of youths to adult criminal court.

METHODS OF JUVENILE TRANSFERS

Although juvenile transfer policies have changed extensively since 1992, they have existed since the development of the juvenile justice system. Early juvenile judges used this authority to transfer to adult courts older juveniles who were charged with more serious offenses (Feld, 1999). Despite the small number of juveniles waived to criminal court each year (approximately 1 percent), the process provided a safety valve to preserve the court's jurisdiction over the remaining juveniles and to protect it from political criticism of coddling young criminals (Feld, 1999, 2000).

Currently, there are three methods of transferring juveniles to adult court: judicial waiver, concurrent jurisdiction (also known as prosecutorial waiver, prosecutorial discretion, or direct file), and statutory exclusion (also known as legislative exclusion). Targeting both violent and nonviolent offenders, the major difference between the three methods is who is responsible for deciding whether a juvenile should be prosecuted as a delinquent or criminal (Griffin, Torbet, & Szymanski, 1998; Feld, 1999). Judicial waivers, the oldest and most common type of transfer method, give juvenile court judges the discretion to transfer jurisdiction of juvenile cases. Waiver hearings are required in which a juvenile judge considers factors such as seriousness of the offense, amenability, and risk to public safety, and the prosecution bears the burden of proof that a juvenile should be sent to adult court. Judicial waivers may be presumptive or mandatory. Presumptive judicial waivers involve cases that are designated as appropriate for transfer waiver to criminal court (Griffin et al., 1998). Although waiver hearings must be conducted, in these cases the juvenile rather than the prosecution bears the burden of proof. Mandatory judicial waivers require the transfer of cases that meet certain age, offense, or other criteria (Griffin et al., 1998). Although these proceedings originate in juvenile court, the juvenile court's role is only to confirm that the statutory requirements for mandatory waiver are met.

A more recent method of juvenile transfer, concurrent jurisdiction, allows prosecutors to determine whether to try a juvenile as a delinquent or adult. Although few states allow this type of transfer, many juveniles are tried as adults in this way (Griffin et al., 1998). The criteria for concurrent jurisdictions vary greatly among the states; however, the minimum level of offense seriousness necessary for a prosecutor to transfer a case to adult court appears to be lower than that required for statutory or legislative exclusion or mandatory or presumptive judicial waiver (Griffin et al., 1998).

Last, statutory or legislative exclusions grant criminal courts original jurisdiction over certain juvenile cases and account for the largest number of juveniles tried as adults in criminal court (Griffin et al., 1998). Many states exclude certain serious offenses from juvenile court jurisdiction, set age limits for excluded offenses, and exclude juveniles charged with felonies if they have prior felony adjudications or convictions. Offenses most often excluded are capital crimes and murders and other serious offenses against persons. State provisions also can permanently terminate juvenile court jurisdiction over individual juveniles who have been tried or convicted as adults (e.g., once an adult/always an adult).

ARGUMENTS OF RACIAL AND ETHNIC DISPARITY

Research consistently shows that minority youths are the victims of discriminatory and disparate treatment in the juvenile justice system. These racial and ethnic differences increase as youths move through the juvenile justice process and are more prevalent than those that exist in the adult criminal justice system (Dorfman & Schiraldi, 2001; Feld, 1999; Males & Macallair, 2000; Zimring, 1998). Research examining racial and ethnic differences in the transfer of juveniles for adult prosecution, especially variations among different transfer methods, is fairly limited (see Bortner et al., 2000). Arguments of racial and ethnic disparity regarding juvenile transfer methods, however, largely address four issues: the purpose of the juvenile court, public perceptions, the decision making of juvenile justice officials and lawmakers, and the differential application of juvenile transfer provisions and laws.

Purpose of the Juvenile Court

The establishment of the juvenile court in 1899 represented the culmination of reform efforts that defined the social and legal status of juveniles in American society. No longer viewed as miniature adults, juveniles were not held as accountable for delinquent and criminal behavior. Acting in the best interest of the child, the juvenile court served as a nonadversarial and nonlegalistic system where juveniles were treated and rehabilitated in individualized programs that were geared toward their specific needs.

Although the juvenile court is credited with saving juveniles from social disorder and the adult criminal justice system, some argue that it was originally intended and designed to regulate the behaviors of poor and immigrant youths (Feld, 1999, Jackson & Pabon, 2000; Platt, 1969; Rothman 1980; Zimring, 1998). In fact, the crimes specifically designated for the new juvenile court (e.g., begging, sexual crimes, frequenting vice establishments, loitering, staying out all night) were all behaviors that were associated with the urban poor (Platt, 1969). Nearly three-quarters of the juveniles who appeared in the Chicago and Milwaukee juvenile courts in the late 1900s were poor and immigrant youths (Feld, 1999). The individualized treatment of juveniles also encouraged class and ethnic disparity by allowing decisions to be based on social status rather than delinquent behavior. Consequently, a dual system of juvenile justice existed in which middle- and upper-class youths were treated (e.g., placed on probation or sent home), and poor and immigrant youths were punished (e.g., placed in juvenile institutions) (Feld, 1999, 2000). Thus, the premise of saving juveniles was actually a promise of protecting society from poor and immigrant youths (Feld, 1999).

The punitiveness of current juvenile justice policies is posited to be a continuation of the tradition of protecting society from other people's children (Feld, 1999; Jackson & Pabon, 2000; Zimring, 1998). Rather than the immigrant youths of the nineteenth century, other people's children now represent minority youths who primarily reside in our urban centers. The growing trend of transferring juvenile offenders to adult criminal court points to a heighten fear of these youths that is grounded in political, historical, and racial factors as well as purposeful design (Brown, 2002; - Feld, 1999; Jackson & Pabon, 2000; Weick & Angulo, 2000). Feld (1999, pp. 208–225) specifically argues that contemporary get-tough juvenile justice policies are reactions to public and political perceptions of serious juvenile crime as *black* crime. These perceptions (which will be discussed more fully in the next two sections) have been used to justify a dual system of juvenile justice in which minority youths are punished (e.g., sent to the adult criminal justice system) and majority youths are rehabilitated (e.g., treated in the juvenile justice system). Thus, the phrase *getting tough on juvenile offenders*, the current theme of transfer and other juvenile justice policies, has meant getting tough on African American and other minority youths.

Public Perceptions

Public perceptions of juveniles play a major role in juvenile transfer policies. Both criminal justice officials and lawmakers depend on public approval for the passage of transfer legislation, the initiation and enforcement of transfer provisions, and for career success. As a result of the growing emphasis on punishment, no elected official or candidate can risk being perceived as soft on crime. For example, Palm Beach prosecutor, Barry Krischer, who was running for reelection when he was handling the Nathaniel Brazill case in 2000, commissioned a private poll asking whether juveniles accused of murder should be charged as adults (Elsner, 2001). Brazill, a thirteen-year-old African American honor student, was charged and convicted of killing his seventh grade teacher who would not allow him back into class after he had been suspended for throwing water balloons. Brazill was sentenced to twenty-eight years in prison.

Generally, the public supports adult prosecution of serious juvenile offenders. Research suggests, however, that public sentiment toward transfer policies is based on more than legal factors. Feiler and Sheley (1999, pp. 61–62) found that although the seriousness of the offense and a juvenile's age influenced the public's desire to waive a juvenile case to adult court, both African American and white citizens were more likely to support waivers if the juvenile in question was African American. This finding was attributed to the association of violence and other serious crime with race and gender and society's image of African Americans as the cause of crime and other social ills in American society. Although the social class status of the respondents was not analyzed, as noted previously, it may be an important factor in understanding the attitudes and perceptions of African Americans. The image of African Americans as social deviants is both historical and political. Since slavery, African Americans, especially African American males, have been portrayed as predators, socially inferior, and immoral. These images have served as a justification for their social, economic, and political status and are currently being used to rationalize punitive juvenile justice policies (see Brown, 2002; Fishman, 2002; Russell, 1998).

Public support for the transfer of African American and other minority youths for adult prosecution are clearly associated with information that is obtained from the media. The media provide knowledge about the nature and extent of crime, strategies that should be taken to ensure public safety, and because of the segregation of American society, information on minority crime. Most importantly, the media bring juvenile and criminal justice issues to the public's attention (Brown, 2002; Dorfman & Scharldi, 2001; Russell, 1998).

The media, however, misrepresent the picture of crime and violence in American society. Analyzing peer-reviewed studies that examined the content of crime news, Dorfman and Scharldi (2001) found that crime, especially violent crime, was reported out of proportion to its actual occurrence and that the media's coverage of crime had increased while real crime rates had fallen. The media also grossly associated race with crime. African Americans were more likely to be portrayed as perpetrators of violence and less frequently shown as crime victims than white Americans. African American perpetrators often were indistinguishable from noncriminal African Americans, and youths of color were more likely to appear in crime news than white youths, who primarily appeared in health or education stories. In short, the media suggest that crime and violence are rising, that the perpetrators of these incidents are African Americans and other minorities, and that the victims are whites. The impact of this imagery on public perceptions and attitudes is significant. Research shows that 60 percent of the people watching a news story without an image of a perpetrator falsely remember seeing one, and in 70 percent of these cases, they remember the perpetrator as an African American, even though they never saw him (Gilliam & Iyengar, 2000). This imagery further increases fear of crime, especially of minority perpetrators, and increases support for tougher crime policies (Peffley, Shields, & Williams, 1996).

In a similar analysis, Zimring (1998) identifies three recurring themes in the print media that promote fear of serious juvenile offenders and galvanize public support for tougher juvenile sanctions. First, serious juvenile offenders are depicted as being qualitatively different from young persons who have violated the law in previous times. According to the print media, these youths have higher rates of offending, and most importantly, commit crimes that are more vicious than youths of past generations. Because of this, they are labeled as *superpredators* and *young criminals* rather than adolescents or children. Second, the print media portray the serious juvenile offenders as being unamenable to treatment and, in turn, the juvenile justice system as being ill equipped to handle serious crime. And third, the print media describe serious juvenile offenders as mature criminals. Simply put, serious crime is not behavior that is associated with childhood.

The racial application of these three themes is illustrated by Brown (2002), who examines the *Atlanta Journal-Constitution's (AJC's)* coverage of serious juvenile offenders tried as adults under Georgia's Senate Bill 440 from 1997 to 1999. Senate Bill 440, also known as the seven deadly sins law, authorizes the state to transfer juveniles as young as thirteen to adult court for certain violent crimes.[3] In 1997, Michael Lewis (also known as Little B), a thirteen-year-old underclass African American youth, was tried and later convicted for the murder of a young African American father in Vine City, a poor inner-city neighborhood of Atlanta. From arrest to conviction, *AJC* characterized Little B as being more dangerous than other youthful offenders, unamenable to treatment, and as a mature criminal. More specifically, he was labeled as *a thug, a repeat offender who had been brought before a juvenile judge twelve times since he was ten,* and as having *committed the crime to prove his manhood.* Lewis was further accused of contributing to the destruction of the black family and the social deterioration of the Vine City area. To rally public support for tougher juvenile laws, *AJC* suggested that society must protect itself from juveniles like Little B, even if it meant locking them up for most of their lives.

AJC's characterization of white youths tried as adults under Senate Bill 440 during this time period is vastly different. Tried and later convicted for the beating death of a middle school youth in 1998, Jonathan Miller, a fifteen-year-old high school student, was never identified as a thug, being unamenable to treatment, or as a mature criminal. Instead, *AJC* referred to Miller simply as a youth who was suffering from attention-deficit disorder and suggested that the punishment (mandatory life sentence for adult conviction for murder) was too harsh. Similarly, in 1999, Anthony T.J. Solomon, age fifteen, was charged with shooting and wounding six students at an Atlanta suburban high school. Solomon was described as a Boy Scout, a disgruntled boy who was upset over breaking up with his girlfriend, and as a youth who was suffering from long-term, untreated, major depression.

In sum, the characterizations of these youths in the print media prompted very different reactions in terms of how they should be perceived and treated by the juvenile justice system. Dangerous mature young criminals who were unamenable to treatment (African American and other minority youths) were to be punished, whereas youths with psychological and/or social problems (white youths) were to be afforded rehabilitative services. Atlantans, both African American and white, were led to fear and despise juvenile offenders such as Michael Lewis and to support tougher juvenile sanctions for this new breed of young criminal.

Decision Making of Juvenile Justice Officials and Lawmakers

The disproportionate transfer of African American and other minority youths to adult court has long been attributed to biased decision making on the part of juvenile justice officials and lawmakers. Judges, prosecutors, and politicians may hold conscious and unconscious biases that are formed as the result of media coverage, little direct contact with racial and ethnic groups, or differences in class status. For example, assumptions are often made about young African American youths who come from inner-city environments, who dress a certain way, and/or who have a certain demeanor that negatively affect how they are treated in the juvenile justice system (Bridges & Steen, 1998; Frontline, 2001). Assumptions also tend to be made about the criminal propensity of these youths. When asked why nearly all of the youths he had prosecuted as adults under Senate Bill 440 in DeKalb County, Georgia, had been African American, District Attorney J. Tom Morgan responded, "They're the ones committing all the crimes" (Brown, 2002, p. 107). Although statutory exclusion laws remove certain offenses from the jurisdiction of the juvenile court, prosecutors still determine whether a juvenile is charged with an excluded offense.

Both prosecutorial and judicial discretion play major roles in disparate juvenile transfer decisions. Prosecutors in concurrent jurisdictions have wide discretionary authority to charge juveniles as delinquents or criminals with virtually no guidance in the exercise of this power. The lack of review procedures and waiver criteria allow prosecutors to treat juveniles charged with the same crime differently. As a result, members of certain unpopular groups can be singled out for harsher treatment in the adult system while equally culpable juveniles, for whom there is cultural loyalty or broader public sympathy, remain in juvenile court (Feld, 2000).

Ironically, disparity in judicial waivers often stem from the discretionary application of waiver criteria associated with the transfer method. The subjectiveness of the criteria, the large number of factors that can be considered, and the emphasis of certain factors over others give juvenile judges broad standardless discretion as to what cases are waived to adult court (Feld, 2000). Judicial waiver criteria, for example, usually involve assessments of dangerousness, amenability, and public safety, factors that cannot be made with any degree of accuracy and that are often negatively associated with African American and other youths of color.

In addition to judicial discretion, disparities in judicial transfer decisions are tied to discriminatory decision making at earlier stages of the juvenile justice system. Podkopacz and Feld (1995) found that differences in judicial waivers were linked to significant differences in the types of offenses with which prosecutors charge minority and white youths. Prosecutors charged most minority juveniles with violent crimes, which involved a greater risk for transfer, and most white offenders with property offenses. Podkopacz and Feld concluded that because judicial waivers constituted the final stages of a cumulative process, discriminatory decisions made at earlier stages of the juvenile justice system influenced which cases were waived to the adult system.

Finally, the role of politics in the decision making of juvenile justice officials and lawmakers cannot be overlooked in examining racial and ethnic disparities in juvenile transfer policies on African American youths and other minority youths. As noted previously, the initiation, passage, and application of juvenile transfer provisions and laws are related to public fear and media attention to violence among minority youths and opportunities for career advancement. The proliferation of statutory exclusion laws adopted by states and the federal government suggests that lawmakers, particularly, have exploited these factors. The political atmosphere, however, is equally as important to juvenile judges. As in the early juvenile court, the waiver of youths who are the most intractable and who pose the greatest threat to public safety creates an effective symbolic gesture regarding the protection of the public and deflects criticism of the entire system (Feld, 1999). Because of the association of race and ethnicity with juvenile crime and violence, minority youths are the most expendable.

Differential Application of Transfer Provisions and Laws

There is a dearth of research examining the racial and ethnic effects of juvenile transfer methods. Bortner, Zatz, and Hawkins (2000) found only fifteen studies published between January 1983 and March 1998 that specifically addressed the issue of race and/or ethnicity. Collectively, this research revealed mixed findings, with only six of the fifteen studies indicating racial and ethnic disparities in the transfer process (Barnes & Franz, 1989; Bortner, 1986; Clarke, 1996; Fagan & Deschenes, 1990; Houghtalin & Mays, 1991; Podkopacz & Feld, 1995).

Males and Macallair (2000) provide some of the strongest evidence of discrimination in the transfer of youths to adult criminal court. Analyzing transfer legislation in Los Angeles County, these researchers tested whether minority youths were disproportionately transferred to adult court and sentenced to incarceration compared with white youths who were similarly situated. Males and Macallair argued that transfer rates should reflect the racial breakdown for violent arrests. Study findings showed that the transfer of minority youths to adult criminal court could not be explained by higher arrests for serious crimes or for the commission of more heinous crimes. Although minority youths in Los Angeles County had higher arrest rates for felony violent crimes, the proportions of minority juveniles transferred to adult court were double that for white youths arrested for felony violent crimes, despite little difference in the severity of the felony arrest. Study findings further indicated that racial and ethnic disparities accumulated as youths moved into the adult system: minority youths were 2.8 times as likely to be arrested for a violent crime, 6.2 times as likely to be transferred for adult prosecution, and 7 times as likely to be sent to adult institutions than white youths in similar situations.

The specifications of juvenile transfer laws can also contribute to differential rates of juvenile transfer to adult court. A prime example of this type of inequitable legislation is Illinois' automatic transfer law for drug offenses. Passed in 1989, the legislation requires that fifteen- and sixteen-year-olds charged with drug sales within a thousand feet of a school or a public housing development be automatically prosecuted as adults. Because almost every neighborhood in inner-city areas lies within a thousand feet of a school zone or public housing, the vast majority of public housing in Illinois is located in Chicago, and almost three-quarters of Illinois' African American juvenile population lives in Cook County (Chicago), this means that the law has a disparate effect on African American youths (Ziedenberg, 2001). Statistics show that from October 1999 to September 2000, 87 percent of the youths prosecuted as adults for drug offenses in Cook County were African American (Ziedenberg, 2001). This is despite evidence that white youths in the state of Illinois use and sell drugs at the same or higher rates than minority youths and that many of the youths transferred to adult court for drug crimes have no previous juvenile conviction or record of juvenile court services (Ziedenberg, 2001).

COLLATERAL CONSEQUENCES

Discussions of racial and ethnic disparity in juvenile transfer policies are incomplete without an examination of the collateral effects of these policies on crime control. In short, what are the unintended effects of these procedures and laws on juveniles and what does this mean for African American and other minority youths and minority communities? Despite the increased use of juvenile transfer methods, research examining the effects of prosecuting juveniles in adult criminal court is still in its infancy. Current juvenile transfer studies primarily have addressed recidivism among transferred juveniles and the adverse experiences and outcomes of being tried as an adult.

As noted earlier, juvenile transfer policies are posited to be a more effective strategy of addressing serious juvenile crime. Research suggests, however, that as a crime control strategy, these policies have neither a general nor specific effect on serious juvenile offending. Both cross-sectional and longitudinal studies indicate higher recidivism rates among transferred youths than youths who remain in the juvenile justice system (Bishop, Frazier, Lanza-Kaduce, & Winner, 1996; Myers, 1999; Podkopacz & Feld, 1996; Stack, 2001; Winner, Lanza-Kaduce, Bishop, & Fazier, 1997). These findings, however, may only be applicable to violent juvenile offenders. Winner, Lanza-Kaduce, Bishop, and Frazier (1997) found that property felons tried in adult court were less likely to re-offend than those tried in juvenile court; however, those who did re-offend did so sooner and more often than property felons tried under juvenile jurisdiction.

Higher rates of recidivism among transferred juveniles have been attributed to the absence of rehabilitative programs in the adult criminal justice system and the effects of formal processing. Despite the premise of getting tough on the worst juvenile criminals, juveniles tried and convicted in adult courts often served less time than youths who were adjudicated in juvenile courts. Stack (2001), for example, found that under

Pennsylvania adult time law, the median sentence for juveniles tried and convicted in adult court was 11.5 months, far less than the five years of jail time suggested by the law. These juveniles returned to the streets more quickly without any of the reform school treatment they would have received in the juvenile system. Other factors that may encourage repeat offending among transferred juveniles include perceptions of unjust transfer to adult court, weakened family and community ties, modeling and learning of criminal behavior from adult criminals, and stigmatization (Bortner et al., 2000; Gainsborough & Mauer, 2000; Stack, 2001; Weick & Angulo, 2000).

Finally, juveniles transferred to adult criminal courts risk the loss of many privileges and rights that are associated with criminal court convictions. Juveniles convicted in criminal court may lose the right to vote and to serve in the military. Unlike juvenile court adjudications, criminal convictions are public records and must be reported on employment applications. In many states, juveniles convicted in adult criminal court are subjected to adult criminal jurisdiction for all subsequent offenses. Also, juveniles convicted in adult criminal courts risk being incarcerated in adult prisons. Adult prisons are ill equipped to address the needs of juveniles, and incarceration in these institutions can lead to abuses by adult offenders (Bortner et al., 2000, p. 309). Because these consequences limit successful reintegration into society and chances for meaningful employment and social opportunities, they may increase recidivism.

What do these unintended effects mean for African American and other minority youths and minority communities? First, African American and other youths of color are less likely to be afforded rehabilitative and educational opportunities that are associated with being tried in juvenile court. The punitive nature of adult criminal courts combined with weakened family and community ties and the lost social and economic opportunities that result from criminal convictions increase the probability of recidivism and the adoption of a life of crime. In short, African American youths and other youths of color who often have been charged with nonviolent offenses and have no previous arrests are not given second chances to correct mistakes and turn their lives around (Brown, 2002; Gonzales, 2000). These factors threaten to create a permanent class of minority youths who are untrained, uneducated, and hardened criminals (Weick & Angulo, 2000).

Second, the unintended effects of juvenile transfer policies negatively affect minority youths by supporting stereotypes and helping to maintain a dual system of juvenile justice. Higher rates of recidivism that are associated with criminal court convictions, for example, may be used to support assumptions that these youths are more dangerous, unamenable to treatment, and should therefore be subjected to adult punishment. They also may be used to justify differential treatment of certain groups or categories of youths. Because they are differentially impacted by juvenile transfer provisions, minority youths are most likely to hold cynical views of the fundamental fairness of the juvenile justice process, views that can lead to more criminal behavior and a self-fulfilling prophecy of higher rates of crime (Weick & Angulo, 2000).

Third, the disproportionate transfer of racial minority youths to adult criminal courts is destructive to the well-being of minority communities. The adverse effects of being tried in adult courts and the higher probability of incarceration in adult prison weaken the social fabric of minority communities by increasing the probability of crime and decreasing the likelihood that the youths in these communities will become productive citizens (Gainsborough & Mauer, 2000; Weick & Angulo, 2000).

ADDRESSING DISPARITY IN JUVENILE TRANSFER POLICIES

The disproportionate effects of juvenile transfer policies on African American and other youths of color have led to allegations of racism and demands that these laws be abolished. In the state of Georgia, Mothers Advocating Juvenile Justice, a grassroots organization, has been organized to address the differential effects of SB 440 on African American youths (Brown, 2002). Composed of African American parents (mostly African American single mothers) with young sons in prison under SB 440 charges, the nonprofit organization seeks to reform or overturn the automatic transfer law. This organization, however, has had a cool reception from African American leaders, legislators, clergy, and other professionals who want little to do with a bunch of women and their condemned children (Brown, 2002, p. 344).

National organizations such as the Leadership Conference on Civil Rights have also recommended that states and the federal government repeal or abandon juvenile transfer policies. In addition to racial disparity, these organizations point to the inconsistency of transfer provisions with traditional juvenile justice policy and practice and the detrimental effects of incarceration and punishment-based crime approaches on juveniles (Weick & Angulo, 2000). These organizations further argue that the juvenile court should be given the necessary resources to handle all but the most exceptional cases in their jurisdiction (Gainsborough & Mauer, 2000).

Research organizations, think tanks, and academic scholars have called for more research to understand the complex role of race and ethnicity in juvenile transfer decisions and to develop effective strategies to address racial disparities (Bortner et al., 2000; Gainsborough & Mauer, 2000; Weick & Angulo, 2000). Research recommendations include the use of qualitative and quantitative research methods to provide insight into the various factors associated with transfer decisions and the examination and comparison of racial and ethnic disparities in all three types of juvenile transfer procedures. The importance of examining the intersection of race, ethnicity, class, and gender, and how transfer decisions affect racial and ethnic minority youths throughout the juvenile and criminal justice systems, have also been noted. These types of analyses extend our understanding of the issue beyond a black/white dichotomy and emphasize the role and salience of all decision points and demographic characteristics (e.g., class, gender) in juvenile transfer procedures (Bortner et al., 2000). Finally, recommendations for research stress the need for an examination of transfer policies within its macrostructural context and the role of politics in racial and ethnic disparities that arise in the transfer process.

CONCLUSION

This chapter examined the effects of juvenile transfer policies on African American and other minority youths. The chapter argues that rather than a response to serious juvenile offending, juvenile transfer procedures and laws are a reaction to the fear of minority youths, the association of serious juvenile crime with race and ethnicity, and the perception of minority youths as other people's children. These perceptions and beliefs have evolved from the negative imagery of minority groups in the United States. The adverse effects of juvenile transfer policies on the well-being of minority youths and minority communities continue to perpetuate this imagery and to justify a dual system of juvenile justice.

Race and ethnic disparities in the transfer of juveniles to adult criminal court call into question the fundamental fairness and legitimacy of the juvenile justice system. More importantly, it erodes public confidence and faith in the rule of the law and provides support for the assumption that the law represents the imposition of one group's values on another (Cole, 1999; Weick & Angulo, 2000). Disparate treatment in the juvenile justice system, however, is reflective of the attitudes, beliefs, and practices of wider society. Thus, in addition to more sophisticated and encompassing research on the issue, efforts to reform juvenile transfer and other juvenile justice policies must include efforts to eradicate race, class, and ethnic divisions in the United States. Only by addressing disparities both within and outside of the juvenile justice system will true equality be achieved for all American youths.

NOTES

1. The estimated cost of both pieces of legislation is tremendous. The juvenile justice bill passed by the House of Representatives calls for an estimated $1.5 billion to arrest, prosecute, sentence, and imprison youths as adults (Randall, 1999). Proposition 21 is estimated to cost California counties more than $100 mil-

lion annually in operating costs and $200–$300 million in one-time construction costs to house juvenile offenders while they await trial in adult court.

2. Only a small percentage (1.4 percent) of all delinquency cases formally processed in juvenile court are waived for adult prosecution. It is difficult, however, to arrive at the total number of delinquency cases moved into the criminal justice system since there are no national data on prosecutorial waivers and statutory exclusion provisions.

3. Senate Bill 440 gives superior court exclusive jurisdiction over children ages thirteen to seventeen who are alleged to have committed one of the following offenses: murder, voluntary manslaughter, rape, aggravated sodomy, aggravated child molestation, aggravated sexual battery, and armed robbery if committed with a firearm. Since the passage of the legislation, about 75 percent of all youths arrested and 90 percent of all youths tried and convicted as adults have been African Americans.

REFERENCES

American Bar Association. (2001). *Youth in the criminal justice system: Guidelines for policymakers and practitioners.* Washington, DC: Author.

Barnes, C., & Franz, R. (1989). Questionably adult: Determinants and effects of the juvenile waiver decision. *Justice Quarterly, 6,* 117–130.

Bishop, D., Frazier, C., Lanza-Kaduce, L., & Winner, L. (1996). The transfer of juveniles to criminal court: Does it make a difference? *Crime & Delinquency, 42,* 171–191.

Black Community Crusade for Children. (2002). *What is the judges' Leadership Council?* Washington, DC: Author.

Bortner, M. (1986). Traditional rhetoric, organizational realities: Remand of juveniles to adult court. *Crime & Delinquency, 32,* 53–73.

Bortner, M., Zatz, M., & Hawkins, D. (2000). Race and transfer: Empirical research and social context. In J. Fagan & F. Zimring (Eds.), *The changing borders of juvenile justice: Transfer of adolescents to the criminal court* (pp. 277–320). Chicago: University of Chicago Press.

Brown, E. (2002). *The condemnation of little B.* Boston: Beacon.

Bridges, G., & Steen, S. (1998). Racial disparities in official assessment of juvenile offenders: Attributional stereotypes as mediating mechanisms. *American Sociological Review, 63,* 554–570.

Clarke, E. (1996). A case for reinventing juvenile transfer: The record of transfer of juvenile offenders to criminal court in Cook County, Illinois. *Juvenile & Family Court Journal, 47,* 3–13.

Cole, D. (1999). *No equal justice: Race and class in the American criminal justice system.* New York: New Press.

Dorfman, L., & Schiraldi, V. (2001). *Off balance: Youth, race, and crime in the news.* San Francisco: Justice Policy Institute.

Elsner, A. (2001). *Tough juvenile sentencing getting second look.* Reuters. Retrieved May 18, 2001, from http://www.crimelynx.com/toughsen.html.

Fagan, J., & Deschenes, E. (1990). Determinants of juvenile waiver deci-
    sions for violent juvenile offenders. *Journal of Criminal Law & Crim-
    inology, 81*, 314–334.
Feld, B. (1999). *Bad kids: Race and the transformation of the juvenile court.*
    New York: Oxford University Press.
Feld, B. (2000). Legislative exclusion of offenses from juvenile court juris-
    diction: A history and critique. In J. Fagan & F. Zimring (Eds.), *The
    changing borders of juvenile justice: Transfer of adolescents to the criminal
    courts* (pp. 83–144). Chicago: University of Chicago Press.
Feiler, S., & Sheley, J. (1999). Legal and racial elements of public willing-
    ness to transfer juvenile offenders to adult court. *Journal of Criminal
    Justice, 27*, 55–64.
Fishman, L. (2002). The black bogeyman and white self-righteousness. In
    C. Mann & M. Zatz (Eds.), *Images of color images of crime* (pp. 177–
    191). Los Angeles: Roxbury.
Frontline. (2001). *Juvenile justice: Is the system racially biased?* Retrieved
    March 5, 2002, from http://www.pbs.org/wgbh/pages/frontline/
    shows/juvenile/bench/race.html.
Gainsborough, J., & Mauer, M. (2000). *Diminishing returns: Crime and in-
    carceration in the 1990s.* Washington, DC: Sentencing Project.
Gilliam, F., & Iyengar, S. (2000). Prime suspects: The influence of local
    television news on the viewing public. *American Journal of Political
    Science, 44*, 560–573.
Gonzales, R. (2000). *Will Proposition 21, "The Gang Violence and Juvenile
    Crime Prevention Act," decrease juvenile crime in California?* Sacra-
    mento, CA: California Budget Project.
Griffin, P., Torbet, P., & Szymanski, L. (1998). *Trying juveniles as adults in
    criminal court: An analysis of state transfer provisions.* Washington, DC:
    U. S. Department of Justice.
Houghtalin, M., & Mays, G. (1991). Criminal disposition of New Mexico
    juveniles transferred to adult court. *Crime & Delinquency, 37*,
    393–403.
Jackson, R., & Pabon, E. (2000). Race and treating other people's children
    as adults. *Journal of Criminal Justice, 28*, 507–515.
Kiely, K. (2002, January 21). Nation's elite political circles lack minor-
    ities. *USA Today.* Retrieved January 21, 2002, from http://www
    .usatoday.com/news/acovmon.htm.
Kopp, E. (2001). Black prosecutors: Dealing with race in the criminal
    justice system. Retrieved June 15, 2002, from http://www.jrn
    .columbia.edu/studentwork/race/2001/justice_kopp.shtml.
Love, D. (2000). *Justice system discriminates against black and Latino youths.*
    The Progressive Media Project. Retrieved May 2, 2000, from
    www.progressive.org/mpblv00.htm.

Males, M., & Macallair, D. (2000). *Color of justice: An analysis of juvenile adult court transfers in California*. San Francisco: Justice Policy Institute.

Myers, D. (1999). *Excluding violent youths from juvenile court: The effectiveness of legislative waiver*. Unpublished doctoral dissertation, University of Maryland, College Park, Maryland.

Peffley, M., Shields, T., & Williams, B. (1996). The intersection of race and crime in television news stories: An experimental study. *Political Communications, 13*, 309–327.

Platt, A. (1969). *The child savers*. Chicago: University of Chicago Press.

Podkopacz, M., & Feld, B. (1995). Judicial waiver, police, and practice: Persistence, seriousness, and race. *Race and Inequality Journal, 14*, 73–95.

Podkopacz, M., & Feld, B. (1996). The end of the line: An empirical study of judicial waiver. *Journal of Criminal Law & Criminology, 86*, 449–492.

Randall, K. (1999). *U.S. youth crime bill: More children to be tried as adults*. World Socialist Organization. Retrieved June 24, 1999, from http://www.wsws.org/articles/1999/jun1999/juvej24.shtml.

Redding, R. (2000). *Deterrence effects of transfer laws*. Charlottesville, VA: Institute of Law, Psychiatry, & Public Policy, University of Virginia.

Rothman, D. (1980). *Conscience and convenience*. Boston: Little, Brown.

Russell, K. (1998). *The color of crime: Racial hoaxes, white fear, black protectionism, police harassment, and other macroaggressions*. New York: New York University Press.

Stack, B. (2001, March 18). Is this justice?: The "adult time" law for juveniles hasn't fulfilled its backers' promises. *Pittsburgh Post-Gazette*. Retrieved March 18, 2001, from http://www.post-gazette.com/regionstate/20010318jintro0318areg2.asp.

Steinberg, L. (2000). *Should juvenile offenders be tried as adults?* Evanston, IL: Center for Poverty Research.

Washington, L. (1994). *Black judges on justice: Perspectives from the bench*. New York: New Press.

Weick, R., & Angulo, C. (2000). *Justice on trial: Racial disparities in the American criminal justice system*. Washington, DC: Leadership Conference on Civil Rights/Leadership Conference Education Fund.

Winner, L., Lanza-Kaduce, L., Bishop, D., & Frazier, C. (1997). The transfer of juveniles to adult court: Re-examining recidivism over the long-term. *Crime & Delinquency, 43*, 548–563.

Ziedenberg, J. (2001). *Drugs and disparity: The racial impact of Illinois' practice of transferring young drug offenders to adult court*. Washington, DC: Justice Policy Institute.

Zimring, F. (1998). *American youth violence*. New York: Oxford University Press.

CHAPTER 10

The Racist Application of Capital Punishment to African Americans

David V. Baker

INTRODUCTION

Racism is integral to capital sentencing in U.S. society. Indeed, the research record on race and capital punishment challenges our society's most basic notions of fairness and equity in criminal sentencing. Yet, nowhere is our societal indifference toward racial injustice more apparent than our patent denial of racial discrimination in capital sentencing. For nearly forty years now, a plethora of distinguished voices have censured the racist administration of the death penalty. In 1967, for example, the President's Commission on Law Enforcement and Administration of Justice declared that the imposition of death sentences in the United States follows discriminatory patterns. "The death sentence is disproportionately imposed and carried out on the poor, the Negro, and the members of unpopular groups."[1] Former U.S. Supreme Court Justice Arthur J. Goldberg asserted a few years later that the Court should declare capital punishment unconstitutional because it is "highly suspect under the standards of degrading severity and wanton imposition."[2] In 1982, the National Minority Advisory Council on Criminal Justice recognized that capital sentencing is a singularly instructive example of how discretion exacts its inequitable toll on nonwhites.[3] Five years later, the American Society of Criminology publicly condemned capital punishment as racist in its application and urged its members to use their professional skills to abolish the penalty. U.S. Supreme Court Justice Harry A. Blackmun asserted after a twenty-year struggle with the issue of capital punishment that the Court must recognize that "the death penalty experiment has failed" and that the

Court should abandon its "delusion" that capital punishment is consistent with the federal Constitution.[4] Most recently, U.S. Supreme Court Justice Sandra Day O'Connor expressed her doubts on equity in death penalty administration.[5]

State and federal governments have largely sidestepped these and other concerted voices, however, and continue in their racist application of the death penalty against black persons.[6] In 1994, for example, Congress rejected the Racial Justice Act that would have afforded condemned prisoners the right to challenge their death sentences as racially motivated.[7] Congress refused to pass the Racial Justice Act mainly because state and federal prosecutors strongly opposed the bill.[8] Government attorneys claimed that the act was unnecessary since racial discrimination in capital sentencing does not exist, but even if it does exist, they nevertheless conceded that it is inevitable and impossible to prevent, detect, or remedy. Leading death penalty researchers believe otherwise, however. Accordingly, "the record of the last twenty-five years demonstrates that the issue of racial discrimination in the use of the death penalty is as susceptible to identification, to adjudication, and to correction as are practices of discrimination in other areas of American life."[9] Yet, even if Congress were to ratify such a bill, white Americans would be outraged and demand its immediate repeal; like a preponderance of state and federal prosecutors, they too believe that racism does not exist in capital sentencing, and even if it does exist, then it is an artifact of individual shortcomings. White Americans labor under a misguided notion that the political reforms arising out of the civil rights campaigns of the 1960s alleviated the arbitrary, capricious, and discriminatory treatment of minorities in the justice system. They summarily reject the idea that racism is systematic and institutionalized in capital sentencing. Nevertheless, the consequences of the racist application of capital punishment in the United States are not obscure and tangential aberrations. Racism is not fragmented and isolated in capital sentencing; rather, it is endemic, integral, and central to its processes. As Randall Kennedy puts it, "alongside notable discontinuities in American race relations are ugly continuities as well, including willful blindness to invidious racial discrimination in punishment."[10]

The purpose of this chapter is to provide a straightforward and candid look at racial bias against blacks in capital sentencing by reviewing the research record. The review shows that social scientists and legal scholars have put forth compelling evidence that state and federal jurisdictions capriciously impose the death penalty on black persons. Moreover, the research finding that blacks that victimize whites consistently have the highest probability of receiving a capital sentence suggests that the death penalty serves the extralegal function of majority group protection. That is, capital punishment jurisdictions have used the death penalty to safeguard whites, which is the least likely class of individuals criminals victimize. This review examines the research record on capital sentencing in the context of three landmark decisions of the U.S. Supreme Court on race and the death penalty, namely, *Furman v. Georgia,*[11] *Gregg v. Georgia,*[12] and *McCleskey v. Kemp.*[13] The review shows that the procedures under which jurisdictions sentence blacks to death remain far removed from the constitutionally prescribed canons of equity, fairness, and impartiality.

THE RESEARCH RECORD ON RACIAL DISCRIMINATION AGAINST AFRICAN AMERICANS IN CAPITAL SENTENCING

Racial discrimination in capital sentencing has a long history in the United States.[14] Since 1930, when the federal government began maintaining an informational index on executions in the United States, death penalty jurisdictions have executed nearly 5,000 condemned prisoners. Of this number, state and federal jurisdictions executed about 2,200 white prisoners and roughly 2,300 black prisoners. These are disturbing numbers because they reveal that death penalty jurisdictions have disproportionately executed black prisoners when compared with their overall representation in the general population. Though blacks constitute about 52 percent of all executed prisoners, they are roughly only 12 percent of the U.S. population. In contrast, whites are 47 percent of the executed prisoner population but 82 percent of the general population. A difficulty with statistics on racial disparities in criminal justice, however, is that distributions showing racial disparity in capital sentencing are not necessarily indicative of racial discrimination in capital sentencing. *Racial disparity* refers to criminal justice outcome differences by race, whereas *racial discrimination* refers to criminal justice outcome differences resulting from racially biased activities of justice administrators. Nakell and Hardy explain that discrimination in the context of capital punishment "involves the question of whether discretion permits the death penalty to be deliberately directed disproportionately against certain qualified defendants, not because of the nature of their crimes, but because they belong to a particular class or group, determined by such considerations as race, sex, nationality, religion, or wealth. Discrimination is deliberate."[15] The studies reviewed in this paper offer persuasive evidence that race discrimination in capital sentencing is *deliberate;* racism has become so entrenched and routinized in capital sentencing that it has developed into a systematic pattern of differential treatment of black defendants.

Furman v. Georgia

The importance of *Furman* to the study of race relations in the U.S. criminal justice system is that it not only represents the first time in the

U.S. Supreme Court's history that the Court set aside a death sentence, but it is also the first instance in which the Court considered the question of racism in capital sentencing. The case involved the death sentence of William Henry Furman, a black man, who killed William J. Micke, Jr., a white Coast Guard petty officer, while burglarizing Micke's home. When Micke discovered Furman in the house, Furman tripped and fell, and the gun that he was carrying went off and killed Micke. A jury convicted Furman of murder and sentenced him to death. Furman argued on appeal that his death sentence should be set aside because the jury had such complete and unbridled discretion in imposing the death penalty that it violated his constitutional rights to the equal protection of the law and against cruel and unusual punishment as prescribed by the Fourteenth and Eighth Amendments, respectively. The Court agreed and commuted Furman's death sentence to life imprisonment. Correctional authorities paroled Furman in 1985, and he is now a construction worker living in Macon, Georgia.[16]

The aftermath of *Furman* saw the Court vacate 120 cases immediately before it and some 645 other cases involving death row inmates. The decision rendered defective the death penalty statutes of thirty-nine states, the District of Columbia, and the federal government. There was no single opinion of the Court in *Furman*, which many scholars hallmark as an exceedingly complex opinion, with each of the nine justices writing separate concurrent or dissenting opinions of the Court's judgment. A majority of the justices held that Georgia's process of sentencing defendants to death was so capricious and discretionary that it systematically denied condemned prisoners equal protection of the law and was tantamount to cruel and unusual punishment. The Court was concerned with the extent to which standardless sentencing had informed capital cases. The justices made it clear that death penalty jurisdictions had to devise procedural strategies to restrict the unbridled discretion of juries remanding prisoners to death. Initially, many scholars interpreted *Furman* as the abolition of the death penalty in the United States, but nowhere in the decision did the Court hold capital punishment per se unconstitutional.[17] Rather, it was the *process* under which jurisdictions applied the death penalty to capital offenders that the Court found constitutionally challenging.

By the time the Supreme Court heard the *Furman* case in 1972, social scientists and legal scholars had amassed an impressive research record on racial bias in capital sentencing. The pre-*Furman* studies on race and capital sentencing clearly demonstrate that jurisdictions have applied the death penalty to black defendants in a blatantly discretionary and discriminatory manner. The research record reveals that even in the earliest studies on race and capital punishment, the race of the defendant and the race of the victim were significant factors in jurisdictions imposing the death penalty. For example, Brearley found that the racial animus of white jurors and court officials toward black defendants in the 1920s in South Carolina resulted in significantly higher conviction rates for blacks in homicide cases than for whites.[18] Swedish social scientist Gunnar Myrdal studied racial disparities in capital sentencing in several southern court systems in the 1930s and determined that not only were death penalty jurisdictions more than twice as likely to sentence black defendants to death than white defendants, but they were also more likely to actually execute black defendants than white defendants.[19] In the 1940s, Mangum reported similar disparities in capital cases in Missouri, Oklahoma, South Carolina, Tennessee, Virginia, and Texas.[20] Guy Johnson recognized that southern jurisdictions treated blacks that victimized other blacks with *undue leniency*, but that jurisdictions treated with *undue severity* blacks that victimized whites. One reason for Johnson's conclusion concerning the differential treatment received by black defendants was that these authorities had never imposed the death penalty on a white defendant who had victimized a black person.[21] Elmer Johnson's study of the death penalty from 1909 to 1954 in North Carolina is important because it represents one of the first empirical investigations of antiblack animus in capital rape cases. Johnson found that North Carolina demanded far more judicial accountability of black persons convicted of rape than white persons convicted of rape.[22] Rupert Koeninger found similar racial disparities for murder and rape in Texas between 1924 and 1968. Moreover, Koeninger points out that in instances where whites and blacks were codefendants, "the white was sentenced to life imprisonment or a term of years, and the Negro was given the death penalty."[23]

Scholars have criticized much of the early capital sentencing research as too narrowly focused on southern jurisdictions. In his evaluation of pre-*Furman* studies, for example, Kleck argued that even though there are conclusive patterns of racial discrimination against blacks in the use of the death penalty, the patterns in capital sentencing are mostly restricted to southern judicial districts.[24] Kleck is somewhat misguided on this point, however. Certainly, many of the early researchers conducted studies on race and capital sentencing in southern judicial districts. But the South is where early researchers would have logically focused their studies on racial disparities in capital sentencing since traditionally blacks have disproportionately populated southern states, and as a result, the vast majority of black executions have taken place in southern judicial districts. In fact, historically based death penalty data show that southern jurisdictions have executed roughly 85 percent of all condemned black prisoners in the United States.[25] Even so, several other studies have shown that the patterns of racial discrimination in capital sentencing decisions have not been restricted to southern jurisdictions. The Ohio Legislative Service Commission, for example, found that state authorities were far more likely to commute the death sentences of white defendants to life imprisonment than the death sentences imposed on blacks.[26] Marvin Wolfgang found it significant that while only 11 percent of black murderers in Pennsylvania between 1914 and 1958 received commuted sentences to life imprisonment, 20 percent of the white murderers had their sentences similarly commuted.[27] In Philadelphia, Frank Zimring and his associates found that of 204 homicides in 1970, authorities sentenced to death or life imprisonment 65 percent of all black defendants convicted of killing whites.[28] But of those felony defendants convicted of killing blacks, authorities sentenced only 25 percent to death or life imprisonment. Another study found that 22 percent of all California executions between 1938 and 1963 were of black defendants.[29] And in a study of criminal convictions in New Jersey from 1937 to 1961, Edwin Wolf found that authorities were more likely to sentence to death black defendants convicted of capital murder than white defendants.[30] As a result of these and other findings, Gross and Mauro called Kleck's observations directly into question when they noted that "to say there is no racial discrimination in capital sentencing, except in the South, is a bit like saying that there is no housing discrimination in a metropolitan area, except in the major residential district."[31] What is more, racial bias in capital sentencing is not only a national characteristic, but its discriminatory roots are traceable to the earliest periods of criminal justice history in the United States.[32]

Researchers have also conducted studies on racial bias in capital sentencing during the period after the U.S. Supreme Court decided *Furman*, but before the Court handed down its decision in *Gregg* in 1976. The purpose of these studies was to determine whether *Furman* had an effect on state capital sentencing schemes. Research conducted during this period generally shows that the U.S. Supreme Court's holding in *Furman* had no diminishing effect on the extent to which jurisdictions subject black capital offenders to racial bias in imposing capital punishment. Studies show that jurisdictions continued to excessively convict and impose death sentences on black defendants that victimized white persons when compared with other defendant–victim racial classifications.

Marc Riedel conducted one of the most important of these studies when he compared the racial composition of offenders under a death sentence in December 1971 (pursuant to pre-*Furman* capital statutes) with offenders under a death sentence in December 1975 (pursuant to post-*Furman* capital statutes).[33] Riedel found that not only did the racial disparity affecting death row inmates in the pre-*Furman* era remain unchanged in the post-*Furman* period, but also that black defendants with white victims still had the highest rate of capital sentencing. Riedel reported that 53 percent of the death row inmates in December 1971 were nonwhite and that this figure rose to 62 percent in December 1975. Though the racial disparity of southern death row populations had declined from 67 percent to 63 percent during the period, western jurisdictions had increased racial disparity of black–white death row inmates from 26 percent to 52 percent. Riedel also found that 87 percent of the death sentences were for white-victim murders and that 45 percent were for the murder of white victims by black defendants. From these figures, Riedel concluded that the statutes enacted before and after *Furman* produced the same degree of racial disproportionality in death sentences.[34]

Gregg v. Georgia

The Supreme Court reaffirmed the constitutionality of capital punishment for aggravated murder in *Gregg v. Georgia*. The question presented to the Court in this case was whether the imposition of capital punishment under Georgia's revised death penalty statute was prohibited under the Eighth and Fourteenth Amendments to the federal Constitution. The case stems from Troy Leon Gregg's participation in the armed robbery and murder of Fred Simmons and Bob Moore in 1973, wherein Gregg admitted to police that he killed Simmons and Moore by shooting them in the head and then robbing them and stealing their car. A jury convicted Gregg of murder and sentenced him to death. On appeal, the U.S. Supreme Court affirmed Gregg's conviction and death sentence because Georgia's revised death penalty statute provided for bifurcated trials, consideration of mitigating circumstances of the defendant and the crime, and appellate review of capital sentences. The Court affirmed these guidelines because Georgia intended them to prevent arbitrary and discriminatory imposition of the death penalty. Moreover, in other cases decided the same day as *Gregg*, the Court declared North Carolina and Louisiana's death penalty statutes unconstitutional because the provisions "allowed no room for consideration of individual mitigating circumstances," and because "the jury's power to determine the degree of the crime in light of the mandatory penalty for first-degree murder did not safeguard against the arbitrary and capricious imposition of the death sentences."[35] Gregg died in prison years later.

Analyses conducted since *Gregg* reveal that the guidelines established in the case have failed to eliminate racial disparities in capital cases. Bowers and Pierce conducted an extensive post-*Gregg* investigation of the patterns of capital sentencing in Florida, Texas, Ohio, and Georgia from 1972 to 1977.[36] The researchers found that the decision to execute condemned prisoners in these states reflected the same arbitrariness and discrimination that characterized the imposition of the death penalty in pre-*Furman* cases. In each state, the researchers found that authorities were more likely to impose the death penalty on black defendants with white victims than white defendants with black victims. To these researchers, the guidelines established in *Gregg* became the "instrumentality" of arbitrariness and discrimination and not its "cure."

In another study, Radelet examined whether race remained a significant factor in the processing of post-*Gregg* homicide cases in Florida between 1976 and 1977.[37] Radelet discovered that Florida jurisdictions were more likely to sentence to death blacks accused of murdering whites than blacks accused of murdering other blacks. Radelet explained this trend as due primarily to a high probability of state prosecutors indicting blacks accused of murdering whites for first-degree murder. To Radelet, "relative equality in the imposition of the death penalty appears mythical as long as prosecutors are more likely to obtain first-degree murder indictments for those accused of murdering white strangers than for those accused of murdering black strangers." Thus, Radelet's study indicates that racial discrimination continued to pervade Florida's criminal justice system to the extent that state prosecutors placed a much lower value on the lives of blacks than they placed on the lives of whites.[38]

Another important study conducted during the post-*Gregg* period involved an examination of whether the Florida Supreme Court had achieved the goals touted in *Gregg* of evenhandedness in capital sentencing in appellate review of capital cases.[39] Here, Radelet and Vandiver were concerned with whether the extralegal factors of the defendant's race and/or the victim's sex correlated with the court's decision to uphold death sentences of convicted capital offenders. They concluded that the Florida Supreme Court was slightly more likely to render a favorable decision in cases involving white defendants than black defendants and that the court was slightly more likely to render favorable decisions in cases involving defendants with male victims than female victims. Accordingly, the findings indicate that the Florida Supreme Court failed to correct for the disparities of trial courts on direct appeal in cases involving black defendants and female victims. Radelet and Vandiver argued that Florida's highest appellate court simply reinforced the judicial bias already in place against black defendants.[40]

McCleskey v. Kemp

In 1978, a Fulton County jury in Georgia convicted a black man named Warren McCleskey for murdering a white police officer during an armed robbery of a furniture store. McCleskey's conviction conformed to Georgia's capital statute under which a jury was not permitted to sentence a defendant to death for murder without first finding that the defendant had aggravated the crime by at least one of ten circumstances. McCleskey failed to present any mitigating evidence to the jury that subsequently sentenced him to death. On appeal to the U.S. Supreme Court, McCleskey claimed that Georgia administered its capital sentencing process in a racially discriminatory manner in violation of the Eighth Amendment protection against cruel and unusual punishment and that the discriminatory system violates the Fourteenth Amendment guarantee to the "equal protection of the law." In support of his claim, McCleskey proffered the results of one of the most methodologically powerful studies of racial bias in capital sentencing to date. In this study, Iowa University Professor David Baldus and his associates analyzed 2,484 murder and nonnegligent manslaughter cases in Georgia between 1973 and 1979. Baldus had controlled for some 230 nonracial variables and found that none of the variables could account for disparities in capital sentences among different defendant–victim racial categories. Baldus maintained that state jurisdictions were 4.3 times more likely to sentence killers of whites to death than killers of blacks, and these jurisdictions were 1.1 times more likely to sentence black defendants to death than other defendants. Accordingly, McCleskey claimed that race had infected the administration of the death penalty in Georgia in two distinct ways: (1) jurisdictions were more likely to sentence murderers of whites to death than murderers of blacks and (2) jurisdictions were more likely to sentence black murderers to death than white murderers. McCleskey alleged that Georgia's system of imposing the death penalty discriminated against him as a black man who killed a white man.

In April 1987, Justice Powell, joined by Justices Rehnquist, White, O'Connor, and Scalia, delivered the opinion of the U.S. Supreme Court concerning McCleskey's claims. Justices Brennan, Blackmun, and Stevens filed dissenting opinions, with whom Justice Marshall joined, in part. The question before the Court in *McCleskey* was whether the presence of racial disparities in capital sentencing, as revealed by a complex statistical study employing aggregate data from a number of capital trials, can be used to prove violations of the Eighth and Fourteenth Amendments in capital cases. Justice Powell held that the Baldus study does not prove that Georgia's capital punishment system is unconstitutional. The Court held that a defendant who alleges an equal protection violation has the burden of proving the existence of "purposeful discrimination" and that the purposeful discrimination had a "discriminatory effect" on him; that is, McCleskey had to prove that the jury in his particular case acted with a discriminatory purpose. To establish only that a pattern of racial discrimination in imposing the death penalty to a select group of defendants is not sufficient to support an equal protection claim. Furthermore, the Court held that McCleskey's claim of cruel and unusual punishment fails because McCleskey cannot prove a constitutional violation by demonstrating that other defendants who may be similarly situated did not receive the death penalty. The Court found that Georgia's sentencing procedures were sufficient to focus discretion on the particularized nature of the crime and the particularized characteristics of the individual defendant and that it cannot, therefore, be presumed that McCleskey's death sentence was "wantonly" and "freakishly" imposed. The essence of the Court's holding in *McCleskey* is that there are acceptable standards of risk of racial discrimination in imposing the death penalty. Accordingly, empirical studies simply showing that a discrepancy appears to correlate with race in imposing death sentences do not prove that race enters into any capital sentencing decisions or that race is a factor in the petitioner's case. The Court was also concerned that a finding for the defendant would open other claims that could be extended to other types of penalties and to claims based on unexplained discrepancies correlating to membership in other minority groups and even to gender.

The dissenting justices claimed that McCleskey had clearly demonstrated that his death sentence was imposed in violation of the Eighth and Fourteenth Amendments and that nothing could convey more powerfully the reality of capital sentencing in the United States "that the effort to eliminate arbitrariness in the infliction of that ultimate sanction is so plainly doomed to failure that it and the death penalty must be abandoned altogether." The dissenters argued that whether McCleskey can prove racial discrimination in his particular case is totally irrelevant in evaluating his claim of a constitutional violation because the Court has long recognized that to establish that a pattern of substantial risk of arbitrary and capricious capital sentencing suffices for a claim of unconstitutionality. The dissenting justices also called into question the effectiveness of the statutory safeguards designed to curb discretionary use of the death penalty. Justice Brennan specifically argued that "(w)hile we may hope that a model of procedural fairness will curb the influence of race on sentencing, we cannot simply assume that the model works as intended; we must critique its performance in terms of its results." The dissenting justices were particularly dismayed by the Court's fear that finding McCleskey's claim sufficient would "open the door to widespread challenges to all aspects of criminal sentencing." To Justice Brennan, the Court's rejection of McCleskey's evidence of racial discrimination in the imposition of the death penalty on the basis that it would open further challenges to criminal sentencing "is to ignore both the qualitatively different character of the death penalty and the particular repugnance of racial discrimination." As one commentator on the *McCleskey* decision put it, "It is unimaginable that the U.S. Supreme Court, an institution vested with the responsibility to achieve equal justice under the law for all Americans, could issue an opinion that accepted the inevitability of racial bias in an area as serious and final as capital punishment." Georgia executed McCleskey by electrocution in September 1991.

A review of the research record on capital sentencing since *McCleskey* shows a continued pattern of racial discrimination in capital punishment. The record reveals that death penalty jurisdictions continue to sentence black defendants to death at significantly higher rates than white defendants and that black defendants are particularly at risk of capital sentencing and actual execution when they victimize white persons. Prosecutorial discretion in the selective prosecution of capital cases, prosecutorial misuse of peremptory challenges to systematically exclude blacks from juries involving black capital defendants, judicial override by trial judges in capital cases with black defendants, prosecutorial misconduct, and the ineffective assistance by defense counsel are the most important reasons why black defendants with white victims are denied fairness and evenhandedness in capital sentencing.

Prosecutorial Discretion

A growing consensus among legal scholars of capital sentencing in the United States is that the unbridled discretion of predominantly white prosecutors is one reason why racism remains so pervasive in capital punishment.[41] Unquestionably, state prosecutors possess unrestrained discretion in filing criminal charges against persons accused of capital crimes; the charging discretion of prosecutors remains largely unregulated, unreviewable, and for the most part, there is no public accountability.[42] All jurisdictions consign the decision to seek the death penalty exclusively to the discretion of prosecutors, and no jurisdiction has implemented guidelines or regulatory mechanisms to control how prosecutors go about deciding whether to seek the death penalty in murder cases.[43] Local district attorneys establish their own criteria in determining whether to seek the death penalty.[44] Indeed, the prosecutor's decision whether to charge and what to charge is the broadest discretionary power in criminal justice administration.[45] Additionally, the U.S. Supreme Court has clearly announced its reluctance to interfere with prosecutorial discretion and has made it virtually impossible for a criminal defendant alleging selective prosecution to seek judicial remedy.[46] Furthermore, individuals who decide whether a defendant is eligible for the death penalty are almost exclusively white. Jeffrey Pokorak found in a recent survey that roughly 98 percent of all death penalty state prosecutors are white, 1 percent is black, 1 percent is Latino, and in eighteen of the thirty-eight death penalty states, prosecutors are exclusively white.[47] In California, for example, the panel of prosecutors responsible for deciding whether the Orange County District Attorney's Office will seek the death penalty in any particular case is composed exclusively of white males.[48]

That prosecutorial decision making may be fraught with racial bias challenges the notion that predominantly white prosecutors seek the death penalty *objectively*. Prosecutors generally deny that racial bias imbues prosecutorial decision making. However, in conceding that state prosecutors are a major source of the racism in the criminal justice system, Kenneth Nunn explains:

Though prosecutors assert that there is no racial bias in the exercise of prosecutorial discretion, they have done little to verify this belief, or dispel the concerns of others. Prosecutors have rarely commissioned studies, promulgated internal guidelines, or made attempts to keep voluntary statistics on prosecutorial racial bias. Few prosecutors have taken it upon themselves to maintain a dialogue on these issues within their offices. There is little effort to sensitize prosecutors or provide diversity training. Even more disappointing than the lack of prosecutorial effort to determine the extent of racial bias in prosecutorial decision making, is that prosecutors actively oppose the efforts of others to do so. Prosecutors have vehemently opposed legislative attempts to gather information regarding bias in the imposition of death sentencing and in automobile stops.[49]

Though many commentators are unwilling to admit that conscious racism permeates prosecutorial decision making,[50] other critics concede that prosecutors suffer from an unconscious racism in seeking capital charges against black defendants with white victims.[51] Pokorak explains it this way:

[U]nconscious bias may creep into the prosecutors' decisions to seek the death penalty. The predominantly white prosecutors may perceive violent crimes against whites as more serious than similar crimes against minorities and thus seek the death penalty more frequently against defendants accused of killing white victims. Conversely, white prosecutors may have an unconscious perception of blacks as inferior and may view violent crimes against blacks as less serious and less worthy of the death penalty than similar crimes against whites.[52]

The stark contrast in racial dissimilarity between prosecutors and the nation's death row population, and the racial similarity between prosecutors and the nation's victim population, stand as crude indicators of the pervasiveness of prosecutors to seek the death penalty against black defendants with white victims. Criminal justice statistics reveal that of the 3,711 condemned inmates presently residing on death rows across the nation, roughly 46 percent are white and about 43 percent are black. In contrast, roughly 81 percent of all capital cases tried by prosecutors involve white victims, yet nationally only half of all murder victims are white.[53] Execution data show similar disparities. Death penalty jurisdictions have executed twelve white defendants convicted of murdering blacks since 1976, but authorities have executed 172 black defendants convicted of murdering whites.[54] These figures reveal that execution authorities are some fourteen times more likely to execute black defendants with white victims than they are to execute white defendants with black victims. Historically, there are only thirty-five cases in the United States where death penalty jurisdictions have executed a white prisoner for killing a black victim.[55]

Capital sentencing researchers continue to find in the post-*McCleskey*

era that the race of the victim and the race of the defendant remain powerful predictors of for whom state prosecutors will seek the death penalty.
A comprehensive review of capital sentencing research by the U.S. General Accounting Office (GAO) reveals that in 82 percent of the studies, the
race of the victim was found to influence the likelihood of a defendant
being charged with capital murder or receiving the death penalty. That is,
persons who murdered whites were found more likely to be sentenced to
death than persons who murdered blacks.[56] In a more recent report expanding on the GAO's review, researchers found that in almost all capital
punishment states the race of the victim correlated with whether the jurisdiction sentenced the defendant to death.[57] The report also indicated
that in nearly half of all states the race of the defendant is a predictor of
who received death sentences. Baldus and his associates found that prosecutors seek the death penalty in 70 percent of all cases involving a black
defendant and a white victim, but in only 15 percent of all cases involving
a white defendant and a black victim do prosecutors seek the death penalty.[58] Sorensen and Wallace also studied prosecutorial discretion in capital
cases and found that prosecutors are far more likely to charge black defendants with aggravated murder and try them as capital offenders when
their victims are white. To these researchers, prosecutorial discretion
amounts to *intentional discrimination* against black defendants with white
victims.[59] North Carolina researchers found that jurisdictional authorities
are nearly four times more likely to sentence to death defendants whose
victims are white than defendants whose victims are nonwhite.[60] And in
a very recent report by the U.S. Justice Department, researchers found that
federal prosecutors are nearly twice as likely to recommend death for a
black defendant when the victim is nonblack than when the victim is
black.

Peremptory Challenges

The peremptory challenge is a procedural device that allows prosecutors to remove potential jurors during *voir dire* for unexplained reasons.
The arbitrary nature of peremptory challenges, however, effectively masks
racial discrimination in jury selection by allowing prosecutors to intentionally discriminate against black jurors.[61] Prosecutors prefer white jurors
to black jurors in capital cases because predominantly white juries are
more prone to convict black defendants.[62] Randall Kennedy has characterized the peremptory challenge as "a creature of unbridled discretion
that, in the hands of white prosecutors and white defendants, has often
been used to sustain racial subordination in the courthouse."[63] Despite
arguments that the federal Constitution prohibits racial discrimination in
the exercise of peremptory challenges, studies reveal that prosecutors consistently exclude blacks from jury participation in capital cases.[64] The

Texas Defender Service found that prosecutors use peremptory challenges to strike black jurors at almost five times the rate of white jurors.[65] In Alabama, some 77 percent of state prosecutors' strikes are used to exclude black jurors in murder cases.[66] Philadelphia prosecutors go so far as to use video training tapes to instruct assistant district attorneys how to exclude black jurors, especially "young black women" and "blacks from low-income areas." Georgia prosecutors use 83 percent of their peremptory challenges against black jurors.[67] In the federal judicial system, prosecutors repeatedly use peremptory challenges to exclude black jurors in capital cases.[68] It remains extremely difficult, however, for black criminal defendants to make out a case of racial discrimination when prosecutors misuse peremptory challenges.[69] In *Batson v. Kentucky*, Justice Marshall called for the elimination of peremptory challenges because he doubted that prosecutors could ever overcome their racist use of the device. He argued that

[a] prosecutor's own conscious or unconscious racism may lead him easily to the conclusion that a prospective black juror is sullen, or distant, a characterization that would not have come to his mind if a white juror had acted identically. Prosecutors' peremptories are based on their seat-of-the-pants instincts as to how particular jurors will vote. Yet seat-of-the-pants-instincts may often be just another term for racial prejudice. Even if all parties approach the Court's mandate with the best of conscious intentions, that mandate requires them to confront and overcome their own racism on all levels—a challenge I doubt all of them can meet.[70]

Judicial Override

The U.S. criminal justice system has traditionally assigned the responsibility of expressing community sentiment on the question of life or death in capital cases to juries. As White explains: "Throughout its history, the jury determined which homicide defendants would be subject to capital punishment by making factual determinations, many of which related to difficult assessments of the defendant's state of mind. By the time the Bill of Rights was adopted, the jury's right to make these determinations was unquestioned."[71] In June 2002, however, the U.S. Supreme Court ruled that the practice of judicial override is unconstitutional; judges can no longer make the ultimate sentencing determination in capital cases.[72] Justice Ginsburg argued for the majority in *Ring v. Arizona* that trial judges violate capital defendants' Sixth Amendment right to a jury trial when judges, rather than jurors, impute death. In part, the *Ring* case stems from death penalty laws in Alabama, Florida, Delaware, and Indiana that had incorporated judicial override into their death penalty schemes. Judicial override allowed trial judges to disregard jury recommendations and to use their own discretion in sentencing a capital offender to life imprisonment or death. In these states capital juries rendered advisory verdicts, but trial judges nevertheless made the ultimate decision to impute death or life imprisonment.[73] Yet, nowhere in *Ring* did the Court concern itself with the factual data showing that state trial judges are noticeably more likely to override jury recommendations in capital cases involving black defendants with white victims. Judicial override has had an adverse effect upon black capital offenders in these states; overall, about 55 percent of all capital defendants sentenced to death because of judicial override have been black and 75 percent of the victims in override cases have been white.[74] Even though some commentators attribute judicial override to the politics of judicial elections,[75] one can easily conclude that these figures are probably more indicative of an antiblack animus of state trial judges. Indeed, several studies have documented specific incidences of state trial judges exhibiting racial bias in capital cases and found it to be a common feature of state court systems.[76]

Despite the Supreme Court's holding in *Ring,* judicial override remains a controversial issue in death penalty cases because it is unclear if the Court will apply its ruling retroactively to include all defendants who have had their death sentences imposed by trial judges rather than juries. It is uncertain if defendants affected by judicial overrides will have their sentences reduced to life imprisonment or receive new sentencing trials with new juries.[77] Death penalty scholars have estimated that the Court's decision could affect as many as 800 condemned prisoners that death penalty jurisdictions have sentenced without the protections extended to capital defendants in *Ring.* The case will surely impact condemned black inmates given that 46 percent of all prisoners on death row in Alabama are black, 53 percent in Delaware are black, 35 percent in Florida are black, and 33 percent in Indiana are black.

Prosecutorial Misconduct

A recent study of some 6,000 capital cases revealed that nearly all capital punishment jurisdictions in the United States have excessive error rates. Kentucky, Maryland, and Tennessee have error rates of 100 percent, followed closely by California (87 percent), Mississippi (91 percent), Montana (87 percent), and Wyoming (89 percent).[78] On retrial, jurisdictions resentenced over 75 percent of all capital defendants to less than death, authorities resentenced some 18 percent of the cases to death, and in 7 percent of the cases jurisdictions found capital defendants innocent of the charges. One of the most common forms of prejudicial error in these cases is prosecutorial suppression of evidence that defendants are innocent of the capital offense or that defendants do not deserve the death penalty. The study shows that state prosecutors frequently suppress exculpatory evidence, knowingly use false testimony, intimidate witnesses, give improper closing arguments, give false statements to the jury, and fabricate evidence. In a Texas study of cases involving serious prosecutorial misconduct, researchers revealed that state prosecutors have "used threats against defendants or their family members to coerce confessions."[79] Undoubtedly, prosecutorial misconduct weighs most heavily against black offenders since blacks are so overrepresented as capital defendants.[80]

Other studies have focused on prosecutors' use of racist remarks while trying capital cases. Though the literature shows that courts are frustrated over the frequency in which prosecutorial misconduct occurs, courts are unwilling to overturn cases on grounds of racial bias and, in the alternative, assess the relative weight of the statements to other evidence or otherwise explain away the prosecutors' remarks.[81] One commentator identified the problem of prosecutorial racism this way:

Many courts refuse to recognize the more discrete and arguably more insidious uses of racism that occur during the criminal trial. Instead, they choose to focus solely on overt expressions of racial bias. Nonetheless, the subtler racial references made by a prosecutor are more difficult to detect, and are precisely those that are most difficult to prove. Thus, in order to protect a defendant's due process right to a fair trial, courts must look beneath the surface to discover the race-based stereotypes on which prosecutors so cleverly rely.[82]

Ineffective Defense Counsel

The U.S. Supreme Court in *Gregg* touted bifurcated trials in capital cases as a procedural device designed to eradicate the capricious and arbitrary imposition of the death penalty that plagued pre-*Furman* cases. Bifurcated trials give defense lawyers an opportunity to present mitigating evidence to persuade juries that it should spare the convicted defendant's life. Yet, as Justice Marshall once noted, federal reporters are filled with stories of lawyers who failed to present mitigating evidence on behalf of their clients simply because the lawyer did not know what to offer, how to offer it, or because the lawyer had not read the state's sentencing statute. Ineffective defense lawyers perpetuate racial discrimination in capital sentencing when they fail to challenge procedures that preclude fairness to black defendants in capital trials. Often, race discrimination claims are unsuccessful for black defendants because defense lawyers fail to raise the claims at required times. Two Georgia capital cases illustrate how the gross incompetency of defense lawyers can summarily deny black defendants constitutional protections. For example, in the case of Johnny Lee Gates, a black man accused of the rape, armed robbery, and murder of a white woman named Katrina Wright, the defense lawyer failed to present mitigating evidence of Gates' impoverished childhood or his inability to function as a normal child.[83] Gates' defense lawyer failed to object to the jury selection process that rendered an all-white jury in a community with a 30 percent black representation. On appeal, the Court did not find Gates' lawyer incompetent or that Gates was denied the ineffective assistance of counsel. Gates remains on Georgia's death row. Defense lawyers also engage in such invidious tactics as making comments that racially disparage their black clients. In the case of Wilburn Dobbs, convicted and sentenced to death for the armed robbery and murder of a white grocery store owner, the trial judge and defense lawyer referred to Dobbs as a "colored boy" and expressed beliefs that blacks generally are inferior to whites morally and intellectually.[84] An appellate court also found this lawyer's conduct permissible. Dobbs remains on Georgia's death row.

Executing Innocent Black Defendants

The pace of executions in the United States has increased dramatically over the last several decades. Death penalty authorities executed eleven prisoners between 1976 and 1983; since then, state and federal jurisdictions have executed another 773 prisoners. Black defendants constitute a disproportionate segment of this population of executed prisoners. Moreover, the escalating rate of executions in the United States significantly increases the possibility that authorities may execute an innocent defendant. That possibility has become so disconcerting to the legal community that the American Bar Association has called for death penalty jurisdictions to halt executions until authorities can ensure fairness and impartiality in its administration.[85] One of the more troubling studies on wrongful executions has identified some 350 cases in which United States jurisdictions have wrongfully convicted capital defendants.[86] Of these cases, authorities sentenced 159 defendants to death, they actually executed another 23 prisoners, and 22 other prisoners came within seventy-two hours of their executions before lawyers established their innocence. Predictably, black defendants constitute a significant proportion of the hundreds of cases of wrongfully convicted defendants. In fact, 43 of the 101 capital defendants released from death rows across the country since 1971 have been black defendants. This number suggests a strong probability that jurisdictions erroneously convict black defendants more than white defendants. Black defendants also spend more years in prison between conviction and exoneration than white defendants; innocent black defendants spend an average of 8.8 years in prison whereas innocent white defendants spend an average of 6.9 years in prison. Undoubtedly, the procedural safeguards established to diminish racism in capital sentencing will prove to be evermore meaningless and ineffectual when the United States executes an innocent black man.

CONCLUDING REMARKS

Proponents of the death penalty often posit the argument that racial disparity in capital punishment knowingly reflects differential offense rates. But social scientists attribute higher levels of violent crimes committed by blacks to the social effects of racial discrimination. As Wolfgang and Cohen point out, "a society that places and holds certain of its citizens in conditions of poverty and disadvantage with respect to occupation and education has itself created the circumstances that leads to criminal violence among the members of its oppressed minority."[87] Indeed, institutionalized discrimination has confined blacks to the lowest strata of the American class structure; blacks are disproportionately represented among the nation's poor, the unemployed, and the undereducated, and confined to the inner cities.[88] Nearly one-third of our nation's young black men are under the direct supervision of the U.S. criminal justice system; they are in jail, on probation, or on parole. In fact, there are more young black men under the control of the criminal justice system than there are young black men enrolled in our nation's colleges and universities. It is also troubling that homicide is the leading cause of death among young black men. Yet, capital sentencing statistics clearly show that the U.S. criminal justice system is not attempting to safeguard the black community with the death penalty. Indeed, it is a rare occurrence in the U.S. criminal justice system that a death penalty jurisdiction executes a black for the murder of another black. Jurisdictions execute blacks far more readily for killing white people. As a result, the U.S. criminal justice system has designed the death penalty to thwart a perceived minority threat against the safety and welfare of the society's dominant white majority.

This review of the research record on race and capital sentencing reveals that the U.S. justice system has fully institutionalized racism in capital sentencing. The death penalty has become an exceptionally effective means by which to oppress blacks and preserve white interests. The most obvious conclusion one can draw from the research record on capital sentencing is that the U.S. Supreme Court has failed miserably in its attempt to eliminate racial bias in capital punishment. The review shows that race-based discrimination continues to typify the imposition of capital punishment in the United States. Even though the Court formally recognized the pervasiveness of racial prejudice in capital sentencing in *Furman* and attempted to create a rational structure of procedural safeguards to curb racial arbitrariness and capriciousness in capital sentencing in *Gregg*, the Court summarily rejected the notions of fairness and evenhandedness in capital sentencing when it rejected in *McCleskey* exceptionally plausible evidence that racially discriminatory patterns remain in capital sentencing. Clearly, the elimination of racial prejudice, racial inequality, and caprice in capital sentencing is not at the forefront of judicial thinking on capital punishment.

NOTES

1. President's Commission on Law Enforcement and Administration of Justice. *The Challenge of Crime in a Free Society* (1967): 143.

2. Arthur Goldberg and Allan Dershowitz. "Declaring the Death Penalty Unconstitutional." *Harvard Law Review* 83 (1970): 1784.

3. National Minority Advisory Council on Criminal Justice. 1982. *The Inequality of Justice: A Report on Crime and the Administration of Justice in the Minority Community* (Washington, D.C.: National Institute of Law Enforcement and Criminal Justice).

4. *Callins v. Collins*, 510 U.S. 1141 (1994).

5. "A Justice's Doubts," *Los Angeles Times*, July 5, 2001; "Death Penalty Experts Welcome O'Connor's Comments on Capital Punishment," *The Associated Press*, 6 July, 2001.

6. David Baldus et al. "Racial Discrimination and the Death Penalty in the Post-*Furman* Era: An Empirical and Legal Overview, with Recent Findings from Philadelphia." *Cornell Law Review* 83 (1998): 1638.

7. For a discussion on the legislative history of the Racial Justice Act see Don Edwards and John Conyers. "The Racial Justice Act: A Simple Matter of Justice." *University of Dayton Law Review* 20 (1995): 699.

8. It's not surprising that the federal government would refuse to pass an effort to rectify racial bias in capital sentencing since this is the same government that on three separate occasions rejected an antilynching law designed to protect blacks from the lethal violence of white lynch mobs during Jim Crow. See W. Fitzhugh Brundage. *Lynchings in the New South: Georgia and Virginia, 1880–1930.* (Urbana: University of Illinois Press, 1993).

9. David Baldus et al. "Racial Discrimination and the Death Penalty in the Post-*Furman* Era: An Empirical and Legal Overview, with Recent Findings from Philadelphia." *Cornell Law Review* 83 (1998): 1638, 1738.

10. Randall Kennedy. *Race, Crime, and the Law.* (New York: Random House, 1997), p. 348.

11. 408 U.S. 238 (1972).

12. 428 U.S. 153 (1976).

13. 481 U.S. 279 (1987).

14. Adalberto Aguirre and David V. Baker. *Race, Racism, and the Death Penalty in the United States.* (Berrien Springs, MI: Vande Vere Publishing, 1991).

15. Barry Naskell and Kenneth Hardy. *The Arbitrariness of the Death Penalty.* (Philadelphia: Temple University Press, 1987), p. 16; Samuel Walker, Cassia Spohn, and Miriam DeLone. *The Color of Justice: Race, Ethnicity, and Crime in America.* (Belmont, CA: Wadsworth Publishing, 2000), pp. 15–18.

16. Robert Bohm. *Deathquest: An Introduction to the Theory and Practice of Capital Punishment in the U.S.* (Cincinnati: Anderson Publishing Company, 1999), p. 23.

17. Samuel Gross. "Race and Death: The Judicial Evaluation of Evidence in Discrimination in Capital Sentencing." *University of California, Davis Law Review* 18 (1985): 1275.

18. Harry Brearley. "The Negro and Homicides." *Social Forces* 9 (1930): 247, 252. See also John Sellin. *The Penalty of Death.* (Beverly Hills: Sage Publications, 1980.)

19. Gunnar Myrdal. *An American Dilemma: The Negro Problem and American Democracy.* (New York: Harper Brothers, 1944).

20. Charles Mangum. *The Legal Status of the Negro.* (Chapel Hill, NC: The University of North Carolina Press, 1940).

21. Guy Johnson. "The Negro and Crime." *Annals of the American Academy of Political and Social Science* 217 (1941): 93. See also E. P. Allredge. "Why the South Leads the Nation in Murder and Manslaughter." *The Quarterly Review* 2 (1942): 123; Harold Garfinkel. "Research Notes on Inter and Intra-Racial Homicides." *Social Forces* 27 (1949): 369.

22. Elmer Johnson. 1957. "Selective Factors in Capital Punishment." *Social Forces* 35 (1957): 165.

23. Rupert Koeninger. 1969. "Capital Punishment in Texas, 1924–1968." *Crime and Delinquency* 15 132. See also Florida Civil Liberties Union. 1964. *Rape: Selective Electrocution Based on Race* (unpublished manuscript); Henry Ehrmann. "The Death Penalty and the Administration of Justice." *Annals of the American Academy of Political and Social Science* 285 (1952): 73; James McCafferty. *Capital Punishment.* (New York: Aldine-Atherton Company, 1972); James Marquart, Sheldon Ekland-Olson, and Jonathan Sorensen. *The Rope, The Chair, and The Needle: Capital Punishment in Texas, 1923–1990.* (Austin, TX: University of Texas Press, 1998).

24. Gary Kleck. "Racial Discrimination in Criminal Sentencing: A Critical Evaluation of the Evidence with Additional Evidence on the Death Penalty." *American Sociological Review* 46 (1981): 783. See also John Hagan. "Extra-Legal Attributes and Criminal Sentencing: An Assessment of a Sociological Viewpoint." *Law and Society Review* 8 (1974): 357; Charles Phillips. "Social Structure and Social Control: Modeling the Discriminatory Execution of Blacks in Georgia and North Carolina, 1925–1935." *Social Forces* 65 (1986): 458.

25. M. Watt Espy and John Smykla. *Executions in the U.S., 1608–1987: The Espy File.* (Tuscaloosa, AL: John Smykla [producer], Ann Arbor, MI: Inter-University Consortium for Political and Social Research [distributor], 1991), machine-readable data file.

26. Ohio Legislative Service Commission. *Capital Punishment, Staff Research Report No. 46.* (Columbus, Ohio Legislative Service Commission, 1961).

27. Marvin Wolfgang, Arlene Kelley, and Hans Nolde. "Comparison of the Executed and the Commuted Among Admissions to Death Row." *Journal of Criminal Law, Criminology, and Police Science* 53 (1962): 301. See also Marvin Wolfgang and Mark Reidel. "Racial Discrimination and the Death Penalty." *Annals of the American Academy of Political and Social Science* 407 (1973): 119.

28. Frank Zimring, Sheila O'Malley, and Joel Eigen. "The Going Price of Criminal Homicide in Philadelphia." *University of Chicago Law Review* 43 (1976): 227.

29. Robert Carter and LaMont Smith. 1969. "The Death Penalty in California: A Statistical Composite Portrait." *Crime and Delinquency* 15 (1969): 63. See also Charles Judson. "A Study of the California Penalty Jury in First-Degree Murder Cases." *Stanford Law Review* 21: (1969): 1302. Compare Harry Kalven. "A Study of the California Penalty Jury in First-Degree Cases," preface. *Stanford Law Review* 21 (1969): 1297.

30. Edwin Wolf. "Abstract to Analysis of Jury Sentencing in Capital Cases: New Jersey: 1937–1961." *Rutgers Law Review* 19 (1964): 56; compare Hugo Bedau. "Death Sentences in New Jersey: 1907–1960." *Rutgers Law Review* 19 (1964): 1; Hugo Bedau. "Capital Punishment in Oregon: 1903–1964." *Oregon Law Review* 45 (1965): 1.

31. Samuel Gross and Robert Mauro. "Patterns of Death: An Analysis of Racial

Disparities in Capital Sentencing and Homicide Victimization." *Stanford Law Review* 37 (1984): 127.

32. For a literature review of the death penalty during colonial and antebellum slavery, see Adalberto Aguirre and David V. Baker. "Slave Executions in the U.S.: A Descriptive Analysis of Social and Historical Factors." *The Social Science Journal* 36 (1999): 1.

33. Marc Riedel. "Discrimination in the Imposition of the Death Penalty: A Comparison of the Characteristics of Offenders Sentenced Pre-*Furman* and Post-*Furman*." *Temple University Press* 49 (1976): 261.

34. See also Steven Boris. "Stereotypes and Dispositions for Criminal Homicide." *Criminology* 17 (1979): 139; Victoria Swiggert and Ronald Farrell. *Murder, Inequality and the Law: Differential Treatment in the Legal Process.* (Lexington, MA: D.C. Heath, 1979); Victoria Swiggert and Ronald Farrell. "Normal Homicides and the Law." *American Sociological Review* 40 (1977): 16; Samuel Gross. "Race and Death: The Judicial Evaluation of Evidence of Discrimination in Capital Sentencing." *University of California, Davis Law Review* 18 (1985): 1275; William Bowers. *Executions in America.* (Lexington, MA: D.C. Heath, 1974); William Bowers. "The Pervasiveness of Arbitrariness and Discrimination Under Post-*Furman* Capital Statutes." *Crime and Delinquency* 63 (1983): 575; Steven Arkin. "Discrimination and Arbitrariness in Capital Punishment: An Analysis of Post-*Furman* Murder Cases in Dade County, Florida, 1973–1976." *Stanford Law Review* 33 (1980): 75.

35. *Woodson v. North Carolina.* 428 U.S. 280 (1976); *Roberts v. Louisiana*, 428 U.S. 325 (1976).

36. William Bowers and Glenn Pierce. "Arbitrariness and Discrimination Under Post-*Furman* Capital Statutes." *Crime and Delinquency* 26 (1980.): 563; William Bowers and Glenn Pierce. "The Pervasiveness of Arbitrariness and Discrimination Under Post-*Furman* Capital Statutes." *Journal of Criminal Law and Criminology* 74 (1983.): 1067.

37. Michael Radelet. "Racial Characteristics and the Imposition of the Death Penalty." *American Sociological Review* 46 (1981): 918.

38. Hans Zeisel. "Race Bias in the Administration of the Death Penalty: The Florida Experience." *Harvard Law Review* 95 (1981): 456; Raymond Paternoster. "Prosecutorial Discretion in Requesting the Death Penalty: A Case of Victim-Based Racial Discrimination." *Law and Society* 18 (1984): 437; Joseph E. Jacoby and Raymond Paternoster. "Sentencing Disparity and Jury Packing: Further Challenges to the Death Penalty." *Journal of Criminal Law and Criminology* 73 (1982): 379.

39. Michael Radelet and Margaret Vandiver. "The Florida Supreme Court and Death Penalty Appeals." *Journal of Criminal Law and Criminology* 73 (1983): 913.

40. See also Samuel Gross and Robert Mauro. "Patterns of Death: An Analysis of Racial Disparities in Capital Sentencing and Homicide Victimization." *Stanford Law Review* 37 (1984): 27.

41. Angela Davis. "Prosecution and Race: The Power and Privilege of Discretion." *Fordham Law Review* 67 (1998): 13; "Race and the Prosecutor's Charging Decision." *Harvard Law Review* 101 (1988): 1520; compare George Cole. "The Decision to Prosecute." *Law and Society Review* 4 (1970): 331; Eric Poole and Robert Regoli. "The Decision to Prosecute in Felony Cases." *Journal of Contemporary Criminal Justice* 2 (1983): 18.

42. James Vorenberg. "Decent Restraint of Prosecutorial Power." *Harvard Law*

Review 94 (1981): 1521, 1555. See also, Robert Heller. "Selective Prosecution and the Federalization of Criminal Law: The Need for Meaningful Judicial Review of Prosecutorial Discretion." *University of Pennsylvania Law Review* 145 (1997): 1309.

43. See Thomas Johnson. "When Prosecutors Seek the Death Penalty." *American Journal of Criminal Law.* 22 (1994): 280; Ronald Tabak. "Racial Discrimination in Implementing the Death Penalty." *Human Rights* 26 (1999): 5; Patricia Ragone and J. Michael Williams. "Conference: The Death Penalty in the Twenty-First Century." *American University Law Review* 45 (1995): 239, 272–273.

44. Stephen Bright. "Discrimination, Death, and Denial: The Tolerance of Racial Discrimination in Infliction of the Death Penalty. *Santa Clara Law Review* 35 (1995.): 433, 451.

45. Bennett Gershman. "The New Prosecutors." *University of Pittsburg Law Review* 53 (1992): 393; Charles Bubany and Frank Skillern. "Taming the Dragon: An Administrative Law for Prosecutorial Decision Making." *American Criminal Law Review* 13 (1976): 473.

46. *United States v. Armstrong,* 517 U.S. 456 (1996).

47. Jeffrey Pokorak. "Probing the Capital Prosecutor's Perspective: Race of the Discretionary Actor." *Cornell Law Review* 83 (1998): 1811, 1813.

48. Stephen Bright. "Discrimination, Death and Denial: The Tolerance of Racial Discrimination in Infliction of the Death Penalty. *Santa Clara Law Review* 35 (1995): 433, 451.

49. Kenneth Nunn. 2000. "The 'Darden Delimma': Should African Americans Prosecute Crime?" *Fordham Law Review* 68 (2000): 1473, 1498.

50. Michael Tonry. *Malign Neglect: Race, Crime, and Punishment in America.* (New York: Oxford University Press, 1995).

51. Sheri Johnson. "Unconscious Racism and the Criminal Law. *Cornell Law Review* 73 (1988): 1016; Angela Davis. "Benign Neglect of Racism in the Criminal Justice System." *Michigan Law Review* 94 (1996.): 1660.

52. Jeffrey Pokorak. "Probing the Capital Prosecutor's Perspective: Race of the Discretionary Actors." *Cornell Law Review* 83 (1998): 1811. See also "Developments in the Law: Race and the Criminal Process." *Harvard Law Review* 101 (1988): 1525.

53. U.S. General Accounting Office. *Death Penalty Sentencing: Research Indicates Pattern of Racial Disparities.* (Washington, D.C : U.S. General Accounting Office, 1990).

54. NAACP Legal Defense and Educational Fund, Inc. "Death Row, U.S.A." [online]. (Criminal Justice Project of the NAACP Legal Defense and Educational Fund, Inc., 2000). Available from the World Wide Web: http://www.death penaltyinfo.org/DEATHROWUSArecent.pdf.

55. Carter Center Symposium on the Death Penalty. *Georgia State University Law Review* 14 (1997): 329–445.

56. U.S. General Accounting Office, 1990.

57. David Baldus and Gary Woodworth. 1997. "Race Discrimination in America's Capital Punishment System Since *Furman v. Georgia*: The Evidence of Race Disparities and the Record of Our Courts and Legislatures in Addressing This Issue." (Chicago: American Bar Association, 1997), cited in Richard C. Dieter, "The Death Penalty in Black and White: Who Lives, Who Dies, Who Decides." (Washington, D.C.: Death Penalty Information Center, 1998).

58. David Baldus et al. "Racial Discrimination and the Death Penalty in the Post-

Furman Era: An Empirical and Legal Overview, with Recent Findings from Phila-delphia." *Cornell Law Review* 83 (1998): 1638. See also Thomas Keil and Gennaro Vito. "Race, Homicide Severity, and the Application of the Death Penalty: A Con-sideration of the Barnett Scale." *Criminology* 27 (1989): 511.

59. Jon Sorensen and Donald Wallace. "Prosecutorial Discretion in Seeking Death: An Analysis of Racial Disparity in the Pretrial Stage of Case Processing in a Midwestern County." *Justice Quarterly* 16 (1999): 559; U.S. Department of Justice. *The Federal Death Penalty System: Supplementary Data, Analysis and Revised Protocols for Capital Case Review.* (Washington, D.C.: U.S. Department of Justice, 2001).

60. Isaac Unah and John Boger. 2001. "Race and the Death Penalty in North Carolina: An Empirical Analysis, 1993–1997," [online]. (The Common Sense Foun-dation, 2001). Available from World Wide Web: http://www.deathpenaltyinfo.org/article.php?scid = 19&did = 246.

61. Patricia J. Griffin. "Jumping on the Ban Wagon: *Minetos v. City University of New York* and the Future of the Peremptory Challenge." *Minnesota Law Review* 81 (1997): 1237; Raymond J. Broderick. "Why the Peremptory Challenge Should Be Abolished." *Temple Law Review* 65 (1992): 369.

62. David Baldus et al. 2001. "The Use of Peremptory Challenges in Capital Murder Trials: A Legal and Empirical Analysis." *University of Pennsylvania Journal of Constitutional Law* 3 (2001): 3; "Discriminatory Use of Peremptory Challenges." *Harvard Law Review* 106 (1992): 240; Barbara Underwood. "Ending Race Discrim-ination in Jury Selection: Whose Right Is It Anyway?" *Columbia Law Review* 92 (1992): 725; Randall Kennedy. *Race, Crime, and the Law.* (New York: Random House, 1997); Sheri Johnson. "Black Innocence and the White Jury." *Michigan Law Review* 83 (1985): 1611; Patricia Griffin. "Jumping on the Ban Wagon: *Minetos v. City Uni-versity of New York* and the Future of the Peremptory Challenge." *Minnesota Law Review* 81 (1997): 1237; Raymond Broderick "Why the Peremptory Challenge Should Be Abolished." *Temple Law Review* 65 (1992): 369.

63. Randall Kennedy. *Race, Crime, and the Law.* (New York: Random House, 1997), p. 214. See also David Baldus et al. "The Use of Peremptory Challenges in Capital Murder Trials: A Legal and Empirical Analysis." *University of Pennsylvania Journal of Constitutional Law* 3 (2001): 3; "Discriminatory Use of Peremptory Chal-lenges." *Harvard Law Review* 106 (1992): 240; Barbara Underwood. "Ending Race Discrimination in Jury Selection: Whose Right Is It Anyway?" *Columbia Law Review* 92 (1992): 725; Randall Kennedy. *Race, Crime, and the Law.* (New York, NY: Random House, 1997); Sheri Johnson. "Black Innocence and the White Jury." *Michigan Law Review* 83 (1985.): 1611.

64. *Georgia v. McCollum,* 505 U.S. 42 (1992).

65. Texas Defender Service. "A State of Denial: Texas Justice and the Death Pen-alty" [online]. (Texas Defender Service, 2000). Available from the World Wide Web: http://www.texasdefender.org/publications.htm.

66. Bryan Stevenson and Ruth Friedman. 1994. "Deliberate Indifference: Judicial Tolerance of Racial Bias in Criminal Justice." *Washington and Lee Law Review* 51 (1994): 509, 520.

67. Steven Bright. "Discrimination, Death and Denial: The Tolerance of Racial Discrimination in Infliction of the Death Penalty." *Santa Clara Law Review* 35 (1995): 433.

68. Samuel Walker, Cassia Spohn, and Miriam DeLone. *The Color of Justice: Race,*

Ethnicity, and Crime in America. (Belmont, CA: Wadsworth Publishing, 2000), 159, 162.

69. Jonathan Mintz. "Note: *Batson v. Kentucky*: A Half Step in the Right Direction (Racial Discrimination and Peremptory Challenges Under the Heavier Confines of Equal Protection)." *Cornell Law Review* 72 (1987): 1026.

70. *Batson v. Kentucky*, 476 U.S. 79, 105–108 (1986) (Marshall, J. dissenting). The *Batson* Court set out a test to establish purposeful discrimination in jury selection that includes proof that the petitioner is a member of a cognizable racial group, that the prosecutor exercised peremptory challenges to exclude members of petitioner's race, and that the facts of the case raise an inference that the prosecutor used peremptory challenges to exclude jurors because of their race.

71. Welsh White. "Fact-Finding and the Death Penalty: The Scope of a Capital Defendant's Right to Jury Trial." *Notre Dame Law Review* 65 (1989): 1, 11.

72. *Ring v. Arizona*, 536 U.S. 584 (2002).

73. Gerald Uelmen. "Crocodiles in the Bathtub: Maintaining the Independence of State Supreme Courts in an Era of Judicial Politicization." *Notre Dame Law Review* 72 (1997): 1133, 1141. See also Fred Burnside. "Dying to Get Elected: A Challenge to the Jury Override." *Wisconsin Law Review* 1999 (1999): 1017.

74. "Judges Ignore Juries to Impose Death," *Los Angeles Times*, June 16, 2002. In Alabama, trial judges override jury recommendations of life and impose a death sentence almost ten times more frequently than they override recommendations of death. In fact, five of the twenty-four prisoners executed in Alabama since 1976 were sentenced to death by judges after juries had recommended life sentences. Florida trial judges also override jury recommendations. In some 224 capital cases tried before juries between 1972 and 1992, Florida trial judges overrode 173 cases for death. Indiana judges have superseded nine jury recommendations for life sentences with death sentences since 1980. And during this same period in Delaware, trial judges ignored jury recommendations for life sentences in seven cases.

75. Stephen Bright and Patrick Keenan. "Judges and the Politics of Death: Deciding between the Bill of Rights and the Next Election in Capital Cases." *Boston University Law Review* 75 (1995): 759.

76. Sherrilyn Ifill. "Judging the Judges: Racial Diversity, Impartiality and Representation on State Trial Courts." *Boston College Law Review* 39 (1997): 95.

77. The Death Penalty Information Center. "Supreme Court Requires Jury Participation in Death Sentences" [press release]. June 24, 2002.

78. James Liebman, Jeffrey Fagan, and Valerie West. "A Broken System: Error Rates in Capital Cases, 1973–1995" [online]. (The Justice Project, 2000). Available from the World Wide Web: www.TheJusticeProject.org. See also James Liebman et al. "Capital Attrition: Error Rates in Capital Cases, 1973–1995." *Texas Law Review* 78 (2000): 1839.

79. Texas Defender Service. "A State of Denial: Texas Justice and the Death Penalty" [online]. (Texas Defender Service, 2000). Available from the World Wide Web: http://www.texasdefender.org/index.html. See also Penny J. White. "Errors and Ethnics: Dilemmas in Death." *Hofstra Law Review* 29 (2001): 1265; Stephen B. Bright. "Discrimination, Death and Denial: The Tolerance of Racial Discrimination in Infliction of the Death Penalty." *Santa Clara Law Review* 35 (1995): 433.

80. Michael Kroll. "Killing Justice: Government Misconduct and the Death Penalty" [online]. (The Death Penalty Information Center, 1992). Available from the World Wide Web: http://www.deathpenaltyinfo.org/article.php?did = 529&scid = 45.

81. Elizabeth Earle. "Banishing the Thirteenth Juror: An Approach to the Identification of Prosecutorial Racism." *Columbia Law Review* 92 (1992): 1212; Andre D. Lyon. "Setting the Record Straight: A Proposal for Handling Prosecutorial Appeals to Racial, Ethnic, or Gender Prejudice During Trial." *Michigan Journal of Race and Law* 6 (2001): 319.

82. V. A. Richelle. "Racism as a Strategic Tool at Trial: Appealing Race-Based Prosecutorial Misconduct." *Tulane Law Review* 67 (1993): 2357.

83. *Gates v. Zant,* 863 F.2d 1492 (1989). See Ronald J. Tabak. "Racial Discrimination in Implementing the Death Penalty." *Human Rights* 26 (1999): 5.

84. *Dobbs v. Zant,* 963 F.2d 1403, 1407 (1991).

85. American Bar Association. Resolution 107. (Chicago: ABA House of Delegates, 1997). See also John C. McAdams. "The ABA's Proposed Moratorium on the Death Penalty: Racial Disparity and the Death Penalty." *Law and Contemporary Social Problems* 61 (1998): 153.

86. Hugo Bedau and Michael Radelet. "Miscarriages of Justice in Potentially Capital Cases." *Stanford Law Review* 40 (1987): 21; Michael Radelet, William Lofquist, and Hugo Bedau. "Prisoners Released from Death Rows Since 1970 Because of Doubts About Their Guilt." *Thomas M. Colley Law Review* 13 (1996): 907. See also Barry Scheck, Peter Neufeld, and Jim Dwyer. *Actual Innocence: Five Days to Execution and Other Dispatches from the Wrongly Convicted.* (New York: Doubleday, 2000).

87. Marvin Wolfgang and Bernard Cohen. *Crime and Race Conceptions and Misconceptions.* (New York: Institute of Human Relations Press, 1970), p. 138.

88. Adalberto Aguirre and Jonathan Turner. *American Ethnicity: The Dynamics and Consequences of Discrimination.* (New York, NY: McGraw-Hill, 2000).

PART III

Seeking Solutions

The urban riots of the 1960s represent a turning point in American policing. As a result of these disturbances and the conspicuous racial differences between the police (who were almost exclusively white) and those being policed (people of color), pressure was exerted on many police agencies to diversify their departments. However, these early affirmative action programs frequently encountered resistance from white-dominated police unions that challenged these court actions (Walker, 1985). In many instances those within the police profession saw racial diversification as a political necessity rather than an opportunity to benefit from the potential contributions that diversity could bring (Maghan, 1993). Opposition to affirmative action probably was a reflection of the fact that police officers were recruited from the white lower-middle and working classes and contained conservative, authoritarian, and racially prejudiced individuals whose views were reinforced by the police subculture (Walker, 1985).

These early experiences notwithstanding, the presence of people of color on U.S. police forces has increased over time. Blacks currently comprise 11.7 percent of all full-time sworn personnel in local police departments (Maguire & Pastore, 2002, table 1.38). With the greater visibility of African Americans in policing, a question emerges: What impact, if any, has black representation had on policing? Helen Taylor Greene addresses this question in chapter 11. She argues that African Americans have been successful in implementing some much needed reforms at the national level, although their impact on local police agencies varies by jurisdiction and circumstances.

Jury nullification has been proposed as a partial remedy for racially disproportionate incarceration. Jury nullification refers to the jury's right to determine both the law and the facts of the case and to act contrary to the law. Albeit controversial, jury nullification is not a new concept. It originated in "medieval England, where juries were called to render a verdict based upon their own knowledge of the facts, not simply sit in impartial judgment of facts as presented" (Farnham, 1997, p. 5). Moreover, early prominent American jurists, such as Alexander Hamilton, John Adams, and Chief Justice John Jay, asserted the principles of jury nullification. Racially based jury nullification has been promoted by George Washington University Law Professor Paul Butler (1995, 1996) as a way of reducing the number of African Americans in prison. Professor Butler (1995, p. 715) advocates the use of racially based jury nullification only in "nonviolent *malum prohibitum* offenses, including 'victimless' crimes like narcotics offenses." In contrast, he does not subscribe to racially based jury nullification in violent crimes such as murder, rape, and aggravated assault.

In chapter 12 Elissa Krauss and Martha Schulman challenge the notion that black jurors regularly engage in jury nullification. They further contend that this myth has been perpetuated in part to reduce the effect of the experiences of people of color on the American criminal justice system. Hiroshi Fukurai, in chapter 13, offers an alternative to jury nullification. Fukurai suggests that the problem is the racial composition of juries, which tends to negate the power of the few minority group members who might be present. He contends that to ensure racial parity in juries, affirmative jury selection principles must guide the jury selection process.

Restorative justice represents yet another proposed tactic to reign in the criminal justice system's overreliance on incarceration as a means of crime control. Although not specifically formulated with the objective of reducing minority incarceration, the restorative justice movement subscribes to the goal that it is preferable to empower people to resolve their own differences than to have the state perform that function. Restorative justice relies heavily on the notions of restitution and victim–offender mediation to accomplish this goal. In direct contrast to adversarial justice, which employs a legalistic view of crime, restorative justice employs a social view of crime and seeks to bring together the offender, victim(s), and other parties affected by the wrongdoing in an attempt to restore harmony and to eventually reintegrate the offender back into the community (Berger, Free, & Searles, 2001, pp. 429–430). In chapter 14, Robert Conners critically examines the restorative justice model to determine its probable impact on African Americans. He concludes that given the status of African Americans in society, the restorative justice model as currently conceived is unlikely to produce greater racial parity than the traditional retributive justice model.

REFERENCES

Berger, R., Free, M., & Searles, P. (2001). *Crime, justice, and society: Criminology and the sociological imagination.* Boston: McGraw-Hill.

Butler, P. (1995). Racially based jury nullification: Black power in the criminal justice system. *Yale Law Journal, 195,* 677–725.

Butler, P. (1996). The evil of American criminal justice: A reply. *UCLA Law Review, 44,* 143–157.

Farnham, D. (1997). Jury nullification: History proves it's not a new idea. *Criminal Justice, 11* (4), 4–10, 12–14.

Maghan, J. (1993). The changing face of the police officer: Occupational socialization of minority police recruits. In R. Dunham and G. Alpert (Eds.), *Critical issues in policing: Contemporary readings* (2nd ed.) (pp. 348–360). Prospect Heights, IL: Waveland.

Maguire, K., & Pastore, A. (Eds.). (2002). *Sourcebook of criminal justice statistics* [online]. Retrieved on August 30, 2002, from http://www.albany.edu/sourcebook.

Walker, S. (1985). Racial minority and female employment in policing: The implications of "glacial" change. *Crime & Delinquency, 34,* 555–572.

CHAPTER 11

Do African American Police Make a Difference?

Helen Taylor Greene

INTRODUCTION

In the foreword to Dulaney's (1996, p. xi) definitive work entitled *Black Police in America*, Reuben Greenberg, Chief of Police in Charleston, South Carolina, notes that African American police can improve the relationship between police departments and African American communities and that they have improved the police profession as well. Although apparent at the macro-level, it may not always be apparent in every locality or agency. Cashmore (1991, p. 101) notes that black police representation has both symbolic value and practical consequences. Symbolically, the presence of black police chiefs is important because they hold powerful positions. From a practical standpoint, black law enforcement officers have been instrumental in decreasing police brutality and increasing minority recruitment. Cashmore nonetheless questions whether black police chiefs have any actual value to the majority of blacks and if they are representative of the working and underclass black population.

Trying to ascertain the effect of African American police on policing is a daunting task. First, these officers are employed in numerous local, state, federal, and private agencies. The type of agency and jurisdiction served will certainly contribute to the effect, if any, of African American police. Additionally, whether African American police have an impact will vary by officer, neighborhood, region, as well as numerous other factors. In communities where black officers are disliked by their (black) peers and shunned by racist colleagues, they may have a minimal impact on black communities and the problem of crime. In others, where they are respected and appreciated, they may make a difference. In still others, good rapport between black police officers and citizens may not be able to overcome socioeconomic factors that contribute to the problem of crime. It is also important to recognize that the impact African American police have is not confined to black communities.

The impact of African American police is due, at least in part, to a dramatic increase in their representation during the past three decades. African Americans represented only 3.6 percent of all sworn officers in the 1960s, 6 percent in the early 1970s, and 7.6 percent in 1982 (Walker & Katz, 2002). By 1997 they comprised 10 percent of local full-time sworn officers (county police, municipal police, sheriffs) and 7 percent of state police officers (Reaves & Goldberg, 1999). Black representation increased from 18.4 percent in 1990 to 20.1 percent in 2000 in large cities (Reaves & Hickman, 2002). There are not only more African American police officers and an unprecedented number of African Americans serving in leadership positions in local agencies, there are also more African American female police officers than white female police officers in some urban agencies (Taylor Greene, 2000). This progress notwithstanding, the ratio of black officers to black citizens continues to be low in large cities. Moreover, blacks are underrepresented in federal agencies. In 2000 blacks comprised 11.7 percent of federal officers. In Department of Justice agencies blacks comprise 6.2 percent in the Federal Bureau of Investigation, 8 percent in the Drug Enforcement Administration, and 7.9 percent in the U.S. Marshals Service (Reaves & Hart, 2001).

The purpose of this chapter is to examine African American police in the United States from the nineteenth century to the present in an effort to determine what difference these officers make in policing. The colonial model provides a theoretical framework for understanding both the effectiveness of and limitations placed upon these police. After a brief summary of the colonial model, a literature review of the history of African Americans in policing, and a discussion of whether African American police make a difference, the chapter concludes with a discussion of future research needs and the role of these officers in the twenty-first century.

THE COLONIAL MODEL

The colonial model provides a useful framework for understanding policing in America and the historical and contemporary role of African American police in our society. Numerous scholars have used the colonial model to explain crime and justice in America (Austin, 1983; Blauner, B., 2001; Blauner, R., 1969, 1972; Staples, 1975; Tatum 1994, 2000; Texeira, 1995). Tatum (1994) describes the colonial model as a sociopsychological approach with several key components, including oppression, racism, subordination (economic, political, and social), and alienation. The colonial model and internal colonialism view the black community as a colony controlled by the racially dominant group. Blauner (2001) uses the term police colonialism to refer to the role of the police in black ghetto communities, especially during the 1960s. According to Staples (1975), the predominantly white police are enforcers of colonial rule who are placed in black communities to protect the colonizers' property, not the residents. Staples (2002, p. 163) cites the findings of the United States Commission on Civil Rights, which reported, "police misconduct often serves as the ultimate weapon for keeping the Negro in his place." Those in the internal colony are repeatedly subjected to *petit apartheid*, a term Georges-Abeyie (2002, p. 237) and others (see Milovanovic & Russell, 2001) use to refer to selectively inhumane and demeaning behavior by police. Palmer (1973, p. 26) summed up the role of the police in the black community as "a direct continuation of the slave overseer . . . [that] functioned like an occupation army in the colonies." Historically, white police participated in lynching, murders of black citizens, and other forms of police abuse (Russell, 1998).

Alienation, one consequence of the colonization process, is defined as a feeling of psychological deprivation resulting in separation of a person from one's self, family, culture, and community (Staples, 1989; Tatum, 1994). Both the colonizer and colonized experience alienation and react in different ways including assimilation, crime or deviance, and protest (Tatum, 1994). Heretofore, the focus has been on how alienation leads to crime and deviance (Staples, 1975; Tatum, 1994, 2000). Yet, alienation may also be important in understanding African American police officers that respond to it by assimilating into policing and the larger society. As agents of the dominant power structure, their role in the black community is to control other African Americans, especially those who are involved in crime. Their alienation of self, significant others, culture, and generalized others may result in violence perpetrated against other colonized individuals (Tatum, 1994). This may be one explanation of earlier findings cited by Langworthy and Travis (2002) that black police are more likely to use deadly force (Fyfe, 1978), are more aggressive (Friedrich, 1977), and are not as lenient with black citizens as white officers (Alex, 1969). Police, regardless of color, are still viewed as an oppressive occupying force in many communities.

Several changes have occurred in our society since the analyses of police in a colonial context offered by Blauner and Staples. Although there is still political subordination, black political empowerment and police ascendancy in many police departments mitigate police colonialism. Black elected officials (and others) appoint African American police to leadership positions, and together they have been instrumental in creating representative bureaucracies, especially in urban areas with large black populations. More representative police agencies provide an opportunity for African American police, who will always be agents of the power structure, to also be agents of positive change, particularly in black communities. Second, the community-policing movement has resulted in police officers and citizens joining together in many jurisdictions to solve problems of crime and disorder.

These changes may help to explain whether African American police make a difference. At the same time, the colonial model is still applicable as the impact of African American police remains related to the broader functions of the police in our society. To better understand the role of policing in American society, a review of the history of African Americans in policing is presented below.

THE HISTORY OF AFRICAN AMERICANS IN POLICING: A REVIEW OF THE LITERATURE

Support for the colonial/internal colony model is pervasive in the history of our country. Williams and Murphy (1990) state that the American legal order sustained slavery, segregation, and discrimination and that the police were bound to uphold that order. As agents of social control the police often treated members of minority communities differently. The police in both the North and South were involved in racial oppression and enforcing racially biased laws such as the Slave Codes and Black Codes. Perhaps the best example of this differential treatment is the slave patrols that were established in the eighteenth century. Designed primarily to control both slaves and free Negroes, slave patrols are considered to be the first truly American style of policing. Undoubtedly the control of slaves must have impacted the structure and functioning of southern police agencies.

The first African American police officers, *free persons of color*, were clearly agents of the colonizers, primarily responsible for controlling the behavior of slaves (Dulaney, 1996). Prior to the Civil War, New Orleans hired blacks on the city guard for a brief period (1805–1830). Other cities employing black officers later in the 1800s include Washington, D.C.; Columbia and Charleston, South Carolina; Clinton, Jackson, and Meridian, Mississippi; and Philadelphia, Pennsylvania. The first black police chief in the nineteenth century was appointed in Jackson, Mississippi, during Reconstruction (Kuykendall & Burns, 1980). In the 1800s most African Americans became police officers during Reconstruction and often were hired to protect blacks from white violence. According to Barlow and Barlow (2000, p. 243), "[W]hite police could not be depended upon to enforce the law against whites terrorizing Blacks, nor could they be counted upon to physically protect blacks from assaults." Black police officers during the nineteenth century were required to enforce segregation laws in what Dulaney (1996) describes as a racist and hostile atmosphere. They were usually limited to policing black communities and were eventually eliminated from most southern police forces after the end of the Reconstruction era (1877).

Williams and Murphy (1990) emphasize that significant developments in policing during the political and reform eras of policing (late 1800s and early 1900s) had virtually no impact on minorities due to their subordination. Some blacks were able to obtain jobs in policing in the early twentieth century in several non-southern cities including St. Louis, Dayton, Berkeley, and Los Angeles (Kuykendall & Burns, 1980). Many of these officers were hired as a result of demands made by the black community. The Negroes' political influence after the 1940s was an important impetus for increasing the number of Negro law enforcement officers in the North and South (Rudwick, 1960).

Early research on blacks in policing focuses primarily on employment trends (Kuykendall & Burns, 1980; Rudwick, 1960). *The Negro Yearbook*, a publication of Tuskegee Institute and *New South*, published by the Southern Regional Council, provided statistics on black police in the South. In 1948 there were 334 black police in 62 southern cities in 12 states (Southern Regional Council, 1949). Nationwide, black police had increased from 47,233 during the decade of the 1940s to 64,489 during the decade of the 1950s (Kuykendall & Burns, 1980). Despite their increased representation, these officers faced overt discrimination in assignments, promotions, access to squad cars, and training. These (overly qualified) officers were systematically denied access to administration and command positions, and institutional racism often facilitated their exclusion. Leinen (1984) noted that whites maintained dominance in the New York City Police Department, relegated blacks to subordinate roles, and discriminated against them for most of the twentieth century. When blacks were given command positions, they were often assigned to units with low status, such as a community relations unit or juvenile unit (Sealy, 1977).

Once again, during the 1960s and 1970s, African American political participation resulted in the increased representation and advancement of black police. Many officers joined the force for economic reasons and to serve their communities. By this time police departments were beginning to accept the social control role black officers could serve. According to Palmer (1973), the function of black police was to serve as pawns of white rulers against black people.

Three federal commissions, the 1967 President's Commission on Law Enforcement and Administration of Justice, the 1968 National Advisory Commission on Civil Disorders, and the 1972 National Advisory Commission on Civil Disorders recommended recruitment of minority-group officers (Sealy, 1977). Federal legislation, affirmative action, and litigation improved access to policing in federal, state, and local agencies. As observed previously, the greatest employment gains were made in large urban areas. Blacks in policing have overcome some, although certainly not all, racial barriers. Unfortunately, many officers, especially in smaller jurisdictions and in many federal and state agencies, are still confronted with institutional racism, racial separation, and resentment.

As a result of the problems they confronted, black officers recognized the need to organize in order to affect change. In 1972 the National Black Police Association (NBPA) was established to bring together African American police associations in order to improve police departments and their relationship with the minority community. In 1976 the National Organization of Black Law Enforcement Executives (NOBLE) was founded at a meeting organized to bring black police executives together to discuss the problem of crime in urban areas. These organizations address numerous issues confronting officers and black citizens, including brutality, crime, discrimination, police–community relations, and recruitment. NBPA and NOBLE continue to influence national and local policies and programs today.

The number of black police executives has increased dramatically. The first African American police chief (director) in a large American city (Newark, New Jersey) was Hubert Williams (Serrill, 1985). In 1982 there were 50 black chiefs; by 1988 there were 130. Five of the largest cities (Atlanta, Chicago, Detroit, Houston, and Washington, D.C.) and six southern cities (Atlanta, Greensboro, Houston, Memphis, Miami, and New Orleans) had black chiefs. Most of these police executives rose through the ranks and targeted affirmative action and crime prevention/reduction programs and policies (Narine, 1988).[1]

In addition to research on employment trends, there have been numerous descriptive studies about black police officers (Alex, 1969; Bannon & Wilt, 1973; Beard, 1977; Campbell, 1980; Dodge & Pogrebin, 2001; Dulaney, 1996; Haarr & Morash, 1995; Kelly & West, 1973; Leinen, 1984; Lewis, 1989; Morash & Haarr, 1995; Palmer, 1973; Stokes & Scott; 1993; Taylor Greene, 2000; Townsey, 1982; Walker, 1983; Zhao & Lovrich, 1998). Although an analysis of these studies is beyond the scope of this chapter, they explore several relevant issues including affirmative action (Lewis, 1989; Stokes & Scott, 1993), black women in policing (Dodge & Pogrebin, 2001; Dulaney, 1996; Martin, 1994; Taylor Greene, 2000; Townsey, 1982), marginality (Alex, 1969; Campbell, 2001), reasons for entering policing (Alex, 1969; Leinen, 1984), racial discrimination (Beard, 1977; Dulaney, 1996; Kelly & West, 1973; Palmer, 1973), and stress and coping strategies (Haarr & Morash, 1995; Morash & Haarr, 1995). Only a few studies assess the impact of these officers (Bannon & Wilt, 1973; Leinen, 1984; Narine, 1988; Walker, 1983; Zhao & Lovrich, 1998). In a study of black policemen in the Detroit Police Department, Bannon and Wilt (1973) found evidence that black policemen make a meaningful contribution to police agencies and black citizens. Walker (1983) attributes this to the similarity between black officers' values and those of the black population. He suggested that black officers better serve core city residents because their values contribute to mutual understanding and empathy. Similarly, Leinen (1984) found that black officers were more effective in black communities because they have a greater interest in its affairs and problems. Zhao and Lovrich (1998) found that whereas the proportion of the population that is black was a major determinant of personnel policies that affect hiring, the presence of black police chiefs was also significant. Furthermore, according to Narine (1988), the presence of black police chiefs is associated with lower crime rates.

DO AFRICAN AMERICAN POLICE MAKE A DIFFERENCE?

Throughout the twentieth century, blacks concerned about crime and policing demanded black police in their neighborhoods. It was believed that these officers would be more concerned about the community and viewed more favorably than white officers. Black citizens were also thought to cooperate with black police more so than with white officers. Despite demands for black police by some segments of the black community, not all blacks viewed black police favorably (Dulaney, 1996). The strain that often exists between black police and citizens defeats the rationale for hiring more blacks: namely, to improve social control and police community relations.

Palmer (1973) asserts that black police can facilitate change if they organize and mobilize themselves in pursuit of the betterment of black people. Many probably agree with Palmer; however, he seems to diminish the power of the police organization. If we consider these officers in the context of their power and capacity to bring about change, it is readily apparent that police chiefs, police in other administrative and command positions, and police officers will vary in the difference they can make. Collectively, black police make a difference both nationally and locally through their professional associations. Despite the lack of research, it is self-evident that black police chiefs can impact policing more than any other black officers. As police leaders they have the power to establish priorities within their agencies and to affect policing on a national level as well. Many have made a noticeable difference in restricting the use of force, recruiting minorities, and implementing community policing.

Shortly after blacks were appointed to the top law enforcement positions during the 1980s, many implemented restrictive use of force policies in their agencies, since blacks were disproportionately the victims of police use of excessive force. They were frequently physically and verbally abused, shot, and sometimes killed by the police at disproportionate rates (Fyfe, 1982; Geller & Karales, 1981; Takagi, 1974). Black chiefs were a part of a nationwide trend in larger police agencies to restrict police use of unnecessary force. It was not until the late 1980s, after the U.S. Supreme Court ruling in *Tennessee v. Garner* (1985) struck down the common law fleeing felon doctrine, that other police departments modified their policies. Black chiefs were also instrumental in NOBLE's development of guidelines that became mandatory standards for the Commission on Accreditation of Law Enforcement Agencies (National Organization of Black Law Enforcement Executives [NOBLE], 2002).

Research documents the positive effect black police executives have had on minority recruitment (Lewis,1989; Zhao & Lovrich, 1998). In an article titled "Top Cops," Narine (1988) found that black officers were instrumental in implementing policies that resulted in hiring more minorities. NOBLE has worked toward affirmative action in hiring minorities by identifying strategies to increase minority recruitment and sponsoring job fairs (NOBLE, 2002).

Palmer (1973) makes a strong case for the importance of shifting power from the police department to the community. Although Palmer never defined what he meant by community, he probably was referring to the black community. Sharing power has occurred in many agencies, especially those that embrace the community-policing approach. Black chiefs have also been at the forefront of the community-policing movement. Lee P. Brown, former leader of the New York City, Houston, and Atlanta police departments, and currently the mayor of Houston, and Hubert Williams, director of the Police Foundation, were advocates of neighborhood/ community policing in the 1980s long before it was as widely accepted as it is today. Brown viewed community policing as an interactive process that involved police and citizens working together to identify and solve community problems (Taylor Greene & Gabbidon, 2000). Many black chiefs embrace community policing because it provides an opportunity to remove the historical barriers between police and the black community. Unfortunately, there are many officers and citizens who do not support community policing, which may undermine its success.

In addition to police chiefs, blacks in administrative and command positions also make a difference in the organization and community. One high-ranking police administrator stated that black administrators are instrumental in expressing the concerns of other black officers and citizens. In the community, they communicate with citizens about what is going on in the police department. Citizens are also more comfortable and willing to share information with black administrators and officers than with white officers (L. Williams, telephone interview, June 12, 2002).

Whether on patrol, enforcing traffic regulations, investigating crimes, working as Drug Abuse Resistance Education (DARE) officers, or attending community meetings, each officer has the potential to make a difference. Since most of what we know is anecdotal, documenting the impact of black officers, whether favorable or unfavorable, is more difficult. As an African American woman, I probably am not alone in feeling a sense of relief when the responding officer is black. At the same time, there are probably others who feel just as anxious with a black officer as they do with a white officer. Sometimes black officers pay a price for making a difference (see Campbell, 2001) or do not strive to make a difference because they have too much to lose (Palmer, 1973).

One example of their potential to make a difference is outlined in a book entitled, *The Slick Boys: A Ten Point Plan To Rescue Your Community by Three Chicago Cops Who Are Making It Happen* (Davis, Martin, & Holcomb,1998). Each author grew up in the projects and now works as a plainclothes officer in these same communities. They espouse 10 principles that are essential to improving police community relations. They are invited to speak around the country, where they share their grass-roots effort to encourage individuals, families, and communities to promote education, hope, and peace.

CONCLUSION AND SUGGESTIONS FOR FUTURE RESEARCH

Compared with a century ago, the status of blacks in policing today is impressive. These officers can favorably impact the black community and policing, but their impact remains equivocal, especially in the context of social control. Black communities still experience too much crime, victimization, police brutality, and racial profiling. Many African Americans have unfavorable attitudes toward the police. Even though the Gallup Organization does not disaggregate opinions of the police by officer race, their findings are disturbing. Whereas 58 percent of blacks hold a favorable opinion of the police, 36 percent of blacks hold unfavorable opinions due to questionable police practices. Even more disturbing is the fact that during the 1960s blacks had more positive ratings of police fairness than today (Newport, 2000). Since the majority of police are white, one might reasonably assume that perceptions of unfairness is primarily directed at these officers. Yet negative attitudes toward officers, regardless of race, adversely impacts crime prevention, control, and recruitment.

The role of African American police in the twenty-first century will be influenced by recent developments that directly impact local, state, and federal law enforcement agencies and their personnel. After the events of September 11, 2001, increased hiring provides an even greater opportunity for African American representation and advancement in federal law enforcement agencies. Concomitantly, local and state agencies are experiencing an exodus of officers that should create hiring opportunities at these levels as well. Many jurisdictions, however, are facing budgetary constraints, and agencies are unable to replace departing officers. Jurisdictions having fewer resources negatively impact crime control efforts, including community policing. Scarce resources are further diverted to security-focused law enforcement in response to terrorist threats. The impact of this on police agencies in the future as they continue to assess their priorities and cope with potential personnel shortages is a largely a matter of conjecture.

African American police leaders, administrators, and officers undoubtedly will be affected by these developments. One distinct possibility is a shift to the yet-to-be-defined homeland security model of policing that focuses on surveillance and intelligence gathering, and not on street crime, which has increased recently. A movement toward a homeland security model of policing may also lead to a deterioration of citizens' rights. During this century, terrorism may well replace race as a critical policing issue. Yet strained relationships between police and citizens remain, and the role of African American police in ameliorating this situation continues to be an important topic for research.

To fully comprehend the role of African American police and their impact, future studies must address several issues. First, we must recognize that there are differences in black police, black citizens, and black communities that must be taken into consideration. Second, researchers must collect data on officers' race/ethnicity, class, gender, age, education, and other demographic variables to elucidate those variables that interact with race. Published reports should also disaggregate information by race and gender. Third, data on the race/ethnicity of police leaders should be collected and made available on a regular basis. With the availability of disaggregated data, several research issues can be addressed, including

- the role of black police executives in reducing biased policing (brutality, profiling, etc.);
- the attitudes and perceptions of black male and female officers;
- the role of black officers in community policing;
- the impact of politicians on black police executives; and
- the employment trends.

Finally, it is important to recognize the strained relationships between police and people of color in other countries. Cross-cultural studies of black police officers in countries where they are either the majority or the minority are essential. African American police can also lend their expertise to police agencies in countries that (1) are experiencing problems between the police and the citizenry, especially minorities, and (2) are seeking technical assistance from African Americans in policing.

NOTE

1. The current number of African American chiefs of police is not readily available at the time of this writing.

CASE CITED

Tennessee v. Garner, 105 S. Ct. 1694 (1985)

REFERENCES

Alex, N. (1969). *Black in blue: A study of the Negro policeman*. New York: Appleton-Century-Crofts.

Austin, R. (1983). The colonial model, subcultural theory and intragroup violence. *Journal of Criminal Justice, 11*, 93–104.

Bannon, J., & Wilt, G. (1973). Black policemen: A study of self-images. *Journal of Police Science & Administration, 1*, 21–29.

Barlow, D., & Barlow, M. (2000). *Police in a multicultural society: An American story*. Prospect Heights, IL: Waveland Press.

Beard, E. (1977). The black police in Washington, DC *Journal of Police Science & Administration, 5*, 48–52.

Blauner, B. (2001). *Still the big news: Racial oppression in America*. Philadelphia: Temple University Press.

Blauner, R. (1969). Internal colonialism and ghetto revolt. *Social Problems, 16*, 393–408.

Blauner, R. (1972). *Racial oppression in America*. New York: Harper & Row.

Campbell, J. (2001). Walking the beat alone: An African American police officer's perspective on petit apartheid. In D. Milovanovic & K. Russell (Eds.), *Petit apartheid in criminal justice* (pp. 15–20). Durham, NC: Carolina Press.

Campbell, V. (1980). Double marginality of black policemen. *Criminology, 17*, 477–484.

Cashmore, E. (1991). Black Cops Inc. In E. Cashmore & E. McLaughlin (Eds.), *Out of order? Policing black people* (pp. 87–108). London: Routledge, Chapman, & Hall.

Davis, E., Martin, J., & Holcomb, R. (1998). *The slick boys: A ten point plan to rescue your community by three Chicago cops who are making it happen*. New York: Simon & Schuster.

Dodge, M., & Pogrebin, M. (2001). African American policewomen: An exploration of professional relationships. *Policing: An International Journal of Police Strategies & Management, 24*, 550–562.

Dulaney, M. (1996). *Black police in America*. Bloomington, IN: Indiana University Press.

Friedrich, R. (1977). *The impact of organizational, individual, and situational factors on police behavior*. Unpublished doctoral dissertation, Department of Political Science, University of Michigan.

Fyfe, J. (1978). *Shots fired: An examination of New York City police firearms discharges*. Unpublished doctoral dissertation, School of Criminal Justice, State University of New York at Albany.

Fyfe, J. (1982). Blind justice: Police shootings in Memphis. *Journal of Criminal Law & Criminology, 83*, 707–722.

Geller, W., & Karales, K. (1981). *Split-second decisions: Shootings of and by Chicago police*. Chicago: Chicago Law Enforcement.

Georges-Abeyie, D. (2002). Race, ethnicity, and the spatial dynamic: Toward a realistic study of black crime, crime victimization, and criminal justice processing of blacks. In S. Gabbidon, H. Taylor Greene, & V. Young (Eds.), *African American classics in criminology and criminal justice* (pp. 227–242). Thousand Oaks, CA: Sage.

Haarr, R., & Morash, M. (1995). Gender, race, and strategies of coping with occupational stress in policing. *Justice Quarterly, 16*, 303–336.

Kelly, R., & West, G., Jr. (1973). The racial transition of a police force: A profile of white and black policemen in Washington, D.C. In J. Snibbe and H. Snibbe (Eds.), *The urban policeman in transition: A psychological and sociological view* (pp. 354–381). Springfield, IL: Charles Thomas.

Kuykendall, J., & Burns, D. (1980). The black police officer: An historical perspective. *Journal of Contemporary Criminal Justice, 1*, 4–12.

Langworthy, R., & Travis, L. (2002). *Policing in America: A balance of forces.* Upper Saddle River, NJ: Prentice Hall.

Leinen, S. (1984). *Black police, white society.* New York: New York University Press.

Lewis, W. (1989). Toward representative bureaucracy: Blacks in city police organizations, 1975–1985. *Public Administration Review, 49*, 257–267.

Martin, S. (1994). "Outsiders within" the station house: The impact of race and gender on black women police. *Social Problems, 4*, 383–400.

Milovanovic, D., & Russell, K. (2001). *Petit apartheid in criminal justice.* Durham, NC: Carolina Press.

Morash, M., & Haarr, R. (1995). Gender, workplace problems, and stress in policing. *Justice Quarterly, 12*, 113–136.

Narine, D. (1988, May). Top cops. *Ebony, 43*, pp. 130, 132, 134, & 136.

National Organization of Black Law Enforcement Executives. (2002). *Information resources.* Retrieved June 5, 2002, from http://www .nobleatl.org/info_resources.htm.

Newport, F. (2000). *Protests by blacks over Amadou Diallo verdict not surprising given long standing perceptions among blacks that they are discriminated against in most areas of their daily lives.* Retrieved February 3, 2001, from http://www.gallup.com/poll/fromtheed/ed0003.asp.

Palmer, E. (1973). Black police in America. *Black Scholar, 5*, 19–27.

Reaves, B., & Goldberg, A. (1999). *Law enforcement management and administrative statistics, 1997: Data for individual, state, and local agencies with 100 or more officers.* Washington, DC: U. S. Department of Justice.

Reaves, B., & Hart, T. (2001). *Federal law enforcement officers, 2000.* Washington, DC: U. S. Department of Justice.

Reaves, B., & Hickman, M. (2002). *Police departments in large cities, 1990–2000.* Washington, DC: U. S. Department of Justice.

Rudwick, E. (1960). The Negro policeman in the south. *Journal of Criminal Law, Criminology, & Police Science, 51*, 273–276.

Russell, K. (1998). *The color of crime*. New York: New York University Press.

Sealy, L. (1977). The dilemma of the black police executives. In H. Bryce (Ed.), *Black crime: A police view* (pp. 141–154). Washington, DC: Joint Center for Political Studies.

Serrill, M. (1985, February 18). The new black police chiefs; updating a long tradition of ethnic groups rising to the top. *Time, 125*, pp. 84–85.

Southern Regional Council. (1949, September). Negro policemen in southern cities. *New South, 4*, 1.

Staples, R. (1975). White racism, black crime, and American justice: An application of the colonial model. *Phylon, 36*, 14–22.

Staples, R. (1989). *The urban plantation*. Oakland, CA: Black Scholar Press.

Staples, R. (2002). White racism, black crime, and American justice: An application of the colonial model. In S. Gabbidon, H. Taylor Greene, & V. Young (Eds.), *African American Classics in Criminology and Criminal Justice* (pp. 161–168). Thousand Oaks, CA: Sage.

Stokes, L., & Scott, J. (1993). Affirmative action policy standard and employment of African Americans in police departments. *The Western Journal of Black Studies, 17*, 135–142.

Takagi, P. (1974). A garrison state in a "democratic" society. *Crime & Social Justice, 5*, 27–33.

Tatum, B. (1994). The colonial model as a theoretical explanation of crime and delinquency. In A. Sulton (Ed.), *African American perspectives on: Crime causation, criminal justice administration, and crime prevention* (pp. 33–52). Boston: Butterworth-Heinemann.

Tatum, B. (2000). Towards a neocolonial model of adolescent crime and violence. *Journal of Contemporary Criminal Justice, 16*, 157–170.

Taylor Greene, H. (2000). Black females in law enforcement: A foundation for future research. *Journal of Contemporary Criminal Justice, 16*, 230–239.

Taylor Greene, H., & Gabbidon, S. (2000). *African American criminological thought*. Albany, NY: State University of New York Press.

Texeira, M. (1995). Policing the internally colonized: Slavery, Rodney King, Mark Furhman and beyond. *The Western Journal of Black Studies, 19*, 235–243.

Townsey, R. (1982). Black women in American policing: An advancement display. *Journal of Criminal Justice, 10*, 455–468.

Walker, D. (1983). Black police values and the black community. *Police Studies, 5*, 20–28.

Walker, S., & Katz, C. (2002). *Police in America: An introduction*. New York: McGraw-Hill.

Williams, H., & Murphy, P. (1990). *The evolving strategy of police: A minority perspective.* Washington, DC: National Institute of Justice.
Zhao, J., & Lovrich, N. (1998). Determinants of minority employment in American municipal police agencies: The representation of African American officers. *Journal of Criminal Justice, 26,* 267–277.

CHAPTER 12

The Myth of Black Juror Nullification: Racism Dressed Up in Jurisprudential Clothing

Elissa Krauss and Martha Schulman

INTRODUCTION

In recent years, African American (and other minority) jurors have regularly been accused of judging cases on preconceived race-based notions about justice rather than on the evidence.[1] Anecdotal accounts of a handful of allegedly race-based acquittals are bolstered by statistics claiming to show higher rates of acquittals and hung juries in jurisdictions where African Americans and other people of color have become the majority. Critics argue that people of color have transformed a color-blind system into one that is color sensitive. The implication is that as juries have become more representative, race has been injected into the justice system where it was previously absent. Such claims strike at the very core of principles of fairness and justice. They are both a shield for racial prejudice and an attack on the American jury system itself. The message of such claims is that rather than following the law and protecting the innocent, the real job of juries is to convict.

This article looks first at changes in the way that courts have treated black participation in the jury system and then moves to an overview of fundamental legal principles underlying jury decision making. We then consider how African American jurors' adherence to these principles has been wrongly characterized as a pattern of nullification that undermines the system. We go on to discuss differences between black and white experiences and attitudes, emphasizing that in a racially divided society only whites have the luxury of claiming to be color blind. In conclusion, we argue that the myth of black juror nullification is a racist attack on the jury system motivated in part by a desire to limit the impact of minority peoples' experiences on the justice system.

THE CHANGING ROLE OF MINORITIES IN THE JURY SYSTEM

This contemporary emergence of broad attacks on black jurors is ironic in light of this country's long history of excluding persons of color from juries.[2] The requirement that jury pools represent a fair cross-section of eligible jurors, though widely acknowledged as a bedrock principle today, is relatively recent. This principle was first articulated by the Supreme Court in the 1940s, and then federally codified in 1968. Increased representativeness of jury pools, however, did not eliminate systematic discrimination, for prosecutors still used peremptory challenges to ensure that juries stayed mainly white.[3]

Only a decade ago, the Supreme Court in *Batson v. Kentucky* (1986) prohibited the discriminatory use of peremptory challenges to accomplish the illegal exclusion of minorities already prohibited at other phases of the jury selection system. *Batson* and its progeny forced those attempting to strip juries of cognizable classes to be more creative in efforts to preserve the all-white jury.[4] Despite these efforts, in some jurisdictions juries have become more representative.[5]

Blacks—along with Hispanics and Asians—now serve on juries in greater numbers than ever before. In some jurisdictions, minorities are the majority in the jury pool, as they are in the broader community. Sometimes they are the majority on a specific jury. One such case was the O. J. Simpson criminal trial. As is well known, that jury's verdict was harshly criticized, and the jurors themselves were subjected to ad hominem attacks.

A groundswell of white public opinion accused the Simpson jurors (nine of whom are African American) of reaching the wrong conclusion. Their relatively brief period of deliberation was often cited as proof that they had not really considered the evidence. Yet their accusers had themselves reached the opposite conclusion in the same short period of time and without any formal deliberation at all.

The Simpson verdict unleashed a host of voices claiming that the jury system was in crisis. Articles in mass media sources, ranging from the *Wall Street Journal* to *The New Yorker* to *Readers Digest*, raised the specter of too many wrongful acquittals and too many hung juries caused by jurors whose narrow focus on their own experiences resulted in excessive skepticism of police and prosecutors. Who are the jurors thought to be causing such havoc? The same ones who until recently were excluded from the process: African Americans.

Black jurors (and sometimes other minorities) have been accused of tainting justice by (a) prejudging based on race, (b) expressing skepticism about police testimony that white jurors and white observers find credible, and (c) empathizing with the troubled lives of some black defendants. The critics imply that these attitudes result in the guilty going free, while the jury system goes to hell. The equation is quite simple: black defendant + black jurors + nonconviction = miscarriage of justice.

THE JURY'S ROLE AND RESPONSIBILITIES

The critique of African American jurors is an attack on the most basic principles of the jury system. Black jurors are being condemned for doing exactly what jurors are supposed to do: demand that the prosecution prove its case beyond a reasonable doubt. All jurors are expected to begin by presuming innocence. However, this hallmark of our system is by no means universally understood or followed. Our surveys, conducted by the National Jury Project in jurisdictions throughout the nation over the last twenty years, consistently find that between 15 percent and 45 percent of juror-eligible respondents believe that a person who is brought to trial is probably guilty; more than 50 percent typically expect defendants to prove their innocence despite judges' instructions to the contrary (Krauss & Bonora, 1996, figures 2.1 and 2.2). It is often difficult to find jurors who understand and will follow the two bedrock principles of our criminal justice system: (1) the defendant is presumed innocent, and (2) the prosecution must prove guilt beyond a reasonable doubt. When jurors who abide by these principles appear on juries, they should be applauded, not condemned.

A defendant remains cloaked in the presumption of innocence until the jury starts deliberations. The jury usually completes its work by finding the defendant either guilty or not guilty.[6] If jurors are not satisfied that the prosecution has met its burden, the jury must acquit. A not guilty verdict does not mean, however, that the jurors believe the defendant is innocent. A not guilty verdict means only that the state has not met its burden of proof.[7]

Post-trial juror interviews conducted by the National Jury Project over many years have shown that in most instances where jurors acquit, at least some of them had the "feeling" that the defendant probably "did it" or at least did "something" wrong, but the government's case did not stand up to reasonable-doubt scrutiny. These acquittals are not the result of juror error or bias, but rather the result of jurors' obedience to their sworn obligation.

Jurors are given a tremendous amount of power to evaluate evidence and judge credibility. Our system expects ordinary citizens to draw on their experiences and reach reasoned conclusions based in part on common sense. The system is organized around the principle that members of the community should decide whether or not a person should be deprived of liberty. This is because, as the Supreme Court has emphasized, "community participation" is "consistent with our democratic heritage" and is "critical to public confidence in the fairness of the criminal justice system" (*Taylor v. Louisiana*, 1975).

In a racially divided country like the U.S., it is not surprising that black and white jurors bring different experiences into the courtroom. One common difference is that black jurors' life experiences lead them to have an easier time imposing as high a standard of credibility on police as on other witnesses and demanding that prosecutors prove guilt *beyond a reasonable doubt*. When they do so, they are accused of nullifying, that is, of deciding cases not on evidence, but on some predisposition or understanding of a higher law. Today, nullification has become a catch phrase to explain the fact that some black jurors reach conclusions unlike those expected or desired by some whites.

PERPETUATING THE NULLIFICATION MYTH

It is rare that the source of a new and widely promoted myth can be pinpointed. In this instance, however, the genesis of the idea that a pattern of black jury nullification is eroding the jury system can be traced to a *Wall Street Journal* article the day after the Simpson criminal trial verdict (Holden & Cohen, 1995). In that article, the authors opine that the justice system is in crisis. They support their claim with statistics and anecdotal reports of individual trials; neither stands up to close scrutiny. The statistics are inaccurate and highly misleading (see Parloff, 1997). The trial anecdotes are incomplete and slanted toward the prosecution. The *Wall Street Journal* article juxtaposes a supposed national acquittal rate of 17 percent, with trial outcome statistics from three jurisdictions. They report that in the Bronx, juries acquit in 47.6 percent of felony trials; in Washington, D.C., 28.7 percent of defendants are acquitted; and in Wayne County, jurors acquit 30 percent of the time.

The statistics simply do not support the authors' position. Roger Parloff (1997) carefully reviewed the available data and concluded that a national acquittal rate of 17 percent is neither accepted by experts, nor is it verifiable. An acquittal rate of about 28 percent is more realistic (p. 6). Hence, Wayne County and Washington, D.C., are right in line with the national average. The "Bronx jury," a phenomenon well-known in New York legal circles, apparently does acquit at a rate above the national average.

To examine the causes and implications of the Bronx statistics, Parloff (1997) wisely followed two investigative paths. First, he asked those who practice in Bronx courtrooms what they have to say about acquittal rates. Second, he tested the black racism hypothesis by comparing the rates of acquittal for black, Hispanic, and white defendants in the Bronx. Parloff found that judges and lawyers who practice in the Bronx do not feel there is a race-based crisis. In fact, practitioners from the bench and from both sides of the bar reported that, in their experience, Bronx jurors are skeptical about police testimony and hold the government to the required high burden of proof. One Bronx district attorney with twenty-four years of experience told Parloff, "Basically the quality of the prosecution will determine whether you get a verdict in a case" (p. 7). Parloff also found virtually identical rates of acquittal by Bronx juries of white, black, and Hispanic defendants.

Thus, the acquittal rate in the Bronx is apparently caused by a combination of two factors: (1) jurors who are doing their jobs well [and] (2) prosecutors who are *not* doing their jobs so well. There is no reason to believe that the Bronx D.A.'s Office is any less competent or efficient than any other urban prosecutor's office. Therefore, if the Bronx example teaches us anything, it is that there is a dangerously high conviction rate elsewhere.

If the national acquittal rate is around 28 percent, then the conviction rate is around 72 percent. Approximately, three out of every four of the very few arrests that actually lead to trial result in conviction.[8] As any seasoned litigator knows, the cases that go to trial are usually the ones where the evidence is not clear-cut. Each side reasonably thinks it has a chance of winning. In most jurisdictions, however, the prosecution routinely does better than the odds. The Bronx outcomes are closer to what would be expected if both sides actually did start out equally. Therefore, the conviction rates elsewhere most likely reflect the pro-prosecution biases held by many jurors.

If the statistics in the *Wall Street Journal* article do not stand up to scrutiny, then we can only rely on the trial anecdotes. However, they, too, wilt under close scrutiny. The cases are presented as if guilt was proven. No information has been given about the police investigation, the credibility or self-interest of police or other witnesses, or on what the defense case was based—surely an incomplete picture of any criminal trial. With such a skewed picture, the reader is led blindly to believe that black jurors are choosing to "disregard the evidence, however powerful" (Holden & Cohen, 1995).

Only enough information is given to reinforce the race-based equation. One case that has become ubiquitous involved the Baltimore trial of a black man accused of murdering a white man (Levine, 1996; Thernstrom & Fetter, 1996; Weiss & Zinsmeister, 1996). Other than a broad outline of the case, the only thing the reader learns is that prior to an acquittal, the sole nonblack juror, a Pakistani-American, sent a note to the judge indicating that race "may be playing a part" in the deliberations (Holden & Cohen, 1995). We are told that several eyewitnesses testified at the trial. No reference is made to questions raised or arguments made by the defense about the eyewitnesses or any other evidence in the case. Nor is there any mention of the widespread understanding today that eyewitness testimony to a crime is extremely unreliable (Loftus, 1979, 1988; Parker, 1980). The reader of the article knows only that a white was killed, a black was charged, there were eleven black jurors, a Pakistani-American juror wrote a note, and the case failed to end in conviction. Black defendant + black jurors + nonconviction = miscarriage of justice.

The "lessons" of the *Journal* article can be found subsequently in *Reader's Digest*, the *ABA Journal*, and elsewhere with the same statistics and similar anecdotal reporting. The anecdotes and statistics are reinforced by references to Professor Paul Butler's (1995) thoughtful and provocative argument, that in a country where so many young black men are under supervision by the criminal justice system, nullifying in some cases is a moral choice. Mere reference by white commentators to Professor Butler's thesis does not, however, tell us if jurors are acting in accordance with his recommendations. In fact, close scrutiny of some published anecdotal accounts reveals that rather than a pattern of nullification, there is a pattern of law-abiding jurors doing their jobs who are being attacked because the authors do not like the resulting outcomes.

The myth of black juror nullification has been perpetuated in other articles that rely primarily on prosecution-biased anecdotal accounts (Haberman, 1995; Rosen, 1997). Clyde Haberman's (1995) *New York Times* column describing the outcome of a trial of two Hispanic defendants is illustrative. After two days of acrimonious deliberations, a multiracial, multiethnic Manhattan jury remained divided seven to five for acquittal. The minority voting to convict, made up of three non-Hispanic whites and two Asians, is characterized as having accepted "on faith" the principle that the system can be "color-blind." The black and Hispanic majority voting to acquit, in contrast, is alleged to have "taken out their social frustrations in deliberations" and to have concluded "right off" that the defendants were "victims of false prosecution."

Lost in Haberman's vignette is any understanding of where the burden of proof lies. The burden is first on the prosecutor and then it is on those favoring conviction. It is never on those advocating for acquittal. Nevertheless, Haberman depicts the jurors who voted to acquit as intransigent and obstructionist. The reality is that by having accepted the presumption of innocence and deciding that the state failed to meet its burden, the jurors fulfilled their obligation. This acquitting majority was, in fact, silenced by an intransigent, conviction-oriented minority, which failed to fulfill its burden of persuading the others.

Apparently, the seven to five division began with the first vote. It is well-established that in nine out of ten cases, a jury's final verdict accords with the verdict supported initially by the majority of jurors (Kalven & Zeisel, 1966, p. 488).[9] But Haberman is quick to convict the minority jurors, who were the majority on this jury, for preventing deliberation. Their crime appears to be a refusal to go along with the minority who agreed with the prosecution.

COLOR BLINDNESS AS A PROP FOR THE NULLIFICATION MYTH

The African American and Hispanic jurors in Haberman's vignette were attacked on the grounds that their actions were color sensitive when they ought to have been color-blind. Thus, Haberman joins a parade of recent commentators holding up color blindness as the ideal for jurors and as a salient feature of the justice system in the days before black jurors injected their race-based perspective. White jurors are assumed to be color-blind. The true history of race-based wrongful convictions (and acquittals) wrought by white supremacy is ignored.

In the past, the concept that color blindness was the desirable way to organize society was inextricably linked to the goal of racial equality. Today, the dream that children would be judged for the content of their character rather than the color of their skin has been co-opted. Color blindness has come to stand for a denial of the existence of race as a factor in American social relations and in Americans' perceptions. This new understanding can be found in many sources, including Republican rhetoric about affirmative action (Gingrich & Connerly, 1997) and in Supreme Court opinions (*City of Richmond v. J.A. Croson Co.*, 1989; *Edmonson v. Leesville Concrete Co.*, 1981; *Fullilove v. Klutznick*, 1980; *Minnick v. California Department of Corrections*, 1981; *Metro Broadcasting v. FCC*, 1990).

Exalting color blindness as the goal of a multiracial society is deeply problematic. Color blindness is impossible because everyone notices racial differences both in daily life and in the courtroom. Contemporary advocates of color blindness seem to hope that upon noticing racial differences, everyone will immediately ignore them. But the reality is that as soon as race is noticed, people attach their preexisting beliefs and assumptions to it (Gotanda, 1991, p. 18). Therefore, calls for color blindness obscure prejudice and become a prop for existing racial injustice. Such calls begin with the premise that race can be ignored. That race affects attitudes and behavior is well-established in social science research which has shown, over and over again, that Americans are not color-blind. For more than fifty years, researchers have found that the facts of race and racial difference affect attitudes and behavior in measurable and sometimes disturbing ways.[10]

Most interesting are unobtrusive studies in which research subjects are not told that racial attitudes or prejudice is being studied (Crosby, Bromley, & Saxe, 1980). Subjects are led to believe that researchers are studying some attitude or behavior not related to race—such as effectiveness of punishment as a teaching tool, helping behavior, or the ways in which jurors interpret different types of evidence. The findings consistently show that both attitudinal and behavioral responses vary in response to the sole change of race.[11] Such variations indicate that bias and prejudice (which often exist below the conscious level) are affecting attitudes and actions.

Studies of the influence of race in jury decision making echo these results. All have found that, in most cases, race has some influence on both black and white research participants (Bernard, 1979; Ugwuegbu, 1979). In many instances, racial prejudice is the only explanation for disparities in white jurors' readiness to convict, impose harsher sentences, predict recidivism, or take into account evidence that they have been told to ignore when considering the fate of minority-race defendants (Gordon, Bindrim, McNicholas, & Walden, 1988; Johnson, 1995; Johnson, Whitestone, Jackson, & Gatto, 1995; Sweeney & Haney, 1992). Race and racism, therefore, affect outcomes even when they are not asked about, not explicitly mentioned, and would probably be denied.

Denying that race or racism exists is possible only for whites whose majority status allows them to assume that they do not have a race (Grillo & Wildman, 1995). Since whiteness is the norm, whites can ignore race until it intrudes, disrupting the fantasy of a color-blind world. Because race and the reality of being minority status are facts of life for people who are not white, they are more willing than whites to name it.

NO TALKING ABOUT RACISM, PLEASE

National Jury Project post-trial interviews and mock-trial research show that minority people are more willing than are whites to discuss race.[12] For an extraordinary example of whites' desire to avoid race and African Americans' willingness to discuss it, consider the case of a white woman suing her employer for wrongful termination. She had a number of claims, including a claim of race discrimination (based on documented expressions of bias by an African American supervisor). In two different mock juries, white jurors ignored her race discrimination claim, reaching verdicts in her favor on the other issues in the case. In each jury, an African American juror reminded the others of the race-discrimination claim, spoke of its credibility in light of his experience, and persuaded the others to find in the plaintiff's favor on the race discrimination claim as they had on her other claims.

The extreme hesitation whites have about mentioning race and racism can result in disapproval of whites who are willing to address these issues head on. A wrongful termination claim by two men, an African American and his white supervisor, is illustrative. The two were fired after the white supervisor refused to follow a directive to fire the African American man. The white supervisor told his boss he believed the termination order was motivated by racism. Rather than being viewed as a hero, the white man

was seen by white jurors in two mock juries as having brought his termination upon himself by bringing up an issue that did not affect him.
The jurors were sympathetic to the black man "who had no choice" and
were critical of the white man who, they felt, could have simply avoided
the problem.

Whites do not like to talk about race, and overt expressions of racism
have become socially unacceptable. But racism, although more covert, is
alive and well.[13] One litmus test question that has been shown over many
decades to successfully uncover racial bias, even in subjects who claim to
be free of such attitudes, has been willingness to accept interracial
marriage. A 1997 Gallup Poll found that 61 percent of whites approve of
marriage between blacks and whites as compared to only 25 percent
in 1972.

While the 1997 poll suggests an improvement, the ramifications of the
continuing disapproval among 39 percent are worth examining. Our National Jury Project research in several different jurisdictions has found that
whites who disapprove of interracial marriage are also less open to a black
person's claim that he has been discriminated against and more likely to
acquit a white police officer accused of brutalizing a black person. Thus,
whites' negative views of interracial marriage continue to be indicators of
other racially biased predispositions.

WHEN THE POLICE ARE NOT YOUR FRIENDS:
BLACK EXPERIENCE WITH THE JUSTICE SYSTEM

Research reminds us what reasonable people, regardless of their race,
should already know. Race affects how you see what you see. People are
not color-blind. What a person living in the United States knows about
the world is shaped in part by that person's race. It is as preposterous to
expect black jurors to leave their experience of race at the courthouse door
as it is preposterous to believe that white jurors have left theirs outside.
It is similarly absurd to presume that race blinds black jurors when, as all
jurors are supposed to do, they rely on their lived experience to evaluate
evidence. One set of experiences pervasive among black jurors and unusual for whites is a history of unjust treatment by police (Gates, 1997).
Numerous polls and studies have shown widespread suspicion of police
among minorities in general and blacks in particular (Gallup Poll, 1997;
Puente, 1995). This should not be surprising; internal and independent
investigations confirm that racial bias and police misconduct go hand-in-
hand in urban police departments.[14] The most recent nationwide poll con-
firms that 60 percent of blacks surveyed think blacks are treated less fairly
than whites by police (Gallup Poll, 1997).

Being stopped by police for no reason other than race is virtually a
universal experience for African Americans (Gates, 1997; Kennedy, 1997).

New stories are constantly reported. In June 1997, Harvard Law Professor Patricia Williams recounted the tale of a forty-year-old black woman lawyer arrested and held in a Manhattan jail for twenty-one hours for having a suspended license and resisting arrest.

When some black jurors' experiences with police leave them skeptical of police claims, that does not make them nullifiers or racists. Such skepticism can enhance deliberations. Though there are few articles describing positive white response to black jurors' skeptical scrutiny of police in the jury room, one such post-O.J. experience was reported by Joan Biskupic (1995, 1996) in the *Washington Post*. She was a member of a mixed-race jury that could not reach unanimity. She came to agree with the questions about eyewitness testimony and police procedure raised by the black jurors.

All jurors are supposed to treat police as they would other witnesses, making individual decisions on their credibility. More whites than blacks find it difficult to hold police to a stringent standard ('Gulf' Separates Races, 1995; Stevenson & Friedman, 1994, p. 509). In fact, our research has found that potential jurors excused for cause, because they would lend greater weight to police testimony than to that of other witnesses, are almost always white.

Many African Americans also have a heightened awareness of racial inequities in the criminal justice system. According to a Gallup Poll (1997), 72 percent believe that blacks are treated more harshly than whites by the criminal justice system.

Careful observers have documented how race, as well as national origin and gender, permeates the justice system, from initial law enforcement decisions to sentencing (Burnett, 1994). Race and ethnicity remain a potent determinant in sentencing. In some cases, nonwhites are likely to receive longer sentences than whites (Zatz, 1987). The disparity in sentencing between blacks and whites actually increased from 1984 to 1990 (Meirhoefer, 1992; Vincent & Hofer, 1994). Today, all sources agree that the U.S. prison population is over 45 percent black (Fisher, 1997; Sentencing Project, 1997).

Racial disparity in sentencing is starkest in the imposition of the death penalty. Numerous studies have found that blacks are disproportionately sentenced to death (Berger, Walthour, Dorn, Lindsey, Thompson, & von Helms, 1989). The most widely known study of this pattern found overwhelming evidence of racial bias in death penalty sentencing in Georgia and formed the basis for black death row inmate Warren McCleskey's appeal (see *McCleskey v. Kemp*, 1987). As is well known and widely deplored, in *McCleskey* the Supreme Court accepted the validity of research findings that grave racial disparities did exist, but they refused to overturn the sentence, concluding that since "apparent" disparities are "inevitable," they are tolerable. Is it any wonder that many blacks feel that the death penalty is itself a form of discrimination, and that every national poll examining the question has found that, while whites overwhelmingly approve of the death penalty, the majority of blacks oppose it (Haney, Hurtado, & Vega, 1994)?

Under these circumstances, Professor Butler's (1995) suggestion that, in some instances, nullification is the moral choice is by no means farfetched. He proposes nullification as a mechanism whereby jurors can affirm their understanding that the actions of some black defendants are "a predictable reaction to oppression" or "a reasonable response to the racial and economic subordination every African American faces every day" (p. 680). His recommendation, however, tells us little about the analysis applied by black jurors who are accused of nullifying. Careful scrutiny of the anecdotes reported in media sources reveals that the jurors in question are not nullifying; instead, they are properly applying the rules. One exploration of the supposed pattern of black juror nullification focuses on cases in Washington, D.C. (Rosen, 1997). Prosecutors and judges there report an increase in the number of juries ending in eleven-to-one votes for conviction, with the lone acquitting holdout being an African American woman. While the author Jeffrey Rosen decries a pattern of "angry woman" nullifiers, he actually describes black jurors demanding high-quality police work.

Three cases are described. The holdouts are characterized as being "irrational, eccentric, or simply angry . . . refusing to listen or to persuade" (Rosen, 1997, p. 56). Each holdout is quoted directly, however, and what she says about the evidence belies these characterizations. One juror rejected the prosecution's case because the police lost the crime weapon. She asked, "How could they lose the knife if there was really a knife?" (p. 58). Rosen would have us believe that since the prosecutor acknowledged that police "messed up," their ineptitude should be excused.

The second, a law school graduate who agonized about her decision to acquit, was castigated for being "uncontrite" because she rejected the credibility of police who told two different stories in describing the same event. Rosen (1997, p. 62) says that "nothing of consequence turned on the discrepancy." He ignores the typical instruction that jurors carefully scrutinize all the evidence including the witnesses' words, demeanor, or behavior in judging the truthfulness, accuracy, and weight of testimony. Jurors are supposed to do this when evaluating any witness's credibility, including police witnesses. If two lay witnesses disagreed about the same event, would it not be appropriate to question their credibility?

In the third case, the prosecution bias is apparent in the case description. A police officer, after hearing a shot, obtained a description of the car from which the shot was believed to have been fired and "pulled it over and found packets of crack and *the gun*" (Rosen, 1997, p. 63, italics ours). The holdout advocating acquittal is dismissed as a conspiracy theorist because she asked "why didn't they dust for fingerprints? Maybe because he hadn't even touched that gun" (Rosen, 1997, p. 63).

One of Rosen's (1997, p. 63) "angry" women felt that she was being asked to "trust whatever the police say." She explicitly rejected this suggestion, as all jurors should. The message in this article, as in others decrying the sorry state of the newly color-sensitive jury system, is that the job of jurors is to convict. Witness the very different treatment of a juror who argued for conviction because, as he said, he was "sick of this going on in my city" (p. 54). This juror is not criticized for bringing extraneous bias to bear in reaching his conclusion. There is, moreover, no reference to the possibility that his comment might reveal a true case of nullification—reaching a decision based on moral outrage at broader social conditions rather than on evidence.

Jurors who resist the moral panic response to crime and insist on closely scrutinizing the prosecutor's case are treated as extremists. Why is it irrational to expect the police to be able to hold onto the crime weapon? What is eccentric about expecting two police officers who say they observed the same event to tell the same story? (Unlike other people, police are trained as observers and witnesses.) Why shouldn't the police and prosecutor have to prove that the gun the police found is actually the one that was fired? Why should blacks be pilloried for acting on their skepticism of a legal system that has been accused by a member of its highest court of harboring "a fear of too much justice"?[15]

CONCLUSION

Black jurors are being attacked by white commentators for drawing on their own experiences, even while the commentators endorse, in theory, the principle that diversity of experience belongs in the jury box. No serious commentator today would suggest that the clock be turned back on community participation in jury panels. Instead, the attacks on black jurors betray an expectation that blacks should deny their own experiences and adopt those of whites.

Surely this is racism—not the old fashioned kind, but the new-fashioned kind, the kind where whites provide seemingly nonracial reasons (e.g., these jurors are not following the law) as the basis for racist opinions. No doubt, the authors of each article criticized here would deny believing that blacks are inferior and whites superior. But how else can we understand the demand that black jurors leave their experiences at the courthouse door?

Jury trial remains a cornerstone of the U.S. justice system. Representative juries, as the Supreme Court has repeatedly emphasized, are a requirement for public confidence in the system. Attacks on black jurors who bring their experiences into this system are attacks on representativeness. These attacks undermine public confidence in the system, erode fundamental rules of the justice system, and pose threats to fairness in future trials.

NOTES

1. Minority groups as a whole are fast becoming the majority.

2. In *Strauder v. West Virginia* (1879), the Supreme Court declared as unconstitutional laws that prohibited black participation in the jury system. However, that opinion was readily sidestepped for many decades. Key man systems, blue ribbon juries, and source lists composed of those who had paid poll taxes and passed citizenship tests were all used to prevent black participation.

3. Prosecutors' purposeful and systematic use of peremptory challenges was recently highlighted by release of a 1986 audio tape of a training session where Philadelphia district attorneys were told that "the blacks from the low-income areas are less likely to convict. . . . [Y]ou don't want those people on your jury" (Former Philadelphia Prosecutor, 1997).

4. Suspicious explanations for systematic use of peremptory challenges to eliminate African American jurors have been routinely upheld (see Johnson, 1988, pp. 1023–1024; *Purkett v. Elem*, 1995; *United States v. Ferguson*, 1991; *United States v. Harrell*, 1988; *United States v. Nichols*, 1991).

5. This is due in part to widespread reforms designed to increase representativeness, including use of multiple source lists and one-day one-trial systems, elimination of exemptions, and increased pay for jurors (Munsterman, 1996).

6. A hung jury is also a legitimate though much-maligned trial outcome.

7. A Simpson criminal trial juror has pointed out that she never found Simpson innocent (Alexander & Cornell, 1997, pp. 57, 71).

8. According to the Department of Justice, Bureau of Justice Statistics, which tracks felony arrests in forty counties, only 6 percent of thirteen thousand such arrests in a given year go to trial—including both judge and jury trials.

9. Although reported thirty years ago, no published research since has replaced these findings. National Jury Project post-trial juror interviews confirm this pattern.

10. Fifty years ago Allport and Postman (1948), while studying rumor, found that 50 percent of the time whites shown a picture of a well-dressed black man conversing with a white man who was holding a razor blade, transposed the races of the two men when asked to describe the picture to another person. In some cases, the black man was even reported to be brandishing the razor threateningly.

11. One such study sheds light on reactions of some whites to the Simpson trial outcomes. White male subjects were led to believe they were inflicting electric shocks on research targets. The race of the man to be shocked was varied. The subject was also led to believe that the man was romantically involved with a woman whose race was also varied. The subjects consistently inflicted the highest level of electric shock on the black targets who they believed were romantically involved with a white woman (Schulman, 1974).

This study may provide a clue to the visceral outpouring of glee celebrating the civil trial outcome. For example, on the day following the civil trial verdict, the

New York Times ran a photo of a group of white men in a bar with glasses raised in a toast, as jubilant over the news of the verdict as if it were a personal victory (Goldberg, 1997).

12. National Jury Project mock trial research is conducted in connection with trial preparation. Mock jurors are carefully selected to reflect the demographic characteristics in the trial jurisdiction. Balanced summary arguments of each side of a case being prepared for trial are presented. Mock jurors then deliberate. Though the research is sponsored by one side, careful attention is paid to having balanced presentations. This is because the research goal is to improve presentation and test for juror comprehension and questions. National Jury Project trial consultants conduct and analyze the research. Elissa Krauss conducted the mock jury research described in this article. National Jury Project research results are shared with counsel and presented in summary form for educational purposes. Work product, privilege, and other rules requiring confidentiality are strictly adhered to in reporting results.

13. Johnson (1988, p. 1027) cites a host of studies of aversive racism, the kind that is largely hidden, denied, and often even unconscious (see also Lawrence, 1987).

14. Independent studies confirming the almost universal experiences of blacks with police include the Christopher Commission, which studied the LAPD in the aftermath of the 1992 riots.

15. See *McCleskey v. Kemp* (1987, p. 339).

CASES CITED

Batson v. Kentucky, 476 U.S. 79 (1986)
City of Richmond v. J.A. Croson Co., 488 U.S. 469 (1989)
Edmonson v. Leesville Concrete Co., 500 U.S. 614 (1981)
Fullilove v. Klutznick, 448 U.S. 448 (1980)
Metro Broadcasting v. FCC, 497 U.S. 547 (1990)
McCleskey v. Kemp, 481 U.S. 279 (1987)
Minnick v. California Department of Corrections, 452 U.S. 105 (1981)
Purkett v. Elem, 514 U.S. 265 (1995)
Strauder v. West Virginia, 100 U.S. 303 (1879)
Taylor v. Louisiana, 419 U.S. 522 (1975)
United States v. Ferguson, 935 F. 2d 866 (9th Cir. 1991)
United States v. Harrell, 847 F. 2d 138 (4th Cir. 1988)
United States v. Nichols, 937 F. 2d 1257 (7th Cir. 1991)

REFERENCES

Alexander, N., & Cornell, D. (1997). Dismissed or banished? A testament to the reasonableness of the Simpson jury. In T. Morrison & C. Lacour (Eds.), *Birth of a nation'hood: Gaze, script, and spectacle in the O.J. Simpson case* (pp. 57–96). New York: Pantheon.

Allport, G., & Postman, L. (1948). *The psychology of rumor.* New York: H. Holt & Co.

Berger, V., Walthour, N., Dorn, A., Lindsey, D., Thompson, P., & von Helms, G. (1989). Too much justice: A legislative response to Mc-Cleskey v. Kemp. *Harvard Civil Rights-Civil Liberties Law Review, 24,* 437–528.

Bernard, J. (1979). Interaction between the race of the defendant and that of jurors in determining verdicts. *Law & Psychological Review, 5,* 103–111.

Biskupic, J. (1995, November 26). I, the juror: Color-conscious justice in a post-O.J. trial. *Washington Post,* p. C3.

Biskupic, J. (1996). Jury verdicts aren't always so black and white. In G. Reynolds (Ed.), *Race and the criminal justice system: How race affects jury trials* (pp. 46–56). Washington, DC: Center for Equal Opportunity.

Burnett, A. (1994). Permeation of race, national origin and gender issues from initial law enforcement contact through sentencing: The need for sensitivity, equality, and vigilance in the criminal justice system. *American Criminal Law Review, 31,* 1153–1175.

Butler, P. (1995). Racially based jury nullification: Black power in the criminal justice system. *Yale Law Journal, 105,* 677–725.

Crosby, F., Bromley, S., & Saxe, L. (1980). Recent unobtrusive studies of black and white discrimination and prejudice: A literature review. *Psychological Bulletin, 87,* 546–563.

Fisher, I. (1997, June 17). Black soldiers wrestle with tangled notions of race and justice in the military. *New York Times,* p. A12.

Former Philadelphia prosecutor accused of racial bias: A tape and dispute in an election year. (1997, April 3). *New York Times,* p. A14.

Gallup Poll. (1997, June 10). *Black/white relations in the United States.* PR Newswire. Retrieved from Westlaw, Allsnews database.

Gates, H., Jr. (1997). *Thirteen ways of looking at a black man.* New York: Random House.

Gingrich, N., & Connerly, W. (1997, June 15). Face the failure of racial preferences. *New York Times,* p. E15.

Goldberg, C. (1997, February 5). Subdued pandemonium, color-coded responses. *New York Times,* p. A1.

Gordon, R., Bindrim, T., McNicholas, M., & Walden, T. (1988). Perceptions of blue-collar and white-collar crime: The effect of defendant race on simulated juror decisions. *Journal of Social Psychology, 128,* 191–197.

Gotanda, N. (1991). A critique of "Our constitution is color-blind." *Stanford Law Review, 44,* 1–68.

Grillo, T., & Wildman, S. (1995). Obscuring the importance of race: The implication of making comparisons between racism and sexism (or other-isms). In R. Delgado & J. Stefancic (Eds.), *Critical race theory:*

The cutting edge (pp. 648–656). Philadelphia: Temple University Press.

"Gulf" separates races in dealings with police. (1995, March 21). *USA Today*, p. A3.

Haberman, C. (1995, November 26). Color blind? Justice, maybe, but not juries. *New York Times*, p. B39.

Haney, C., Hurtado, A., & Vega, L. (1994). "Modern" death qualification: New data on its biasing effects. *Law & Human Behavior, 18*, 619–633.

Holden, B., & Cohen, L. (1995, October 4). Color blinded? Race seems to play an increasing role in many jury verdicts. *Wall Street Journal*, p. A1.

Johnson, J., Whitestone, E., Jackson, L., & Gatto, L. (1995). Justice is still not color-blind: Differential racial effects of exposure to inadmissible evidence. *Personality & Social Psychology Bulletin, 21*, 893–898.

Johnson, S. (1988). Unconscious racism and the criminal law. *Cornell Law Review, 73*, 1016–1037.

Johnson, S. (1995). Black innocence and the white jury. In R. Delgado & J. Stefancic (Eds.), *Critical race theory: The cutting edge* (pp. 152–162). Philadelphia: Temple University Press.

Kalven, H., Jr., & Zeisel, H. (1966). *The American Jury.* Boston: Little, Brown.

Kennedy, R. (1997). *Race, crime and the law.* New York: Pantheon.

Krauss, E., & Bonora, B. (Eds.). 1996. *Jurywork: Systematic techniques.* New York: Boardman.

Lawrence, C., III. (1987). The id, the ego, and equal protection: Reckoning with unconscious racism. *Stanford Law Review, 39*, 317–388.

Levine, D. (1996, June). Race over reason in jury box. *Reader's Digest*, pp. 123–128.

Loftus, E. (1979). *Eyewitness testimony.* Cambridge, MA: Harvard University Press.

Loftus, E. (1988, April). Powerful eyewitness testimony: Lessons from the research. *Trial, 24*, 64–66.

Meirhoefer, B. (1992). *The general effect of mandatory minimum prison terms.* Washington, DC: Federal Judicial Center.

Munsterman, G. (1996, March/April). A brief history of state jury reform efforts. *Judicature, 79*, 216–219.

Parker, L. (1980). *Legal Psychology: Eyewitness testimony: Jury behavior.* Springfield, IL: Thomas.

Puente, M. (1995, March 21). Poll: Blacks' confidence in police plummets. *USA Today*, p. A3.

Parloff, R. (1997, June). Race and juries: If it ain't broke. . . . *The American Lawyer*, p. 5.

Rosen, J. (1997, February 24/March 3). One angry woman. *The New Yorker*, pp.54–62.

Sentencing Project. (1997). *Facts about prisons and prisoners*. Washington, DC: Author.

Schulman, G. (1974). Race, sex, and violence: A laboratory test of the sexual threat of the black male hypothesis. *American Journal of Sociology, 79*, 1260–1277.

Stevenson, B., & Friedman, R. (1994). Deliberate indifference: Judicial tolerance of racial bias in criminal justice. *Washington & Lee Law Review, 51*, 509–527.

Sweeney, L., & Haney, C. (1992). The influence of race on sentencing: A meta-analytic review of experimental studies. *Behavioral Science & Law, 10*, 179–195.

Thernstrom, A., & Fetter, H. (1996, Winter). From Scottsboro to Simpson. *The Public Interest,* (122), pp. 17–27.

Ugwuegbu, D. (1979). Racial and evidential factors in juror attribution of legal responsibility. *Journal of Experimental Social Psychology, 15*, 133–146.

Vincent, B., & Hofer, P. (1994). *The consequences of mandatory minimum prison terms: A summary of recent findings*. Washington, DC: Federal Judicial Center.

Weiss, M., & Zinsmeister, K. (1996, January/February). When race trumps truth in the courtroom. *The American Enterprise,* pp. 54–57.

Williams, P. (1997, June 16). The climates of disbelief. *The Nation, 264,* p. 10.

Zatz, M. (1987). The changing forms of racial/ethnic biases in sentencing. *Journal of Research in Crime & Delinquency, 24*, 69–92.

CHAPTER 13

Embracing Affirmative Jury Selection for Racial Fairness

Hiroshi Fukurai

"You'd almost *have* to be black to understand. All their grievances, all their distrust of the system, all the beliefs people had in the evil of the system. Suddenly, it all turned out to be true."
—Clarence Dickson, the highest-ranking black administrator in the Miami Police Department, in responding to the 1980 acquittal verdict of four white police officers in the murder trial of Arthur McDuffie, a black motorist, by the all-white jury (Porter & Dunn, 1985, p.48.)

"They kill with love."
—Innocent black death row inmate John Coffery, telling the head guard, Paul Edgecome (played by Tom Hanks), before facing his own electrocution in *The Green Mile*.

INTRODUCTION

The fact that an all-white jury that convicts a black defendant or acquits a white defendant against overwhelming evidence of his guilt is deeply disturbing. The fact that a jury is all white has the powerful effect of racializing the jury proceeding. In reality, however, a black defendant in most jurisdictions is often confronted by white police officers, indicted by an all-white grand jury, prosecuted by a team of all-white district attorneys, convicted by a predominantly, if not all, white jury, sentenced by a white judge, denied appeals by white state appellate court jurists and white federal judges, and executed by a team of white prison officials. Such criminal proceedings and jury trials carry a long-lasting impression of racial inequality in the criminal justice system. Race, then, becomes a critical emblem by which members of a minority race carefully assess trial fairness, verdict legitimacy, and the quality and integrity of the criminal justice system.

Social scientists and legal scholars have long recognized the barriers and impediments to overcome the legal system's procedural failings, moral inequities, and judicial injustices (Fukurai, Butler, & Krooth, 1993; King, 1993). Yet, even today, almost all legally prescribed arguments and defense motions that attempt to mount the claim of racial discrimination in jury trials have had a limited scope, dealing only with racial disparities in the composition of the jury pool *before* jurors are ultimately chosen for the final criminal jury. Surprisingly, the U.S. Supreme Court has never discussed or addressed the *necessity* of introducing procedural means or legal arguments to ensure racial equality in the makeup of *final* juries.

In most criminal trials, it is fairly clear that the laws calling for equitable jury selection have been systematically undermined, politically manipulated, and legally entangled in procedures that prohibit defense counsel from initiating actions to compel courts to empanel racially diverse final juries. The result has been the general absence of racial diversity in such juries, leading to discriminatory, racialized trials and convictions. And to date, there has been a litany of abuses, ensuring that final juries will be skewed away from an equitable balance of racial minorities in criminal cases involving minority defendants (generally, see Fukurai et al., 1993). Drawing on the critical race theory, this chapter provides more racially localized remedial strategies and mechanisms to create racially diverse juries. Examined here are four different types of affirmative jury selection strategies, using race for the wider administration of equity and fairness, arguing that the racial components of the jury structure is the sociopolitical and legal expression of power, as well as more profound, underlying conflicts by race, class, and gender. The jury as a potential democratic forum within the frame of this larger political and racialized system is clearly on the cutting edge in the pursuit of essential fairness, equality, and racial justice. And the U.S. Supreme Courts' extremely narrow debates on racial jury composition reflect the social and racial struggle to dominate a body of peers in our time, especially by racial makeup.

Those four methods of empanelling racially diverse juries include the following: (1) the split jury, or the jury *de medietate linguae*, in which half of the jurors come from the majority and the other half from the minority groups; (2) the proportional jury (the Hennepin model), in which the extent of juries' racial representativeness reflects respective proportion of both majority and minority groups in the general population; (3) the quarter jury (the social science model), in which the jury must have at least three minorities in the twelve-member jury to resist successfully the group pressure of the white majority in jury decision-making processes, and

(4) peremptory inclusion, in which the final jury is chosen by affirmatively selecting from the eligible pool those jurors who share the same racial, sociocultural, and other cognizable background characteristics as those of the defendants.

Those affirmative jury selection strategies are not entirely new remedial programs. The first affirmative jury model (jury *de medietate linguae*) appeared in twelfth century England, and the original jury was composed of half English and half Jewish members of the local community. This equitable jury system lasted until the end of the nineteenth century. In the United States, this *medietate* jury, which was brought by colonists, was also extensively used in northeastern states until the beginning of the twentieth century.

Similarly, Hennepin County, Minnesota, recently relied on the affirmative jury selection method to ensure the proportional racial representation in the composition of the final grand jury. The other two models—the quarter jury and affirmative peremptory inclusion—were also proposed by social scientists, legal scholars, and legislators, and their merits and possible applications in the empanelment of the final jury are also currently debated and evaluated in a number of jurisdictions in America.

Those affirmative jury selection methods are designed to neutralize logistical problems and structural biases inherent in the current jury selection methods and to provide an internal check in the criminal justice system to ensure proper and fair performances by governmental agencies, including judges, prosecutors, and the police. The first three types of affirmative jury structures may be seen as the formative configuration of the racialized jury box, whereas affirmative peremptory inclusion is a procedural strategy taken in courtroom to attain the ideal racial balance in the jury box. The following sections provide a detailed account of the four specific types of affirmative jury selection strategies.

THE SPLIT JURY (*DE MEDIETATE LINGUAE*) MODEL

The ancient jury *de medietate linguae* made its historical appearance as a narrowly defined conception of equity, with the judging group composed of representatives of an accused's peers. For the jury *de medietate linguae*, the peers are in most cases defined in terms of the defendant's own racial and national identity.

The concept of the jury *de medietate linguae* first originated in the treatment of Jews in twelfth century England (Constable, 1994). The term literally means jury of the "half tongue" because the jury selection method applied to people who were considered alien or foreign and spoke different languages. The English viewed the Jews as aliens in race, religion, and culture, and considerable animosity existed against the Jews because they were known as the anti-Christ and Christ-killers (Quinley & Glock, 1972, pp. 94–109) and because "they were darker-skinned and spoke a mysterious and foreign language" (Ramirez, 1994, p. 783).

The emergence of the already unpopular Jews as moneylenders in the twelfth and early thirteenth century only added to animosity toward them. When Christian debtors could not or would not repay their debts, they seized upon the unpopularity of the Jews as a convenient means of extricating themselves from their predicament. A riot or massacre might fortuitously destroy the records of the transaction, thereby canceling the debtors' obligations and precluding the King, as owner of the Jews, from claiming retribution (McCall, 1979, p. 281).

Caught between scheming debtors and the King, the Jews relied on the Crown for protection. And in the throes of mass riots and violence in 1190 directed against wealthy and influential Jews who were clearly the King's property, King Richard I enacted a charter on April 10, 1201, giving Jews the right to the jury *de medietate linguae*—a half-Jewish jury (Wishman, 1986, p. 31). Thereafter the jury *de medietate linguae* was granted to Jews to protect the Crown's property interest in Jews and their effects (Massaro, 1986, p.550, n238). Though England subsequently banished all Jews in 1290, foreign merchants from Italy and Germany soon became the King's financial agents replacing the Jews, and the newcomers were given the privilege of a trial *de medietate linguae*—a trial by a jury composed of half of their own countrymen and the other half with Englishmen qualified to serve as jurors.

The *medietate* jury also provided substantive fairness and protection against unfair verdicts derived from prejudice against ethnic minorities in England. Even after the expulsion of the Jews, the mixed jury privilege provided foreign merchants a perception of substantial fairness and equity in disputes involving aliens. The international composition of the jury was intended to ensure foreign merchants a fair trial without the possibility of local prejudice. These courts applied law as they perceived it, almost regardless of the source of law, in order to achieve transnational commercial benefits and fairness.

The *de medietate* concept also had wider applications. For example, when an English university scholar was indicted for treason, felony, or mayhem, the vice-chancellor of the university could claim jurisdiction, and the resulting trial was before the high steward and a jury formed *de medietate*—half from a panel of eighteen freeholders returned by the sheriff and half from a panel of eighteen matriculated laymen returned by the beadles of the university (Oldham, 1983). Similarly under a *writ of jure patronatus* concerning church patronage, the dispute could be tried by the bishop or by a specially appointed commission before a jury of six clergymen and six laymen of the neighborhood (Oldham, 1983, pp. 168–169).

The right of juries *de medietate linguae* in England endured until 1870, when Parliament finally passed the Naturalization Act, which permitted aliens to serve on juries and to acquire, hold, and dispose of property in the same manner as English-born citizens, thereby eliminating the need for the mixed jury privilege (Ramirez, 1994).

Drawing on English tradition, the American colonies and courts also experimented with the use of juries *de medietate linguae* after English settlers developed their sense of equity, justice, and laws. At various times between 1671 and 1911, a number of states, including Kentucky, Maryland, Massachusetts, Pennsylvania, New York, Virginia, and South Carolina, each provided for juries *de medietate linguae*. As early as 1674, the courts in Plymouth colony used mixed juries composed of half Native Americans and half colonists. In 1675, when the Plymouth court tried three native Indians allied with King Philip and accused of murdering an Indian named John Sassamon, the jury of Englishmen and six Indians jointly adjudicated the case, sentencing the defendants to death (Kawashima, 1986, p. 131; Ramirez, 1994). The mixed jury was used in the early colonies as a way to ensure substantive fairness, enhance the legitimacy of jury verdicts, and prevent native upheaval. "[The mixed jury] was important to the colonists as the natives' perception of unfairness may have triggered bloody unrest or, at least, social tension," one jury study notes (Ramirez, 1994, p.790).

Since independence and the passage of the Bill of Rights in 1789, the U.S. Supreme Court has discussed the right to a jury *de medietate linguae* only once, in *United States v. Wood* (1936), in dictum and without analyses, declaring that "the ancient rule under which an alien might have a trial by jury *de medietate linguae*, 'one half denizens and the other aliens'—in order to insure impartiality—no longer obtains."

The application of juries *de medietate linguae* has also been reviewed and discussed. The Massachusetts Supreme Court in 1986 examined the applicability of the jury *de medietate linguae*, having to compare the denizen with the noncitizen alien. Article 12 of the Massachusetts Declaration of Rights drawn from Magna Charta, c.39, entitles denizen defendants to explicit rights, viz. "no freeman shall be taken or imprisoned, or be *disseized* of his freehold, or liberties, or free customs, or be outlawed or exiled, or other wise destroyed; nor will we not pass upon him, nor condemn him, but by lawful judgment of his peers, or by the law of the land." The defendants in this case argued that Article 12 calling for "lawful judgment of peers" afforded them the right to a trial by jury *de medietate linguae*, contending that the statutory requirements of a jury composed by citizenship and command of English were unconstitutional.

The court, however, held that the right to the jury *de medietate linguae* was not of constitutional magnitude in this case, and that the requirement that jurors speak and understand English and be U.S. citizens withstood constitutional challenges raised under the Sixth Amendment and the Constitution's equal protection clause.

Yet, neither the U.S. Supreme Court nor the Massachusetts Supreme Court fully explored the roots of the jury *de medietate linguae* in English common law or statutory history; nor did they discuss the wisdom or practicality of the mixed jury as a jury of peers. Thus, the debate on the jury *de medietate linguae* ceased, and the mandatory mixed jury disappeared from application under American law.

It is important to note that the use of the split jury was not only found in northeastern America, but it was also extensively used in other British colonies as well. When the criminal case involved European or American defendants, the Barbados court, for instance, allowed a racially mixed tribunal that included up to six European or American jurors in the twelve-member jury. The Nigerian courts also relied on the trial *de medietate* in criminal cases with nonnative defendants. The racially mixed jury in Gold Coast and North Borneo similarly permitted the majority participation of nonnative jurors in criminal cases involving nonnative defendants (Ramirez, 1994). As recent as the early 1970s, petit and grand juries in Okinawa were also made up of both Americans and Japanese-Okinawans to adjudicate both civil and criminal matters. The mixed juries were considered to be an important element of increased public awareness and respect in the administration of justice in Okinawa (Japanese Federation of Bar Associations, 1992).

In our time, the equitability of a mandatory balanced jury must not be ignored. The essential feature of the *de medietate linguae* model is that, regardless of the composition of aliens or minority groups in the general population, the composition of the mixed jury is considered to be fixed: half of the jury should come from the majority and the other half from the minority group. Similarly, the fixed measure of the jury's composition is derived from an acknowledgment that *prejudice* has historically existed against the minority group, and an ordinary jury composition using the traditional method of selection would not necessarily produce a fair result (Constable, 1994). The fixed allocation of jury seats is thus viewed as an essential feature of the jury's composition to ensure both the appearance and substance of fairness and equity in jury verdicts. Though the concept and application of the mixed jury principle may have originally developed out of the economic concerns of England during the medieval period, its wisdom and practice in England, the United States, and other former British colonies held broader implications concerning the fundamental notion of fairness in jury proceedings and legitimacy of jury verdicts.

THE PROPORTIONAL JURY (HENNEPIN COUNTY) MODEL

Another model for racially diverse juries is found in the courts of Hennepin County, Minnesota, where, according to the 1990 U.S. Census, approximately 9 percent of the adult population was minority (4.59 percent blacks, 2.22 percent Asian-Pacific islanders, 1.10 percent Native Americans, and 1.12 percent Hispanics). Though the Hennepin County model focuses on the grand jury, this affirmative action principle can easily be extended to the petit jury.

The Hennepin model is different from the juries *de medietate linguae* model in that the allocation of jury seats for the racial minority is derived from the proportional minority composition of the general population. The racial compositional distribution of the Hennepin model is not fixed, but remains changeable depending on the gyrating racial composition in the jurisdiction.

In Hennepin County, the grand jury consists of twenty-three members; thus, 9 percent of the twenty-three grand jurors is specifically reserved for minority groups, requiring that at least two minority grand jurors sit on every twenty-three–member grand jury. The allocation process works as follows:

[If] after randomly selecting the first 21 grand jurors either only one or no minority persons appear on the panel, selection [shall] continue down the list of 55 randomly selected and qualified persons until there are at least two minority persons out of 23 on the grand jury. If no minorities appear in the list of 55 potential grand jurors, another 55 qualified persons should be selected until the goal of at least two minority jurors is obtained. If random selection of the first 21 grand jurors yields two or more minority persons, the selection should simply proceed to the next two persons on the list. (Office of the Hennepin County Attorney, 1992, p. 45)

Besides setting up the proportional allocation of the jury to racial minorities, the task force proposal for the Hennepin model also recommended additional race-neutral reforms to increase the representativeness of grand juries, including (1) integrating lists from the Immigration and Naturalization Service of recently naturalized citizens and from tribal membership rolls into source lists; (2) raising the jury fee to $30 per day; and (3) establishing a day-care center for jurors' children (Smith, 1993, pp. 55–58). The U.S. District Court for the Eastern District of Michigan also maintains a racially stratified venire by sending extra jury questionnaires to areas in which black residents constitute at least 65 percent of the population, as well as removing questionnaires returned by white residents (Saunders, 1997). This stratified method, however, only improves the black jury representation in jury panels, not the final jury itself. Although it is impossible to estimate how widespread such racially proportionate juries are, following the Hennepin County model five states including California do not require that grand juror names be drawn randomly from the grand jury venire and instead allow judges or jury commissioners the discretion to select who will actually serve as final jurors (Fukurai, 2000). Though the *de medietate linguae* model requires the equal distribution of jury seats for both majority and minority groups, the Hennepin model assumes that the mixed jury is created to reflect the minority composition within the general population, thus requiring that varying numbers of minority jurors be selected for the jury box.

THE QUARTER JURY (SOCIAL SCIENCE) MODEL

Besides the two types of mixed juries and racial participation in the Anglo-Saxon tradition of law, social science research offers a different version of racially diverse juries. For the previous two jury models, the central issue is the number of jurors who are similar in race or national origin to the defendant and to which a defendant should be entitled in equity for a fair-minded verdict. The classical jury *de medietate linguae* thus entitles the defendant to six jurors of twelve, or half of the total number of jurors in jurisdictions using smaller juries. But the possible disadvantage of the *de medietate* model is that six jurors of the defendant's race might be difficult to obtain in some areas. In a jurisdiction with a very small minority population, random selection would not secure the presence of a sufficient number of minority prospective jurors in a qualified jury pool for the final jury. A split jury system may also offer an incentive for the state to elect the use of smaller size juries, a change generally deemed undesirable (Kaye, 1980, p. 1004). And the nativist response of denizens to practical difficulties in picking a jury is to limit the defendant's right to one juror similar to the defendant's race. Yet, jury research demonstrates that a single dissenting juror rarely succeeds in either hanging a jury, blocking a verdict, or reversing its predisposition (Kalven & Zeisel, 1966, p. 463).

Recent psychological studies show that without a minimum of three minority jurors, they may not be able to withstand the group pressure of the majority, suggesting that one or two dissenting jurors eventually accede to the majority's opinion (Saks, 1977; Kerr & MacCoun, 1985; see also *Ballew v. Georgia*, 1978). Behavioral studies also suggest that a reasonable compromise between the *medietate* jury and the proportional Hennepin model, especially applied in a jurisdiction with small minority populations, is to secure three minority jurors in order to preserve not only the appearance of fairness, but also the legitimate viability of jury deliberations and verdicts. A minimum of three members of racial minority jurors are thus viewed as necessary to offset the group pressures of the dominant white jurors during jury deliberation, suggesting that one or even two jurors are unlikely to maintain their own judgment of the proper and fair verdict in the face of opposition by the remaining majority jurors (Johnson, 1985, p. 1698).

If representativeness is the key to impartiality, a race-neutral verdict may be expected when at least three minority jurors are selected to judge a criminal or civil case that involves the rights of a defendant with the same minority racial characteristics and backgrounds. Professor Johnson (1985) argues that the Court could create for defendants accused of interracial capital crimes a right to a jury that includes jurors of the defendant's race. If at least three jurors were of the same race as the defendant, one of this group alone could hang a jury otherwise prone to imposing a racially motivated death sentence. As a member of a minority race historically suffering from discrimination, this approach allows the defendant to have a juror-advocate and fight against the majority's group pressure. Proponents of this remedy argue that such guaranteed racial quotas would (1) appease society's dissatisfaction with racially discriminatory peremptory challenges; (2) lead to fairer decisions, on the assumption that minority jurors are better able to correctly judge the character of a defendant with similar racial heritage and experiences; and (3) increase society's faith in the fairness of the jury system (Johnson, 1985, pp. 1706–07).

The equitably balanced jury thus provides the indispensable condition for rendering a just verdict that holds legitimacy in the eyes of both minority communities and the public at large. Three minority members in the jury box do appear to constitute the minimum number of minority jurors needed to maintain the fairness of jury deliberations and to increase potential acceptance of jury verdicts by the general community.

AFFIRMATIVE PEREMPTORY INCLUSION

Now we will slightly switch our perspective. Empanelling racial minorities in the final jury through the race-based exercise of peremptory challenges by the prosecution poses unique methodological problems for the defense. The peremptory challenge is a process used by both prosecution and defense attorneys to remove, without cause, objectionable prospective jurors from serving on juries. In criminal trials with black defendants, prosecutors exhibited the tendency to use peremptory challenges against black prospective jurors, suggesting that the likelihood of black jurors chosen for the final jury remains minimal.

After screening for qualification, eligibility, excuses, and challenges for cause, if peremptory challenges are still procedurally allowed—as they have been under the current jury selection system—black and other minority jurors would likely be systematically eliminated from serving on the final jury. In other words, the formation of affirmative jury structures, such as split, proportional, and/or quarter juries, would require either some restrictive usage, if not the complete abolition, of peremptory challenges so as not to impair the jury representation of racial minorities in the final jury.

Initially proposed by Altman (1986) as an alternative to peremptory challenges to empanel the final jury, this innovative strategy of peremptory choice or inclusion requires that both sides may enlist twelve jurors in order of preference. The judge then initially selects any juror whose name appears on both parties' lists, regardless of how the juror was ranked. Alternating between both lists, the judge proceeds to take the highest-rated juror from each list until a complete panel of twelve is assembled.

Many legal commentators and jury studies advocate the elimination of the peremptory challenge system, suggesting that, if the courts truly mean to eliminate racial discrimination in the jury selection process, the elimination of peremptory challenges is the only effective remedy (Hoffman, 1997; King, 1993; Ramirez, 1994). Once eliminating the discriminatory effects of peremptory challenges on racial minorities' jury representation, affirmative peremptory inclusion is considered to be an important strategic alternative to peremptory challenges.

The proposal for affirmative jury selection is a strategic departure from previous debates, which called for either the complete elimination of peremptory challenges or Altman's peremptory inclusive strategy in favor of an alternative jury selection approach, such as affirmative peremptory inclusion. Rather, this chapter suggests allowing both peremptory challenges and peremptory inclusion to coexist during jury selection. After screening for qualifications, excuses, exemptions, and cause challenges, the proposed method requires that both sides select a fixed number of jurors from the qualified jury pool. A challenge for cause is a process used by a presiding judge to remove a jury candidate, if it is revealed that, for some reason (e.g., deep-rooted racism and/or sexism), a prospective juror is unable or unwilling to set aside preconceptions and pay attention only to the evidence. The specific number of these peremptory inclusions may depend on the availability of targeted potential jurors in the qualified jury pool. For example, in a jurisdiction where the targeted racial minority population in the community is very small, the availability of minority groups in the qualified jury pool would be significantly limited.

As stated earlier, in a jurisdiction with a small number of minority jurors, the number of minority jurors should be at least three in order to ensure viable jury deliberations as proposed by the social science model. From a practical standpoint, the selection procedure requires that both sides prepare a separate preferential list of three potential jurors in the pool, making up a total of six peremptorily chosen and identified jurors by both parties. The remaining jury seats for the six jurors and alternates would then be filled by randomly selecting the jurors from the qualified jury pool. If both sides identified the same jurors in their preferential list, seven or more remaining jurors would be randomly selected from the qualified jury pool. In a trial that may last weeks or more, a large pool of alternate jurors might be necessary and those jurors would also be selected randomly from the qualified jury pool. For the final jury, peremptory challenges can still be exercised in the selection of those remaining jurors as normally done under the current jury selection procedure.

This author also proposes the affirmative selection of three jurors as the minimum number of required jury seats to be filled for each side. The number of peremptory inclusions should thus range from three to six in order to ensure the minimum condition for viable jury deliberations. As the quarter jury model proposes, the inclusion of at least three jurors would ensure a race-neutral verdict to "judge a criminal or civil case that involves the rights" of a minority defendant (Colbert, 1990, p. 124). This suggests that jury representation of three minority persons in the twelve-member jury may be the reasonable compromise between the harm of having one or no racially similar jurors, and the impracticability of obtaining a jury evenly balanced along racial lines (Bell, 1980, pp. 273–274).

Speculative concerns, however, may still exist that affirmative inclusive selection may possibly increase the instances of hung juries. Would the inclusion of a racial minority in a traditionally white-dominated jury increase the incidence of hung juries in those cases where an all-white jury would have acquitted a white defendant? Based on social science studies on group dynamics in jury deliberation, the jury may require at least ten racially similar jurors to make acquittal a predictable jury verdict. In such a case, a unanimous verdict would require both majority and minority members of the jury to work out their differences, possibly preventing wrongful convictions. As happens in most cases involving white defendants, as well as in many criminal cases involving minority defendants, the strength or weakness of the evidence will usually result in a unanimous verdict. It is only in cases where there is marginal evidence that the mixed jury might be more expected to argue with sharply divergent opinions than under the current color-blind system.

The debate on the problematic nature of hung juries is also seriously distorted because challenges for cause presumably will have removed demonstrably biased and prejudiced individuals prior to the system of peremptory inclusion, thereby reducing the likelihood of split jury decisions. Another dominant narrative for potential problems of hung juries also reveals the judicial system's long-standing bias in favor of more homogeneous, all-white juries. Even though such single-race juries may reach unified judgments on a consistent basis and in a shorter period, there is no reason to assume that these outcomes are genuinely fair, lawful, or free of racial prejudice or other biases. Jury research has shown that the small six-member jury is less likely to render hung jury verdicts than the twelve-member jury, because smaller juries are more likely to be homogeneous in race, opinions, and attitudes than twelve-member juries (Cocke, 1979; Kaye, 1980; Roper, 1979). In case of conflict resolution, a hung jury is an expression of substantive or emotive disagreements over the evidence, the testimony, and the nature of the case—not necessarily a negative result. Rather, after jurors reach differing conclusions as they evaluate the same evidence and testimony, a hung jury may provide a truly realistic result, suggesting that there is not a consensus among the community that the defendant is guilty.

The system of peremptory inclusion also provides the positive effect of preventing miscarriages of justice in cases with weak evidence, especially involving members of racial minority defendants. Coke (1994, pp. 385–386) suggests that the prosecution normally makes racialized, calculated decisions and risk assessments about which cases to bring to trial—based in part on their knowledge that most juries are predominantly white and pro-prosecution. The system of peremptory inclusion and racially diverse tribunals will then force the prosecution to assess the merit of the case and the credibility of the criminal charges, or to make efforts to strengthen the state's evidence and testimony, as the government rightfully bears the burden of proving guilt beyond a reasonable doubt.

Peremptory inclusion will likely bring about a small revolution in equity, allowing the defendant to attempt to introduce the internal checks-and-balances mechanism against racialized trial proceedings by forcing the representation of his or her peers on the final jury. Since these peers may look like the accused, perhaps better understand the defendant's circumstances, and respond to the state of mind, conditions, and backgrounds of the defendant, credibility of evidence and strength of testimony *as well as race-neutral preparation and presentation of such evidence* may become critical concerns of both police and prosecutors. For example, police and prosecutors may be deterred from pursuing racially discriminatory investigations, evidence gathering, and overcharging criminal acts by the public's perception of fairness and by empanelling racially diverse juries. In trials monitored by black jurors today, when presenting evidence and putting witnesses on the stand, prosecution's trial strategies may be similarly altered in preparing, introducing, and arguing. Racially diverse tribunals may also exert a significant influence over judges' performance, including evaluations of racial fairness in peremptory challenges, taking the recommendations of jury forepersons, making assessments of culpability, and sentencing determinations.

The peremptory inclusionary approach also enhances the public's perceived legitimacy of the jury composition, its deliberations and verdicts by balancing the defendant's personal rights to a fair trial with the minority community's interests. Another benefit of the peremptory inclusion is that, due to the straightforward process of peremptory inclusion, less time would be spent for jury selection, so that the inclusionary approach would allow more rapid processing and disposition of jury trials than by following traditional jury selection procedures.

SUMMARY AND CONCLUSION

Racial and ethnic minorities continue to be substantially underrepresented on the vast majority of both state and federal courts (Fukurai et al., 1993). The social costs of unrepresentative juries have prompted lawmakers and the courts to consider race-conscious methods to ensure minority representation, and a growing number of courts are beginning to experiment with the use of race-conscious methods to select jurors (Fukurai, 1999). One problem of the race-conscious method to ensure minority representation on juries, however, is that there are no clearly defined formulas to determine the extent of minority participation.

This chapter reviewed the history of the Anglo-Saxon tradition of laws, as well as social science research on jury representativeness. Four specific models of affirmative jury selection methods to create racially diverse juries—the split jury (*de medietate linguae*), the proportional jury (the Hennepin County model), the quarter jury (the social science model), and affirmative peremptory inclusion—were also examined. The chapter argued that an affirmative action mechanism to secure racially diverse juries is essential to the appearance, the substance, and the public's perception of trial fairness and verdict legitimacy in criminal jury proceedings. It was further argued that racially diverse tribunals provide a mechanism of internal checks to ensure fair and proper performance by government agencies, thereby enhancing the legitimacy and integrity of the judicial decision-making process and trial verdicts.

The proposal for race-conscious affirmative jury selection is certainly controversial and unsettling to some. But constructive debates and reasoned disputes about the application of affirmative jury selection may lead to even deeper social and political considerations surrounding the issue. With the public, legislatures, and the legal community discussing the question and its implications, one may envision the emergence of a more equitable jury system through the implementation of procedures that represent the various racial and ethnic segments of our national community.

CASES CITED

Ballew v. Georgia 435 U.S. 223 (1978)
United States v. Wood 299 U.S. 123 (1936)

REFERENCES

Altman, T. (1986). Note: Affirmative action: A new response to peremptory challenge abuse. *Stanford Law Review, 38*, 800–812.

Bell, D. (1980). *Race, racism and American law.* Boston: Little, Brown.

Cocke, A. (1979). Constitutional law—Sixth Amendment right to trial by jury—Five jurors are not enough. *Tennessee Law Review, 46,* 847–864.

Coke, T. (1994). Lady justice may be blind, but is she a soul sister? Race-neutrality and the ideal of representative juries. *New York University Law Review, 69,* 327–386.

Colbert, D. (1990). Challenging the challenge: Thirteenth amendment as a prohibition against the racial use of peremptory challenges. *Cornell Law Review, 76,* 1–128.

Constable, M. (1994). *The law of the other.* Chicago: University of Chicago Press.

Fukurai, H. (1999). The representative jury requirement: Jury representativeness and cross sectional participation from the beginning to the end of the jury selection process. *International Journal of Comparative & Applied Criminal Justice, 23,* 55–90.

Fukurai, H. (2000). Where did Hispanic jurors go? Racial and ethnic disenfranchisement in the grand jury and the search for justice. *Western Criminology Review, 2.* Retrieved May 15, 2001, from http://wcr .sonoma.edu/v2n2/fukurai.html.

Fukurai, H., Butler, E., & Krooth, R. (1993). *Race and the jury: Racial disenfranchisement and the search for justice.* New York: Plenum.

Hoffman, M. (1997). Peremptory challenges should be abolished: A trial judge's perspective. *University of Chicago Law Review, 64,* 809–871.

Japanese Federation of Bar Associations. (1992). *Okinawano baishin saiban (Jury trials in Okinawa).* Tokyo: Takachiho Shobo.

Johnson, S. (1985). Black innocence and the white jury. *Michigan Law Review, 83,* 1611–1708.

Kalven, H., Jr., & Zeisel, H. (1966). *The American jury.* Boston: Little, Brown.

Kawashima, Y. (1986). *Puritan justice and the Indian: White man's law in Massachusetts, 1630–1763.* Middletown, CT: Wesleyan University Press.

Kaye, D. (1980). And then there were twelve: Statistical reasoning, the Supreme Court, and the size of the jury. *California Law Review, 68,* 1004–1048.

Kerr, N., & MacCoun, R. (1985). The effects of jury size and polling method on the process and product of jury deliberation. *Journal of Personality & Social Psychology, 48,* 349–363.

King, N. (1993). Racial jurymandering: Cancer or cure? A contemporary review of affirmative action in jury selection. *New York University Law Review, 68,* 707–776.

Massaro, T. (1986). Peremptories or peers? Rethinking Sixth Amendment doctrine, images, and procedures. *North Carolina Law Review, 64,* 501–564.

McCall, A. (1979). *The medieval underworld.* London: H. Hamilton.

Office of the Hennepin County Attorney. (1992). *Final report: Task force on racial composition of the grand jury.* Minneapolis: Hennepin County Attorney.

Oldham, J. (1983). The origins of the special jury. *University of Chicago Law Review, 50,* 137–213.

Quinley, H., & Glock, C. (1972). *Anti-Semitism in America.* New York: Free Press.

Porter, B., & Dunn, M. 1985. *The Miami riot of 1980: Crossing the bounds.* Lexington. MA: D.C. Heath.

Ramirez, D. (1994). The mixed jury and the ancient custom of trial by jury de medietate linguae: A history and a proposal for change. *Boston University Law Review, 74,* 777–818.

Roper, R. (1979). Jury size and verdict consistency: "A line has to be drawn somewhere"? *Law & Society Review, 14,* 977–995.

Saks, M. (1977). *Jury verdicts: The role of group size and social decision rule.* Lexington, MA: Lexington Books.

Saunders, K. (1997). Race and representation in jury service selection. *Duquesne Law Review, 36,* 49–77.

Smith, L. (1993). Final report of the Hennepin County attorney's task force on racial composition of the grand jury. *Hamline Law Review, 16,* 879–921.

Wishman, S. (1986). *Anatomy of the jury: The system on trial.* New York: Times Books.

CHAPTER 14

How "Restorative" Is Restorative Justice? An Oppression Theory Critique

Robert Conners

In the past two decades, a trend in U.S. jurisprudence known as restorative justice has risen to challenge the two-century supremacy of traditional retributive justice. Unlike retributive proceedings in which the offender is viewed as accountable primarily to the state, a restorative justice proceeding would make the offender accountable primarily to the victim of his/her offense, to the victim's primary social circle, and to the community. In the ideal restorative justice scenario, a process of facilitated negotiation among the victim, the offender, and community representatives would restore economic, social, and emotional equilibrium to the victim by reparative action made by the offender both to the victim and to the community (e.g., Bazemore, 1996; Bazemore & Umbreit, 1998; Hudson, Galaway, Morris & Maxwell, 1996; Young, 1995; Zehr, 1990).

Undoubtedly, restorative justice represents a paradigm shift in justice philosophy (Van Ness, 1993), offering "an entirely new framework for understanding and responding to crime and victimization within American society" (Umbreit, 1998a, p. 1). As an alternative to the more impersonal proceedings and punishment-oriented sanctions of traditional justice, many believe restorative justice, with its emphasis on human relationships and community building, has greater capacity to "heal [the wounds] and put right the wrongs" of crime (Zehr, 1998).

On the surface, then, restorative justice would appear to be a more participatory, more inclusive, more democratic philosophy of justice. However, despite a more human face, it is also worth noting that the optimistic reception the restorative justice model has received among practitioners and scholars alike originates almost exclusively from a mainstream (i.e., white majority) perspective, notwithstanding philosophical claims of kinship to North American aboriginal customs (Griffiths & Patenaude, 1990). If this proposition is true, it suggests a fair and thorough treatment of the topic of restorative justice must also include more culturally and politically diverse critical frameworks.

It was this observation that led to the question posed by this critique: How would restorative justice withstand the scrutiny of so-called minority intellectual discourse, or "counter-discourse," as West (1982) has labeled it? For example, in selectively limiting the context of restorative accountability as a case of offender accountability to the victim and to the community, and in substantively ignoring the role of institutionally enforced economic, social, and political inequality as a context for some categories of crime, is it possible that restorative justice, as presently practiced, is just as vulnerable to the charges of group-based self-interest as the traditions of distributive and retributive justice it claims to challenge?

A framework of minority intellectual discourse that addresses these issues of context and societal inequality is the general category I have labeled *oppression theory*. Minimally, such a framework would pose the following questions to restorative justice practitioners:

1. For some offenders, when considering what must be restored, when and why must we consider the effects of one's economic, social, and political context that remain as the uncorrected historical legacy of group-based inequalities he/she did not create?

2. How would this expanded economic, social, and political context of decision making alter both the theory and practice of restorative justice?

Since these questions deal with the interplay of economic, social, and political context and the appropriate role of restorative justice in determining what is just, what must be restored, and to whom, before addressing them it is useful to examine restorative justice discourse to date for any substantive acknowledgment of the role of oppression as a determinant of individuals' societal context.

RESTORATIVE JUSTICE, CRIME, AND ISSUES OF SOCIETAL CONTEXT: A BRIEF OVERVIEW

With justification, restorative justice has been praised for bringing many creative reforms to the practice of criminal justice, particularly in strengthening the role of the victim and the community in creating restorative sanctions for the offender (Bazemore, 1996; Griffiths & Hamilton, 1996; Zehr, 1998). On the other hand, a few commentators (e.g., Zehr, 1998; Umbreit, 1998b; and McCold, 1996) have suggested that more attention should be given to the relationship between economic, social, and political inequality and its influence on both crime and the determination of re-storative sanctions. For instance, when one examines the so-called guiding principles of restorative justice advanced by major figures in the field such as Bazemore and Umbreit (1998) or Van Ness and Strong (1997), it is clear these principles do not address the restoration of economic, social, and political equality to those who are today's victims of uncorrected historical oppression. Moreover, a review of 552 citations in McCold's (1997) excel-lent annotated bibliography of restorative justice literature reveals only eight references to social justice issues in general and only White (1994) and (arguably) Zehr (1990) seem to have addressed the issue of societal inequality in any substantive theoretical way.

This is not to suggest that the scholarly discourse of restorative justice has been either irresponsible or intentionally mute on the topic of op-pression and inequality. Zehr (1990), for example, considered oppression in the biblical context of "Shalom community," observing that "the Bible makes it clear that oppression and injustice . . . do not represent right relationships, that they must not be allowed to exist . . . [and that people must live] in just economic and political relationship with one another . . . [without] marked divisions in material conditions and in power . . . " (Zehr, 1990, pp. 130–131). Presumably, when such conditions prevail, "so-ciety or the social structure is the culprit. . . . [Therefore,] for punishment to seem fair, outcome and process need to relate to the *original wrong*. . . . [That is,] there is a larger question of social, economic, and political jus-tice" (Zehr, 1990, p. 131).

So there is, indeed, concern among practitioners that some offenders from historically oppressed minority communities rife with crime, pov-erty, and high unemployment are, themselves, victims of historical in-equality. On the other hand, Umbreit (1998b) has puzzled over the practical conundrum of balancing the needs of the victim with the needs of such an offender when the mediator "observes the offender's broken-ness," hears the offender's comments that the system is oppressive and that the offender needs to get his/her "little piece [of the 'pie']." Similarly, McCold (1996) has challenged the feasibility of successfully reintegrating an offender into a crime-ridden community as a productive and law-abiding member without addressing the "existing social structures [which he believes to be] . . . the root causes of the criminal conflict. . . . " McCold (1996, p. 95) concludes, "System reform is embedded in restorative justice."

To summarize this discussion, it is fair to say there has been substantive acknowledgment among restorative justice commentators of the impor-tance of economic, social, and political inequality as a consideration within the practice of restorative justice, but equally accurate to say there is no general acknowledgment of a system of oppression, per se, as its cause. Although issues of social justice as they affect some minority of-

fenders have been raised, the most expansive economic, social, and political context of restorative justice, as currently practiced, is one that may
foresee greater community involvement and community ownership for
problem solving, but one that does little in practice to address Zehr's
(1990, p. 210) lingering concern that fairness in the disposition of an offender must also consider the fairness of the larger societal context, or,
more specifically, what Tetreault (1993) refers to as the economic, social
and political "positionality" of all involved in the restorative justice
proceeding.

It is reasonable to excuse this shortcoming, in part, as a function of the
youth of the field. However, a counterdiscourse critique must also remain
skeptical in that such conceptual shortcomings more likely represent a
failure of the general framework of criminal justice discourse, including
restorative justice discourse, that is, a framework that is conceptually inadequate to the task of restoring equality to the victims of historical inequality. To address this conceptual inadequacy, this analysis of
restorative justice proposes the counterdiscourse framework of oppression theory to expand the elite discourse (van Dijk, 1993) of mainstream
criminal justice (Close, 1997).

OPPRESSION THEORY'S CHALLENGE TO THE
ELITE DISCOURSE OF RESTORATIVE JUSTICE

Van Dijk (1993) coined the term *elite discourse* to characterize the economic, social and political arena of ideas that is the well-spring of a society's cherished beliefs, values, and lore, setting the parameters of what
constitutes a society's official knowledge. The framework of discourse established by the elite are those rules of reasoning and evidence governing
what a society holds and inculcates as true and false, as legitimate and
illegitimate, as acceptable and unacceptable. Van Dijk (1993) argues that
this elite tends to be populated by representatives of a fairly culturally
and economically homogeneous group who are in a position to influence
and direct a society's economic, social, and political discourse, intercourse,
institutions, and policy. In the case of the United States, the elite is made
up of those who trace their ancestry largely to Northern European traditions and cultures.

That this same group dominates the decision-making institutions in U.S.
society (e.g., the universities, the official halls of political decision making,
major institutional boardrooms, and the popular media) is not only indisputable, but, the elite discourse hypothesis asserts, it is also a predi-
cable outcome of a *particular* social order reflecting a *particular* agenda of
group self-interest. Consequently, elite discourse is notable for the absence
of the perspectives and worldview frameworks of other, historically subordinated minority groups whose disenfranchisement has been not only

economic, social, and political, but also cultural, and, according to post-modern, poststructural thinkers such as Freire (1997), Foucault (see Drey-fus, 1983), and Nandy (1987), perhaps even epistemological.

Oppression theory, as one such category of counterdiscourse, seeks to challenge the group self-interest of elite discourse. There are several op-pression theory frameworks (e.g., Andrzejewski, 1996; Sidanius and Pratto, 1990; van Dijk, 1993), many of which, predictably, have their ori-gins in ethnic, racial, or feminist minority intellectual traditions. Generally, an oppression theory framework is one that would not simply recognize the unequal economic, social, and political context of some minority of-fenders; it is one that would also assign culpability and responsibility for the correction of that historical inequality to those who created it in the first place and who continue to benefit from it today. One such framework drawing largely on philosopher and religion scholar William R. Jones's analytic model of oppression (Jones, 1990a) will inform the method of counterdiscourse employed here to evaluate the group interests of restor-ative justice.

The Jones Analytic Model of Oppression: Four Features

Oppression can be defined as the systematic exploitation of an individual or group based on the economic, social, and political status of one's des-ignated reference group. The idea of designated status is meant to convey the notion that another, more powerful group is in charge of a society's institutions of social control, operated largely for the purpose of enhanc-ing its survival and well-being, usually at the expense of subordinated group members.

For this evaluation of restorative justice, I will select four features of the Jones model. First, I will establish that human society oppression is an unassailably universal feature of culture. Second, I will present a theo-retical framework for evaluating the oppression potential of social policy, in general, and restorative justice, specifically. Third, to address the ques-tion posed in the title, "How 'Restorative' Is Restorative Justice?", I will examine the role of economic, social, and political context and its influence on individual opportunity. And, finally, I will address the group self-interest implications of restorative justice by exploring what Jones calls "oppression legitimation" (Berger, 1965; Jones, 1990c, 1990d) and its role in restorative justice practice.

Human Society Oppression as a Cultural Universal

Jones (1990c, 1990d) appropriates sociologist Peter Berger's (1965) views on the role of culture and its institutions as enterprises that legitimate the economic, social, and political agenda of a society's dominant group(s) to assert the universality of societal oppression. This is not to suggest that hierarchy is an absolute condition of human being, as did Sidanius and Pratto (1990), but that some form of hierarchy, based on a differential in power, has been a universal component of all economic, social, and political relationships at the societal level.

According to Jones, the roots of human society or "intraspecies" oppression are to be found in the ontological choice to survive: That is, at the most basic level of existence, in order for any living thing to survive, it must kill and consume something else. It follows, therefore, when human beings make the choice to survive (i.e., there is always the option of suicide), we establish an ontological hierarchy, giving primacy to our continuation and, by necessity, placing lesser value on the survival of that which is consumed. Jones argues for the universality of oppression as a generic cultural feature by first describing the dynamics of this ontological relationship and then by proving that these same dynamics have operated in every hierarchically arranged society throughout human history.

However, unlike the extraspecies relationship, in which oppression is absolutely inherent in survival, human survival is not contingent upon the oppression of other human beings. This distinction is theoretically important because it suggests that human society oppression is not only not an immutable, ontological feature of the human condition, but that it must be a choice[1] made by those who possess a surplus of a society's economic, social, and political power and resources: that is, to maintain their position nearer the top of the societal hierarchy, the dominant (or surplus) group must oppress others who are in a deficit resource and power position.

Since culture provides the means of maintaining and legitimating human hierarchy, any product of a group-based hierarchical economic, social, and political arrangement must be critically analyzed to determine if it advances the economic, social, and political interests of those at the top of the group hierarchy to the detriment of those at the bottom of the hierarchy.[2] It follows that restorative justice, conceived as it has been within a group-based hierarchical arrangement, must also account for itself and its philosophy by submitting to the litmus test of oppression theory.[3]

The Binary Logic of Oppression: A Litmus Test of Social Policy

Oppression theory poses the fundamental question: How do we correct inequality produced by historical oppression? For historically disenfranchised groups whose legacy is one of race-based, economic, social, and political subordination, the logic of oppression is binary, that is, any policy, law, institution, philosophy, or remedy has the effect of either correcting the present-day economic, social, and political inequality that is the product of historical oppression by promoting, or progressing toward, relative economic, social, and political equilibrium among groups, or it preserves the status quo arrangement of group-based inequality. These categories are mutually exclusive (i.e., binary). In a society organized around group-based inequality, a correction policy can be defined as any policy leading to a systemic transfer of economic, social, and political power or resources from the dominant group to a subordinated group. A policy that does not do this in some way may well represent a change of the status quo (e.g., a passive affirmative action program that merely recruits qualified minority applicants, but does not guarantee that qualified minorities will be hired), but it is not, from the perspective of oppression theory, a correction of societal inequality (e.g., aggressive, quota-based affirmative action that both promotes and guarantees equality of result over equality of access).[4]

Applying the binary logic principle to the practice of restorative justice, any restorative justice disposition involving minority offenders from historically oppressed commentators must, in some way, move to restore equality to the economic, social, and political inequality created by historical oppression, or it is, by definition, not a corrective. I will address the notion of correction in greater detail later in a discussion of the binary logic of the restorative justice practice of reintegrative shaming.

The Role of Economic, Social, and Political Context in Oppression

Philosophers such as Jones and scholar and theologian Cornel West (1982) believe equal-opportunity policy has failed to achieve equality of result because equality of access, as a legal construct defined by antidiscrimination legislation and the landmark reforms of the civil rights era, has been confused with the more theoretical and ill-defined ideal of equality of opportunity. To appreciate the distinction, one need only ponder the following question: What if, suddenly, complete and equal access to housing, jobs, and educational institutions were made available to historically oppressed minorities who were systematically denied such access during three centuries of oppression, but without also accommodating the transgenerational and cumulative economic, social, and political competitive advantage in relation to economic resources and institutions of social control that accrued to white Americans, on one hand, and the commensurate cumulative disadvantage that accrued to minorities, on the other? This is, in fact, what has occurred in the guise of equal opportunity. According to van Dijk (1993, pp. 192–193), for historically oppressed minorities, these reforms merely replaced their "unequal treatment . . . in an unequal situation with their equal treatment in [what remains] an unequal situation." Either way, the result is likely to be the same.

To underscore van Dijk's point, two visible economic effects of majority advantage and minority disadvantage resulting from historical oppression can be examined relative to home-ownership patterns in the United States. Currently, white median family income is two-thirds greater than African American median family income (i.e., $49,023 for white Americans compared with $29,404 for black Americans) (U.S. Bureau of the Census, 2000, p. 470). The average white family also claims $74,000 in asset wealth compared with $17,000 for the average African American family (Littman, 1998, p. 80). As only two indices of race-based inequality, these economic disparities alone portray an overwhelming competitive advantage for white Americans, influencing access to better public schools or to the economic availability of such resources as information technology, both of which profoundly influence one's preparation for competition in the modern information age.

However, the advantage for white Americans is not only on the playing field of the present. It even extends to future generations, since, over the years, the majority has had far greater freedom to accrue equity wealth through access to home mortgages long denied minorities. For the majority's middle class, especially, this has meant that wealth could be passed to the next generation to ensure white America's advantage as a birthright. According to Jones (1990a, 1990b), until this disparity has been corrected, simply removing the barriers to the competitive playing field (i.e., providing equal access) can never guarantee equal competition in a group-based, unequal status quo (i.e., equal opportunity).

In light of such obvious disparities, the question posed by oppression theory is, Why would we confuse equal access with equal opportunity in the first place? Put simply, most white Americans, relative to others, *do* inhabit an equal-opportunity world, relatively unfettered by limitations of historically imposed economic, social, and political deficit and disadvantage. It is a world informed by a dominant group worldview (Gordon, 1995; Howard, 1999; van Dijk, 1993)[5] in which the ultraindividual and his/her potential are unrestrained by uncorrected, group-related systemic limitations of opportunity and competitive disadvantage. It is this biased, acontextualized account of the individual that also belies the dominant group's myopia when it comes to an appreciation for how historical racism continues to generate modern day racial inequality. Jones (1990e) refers to this myopia as "oppression denial." Oppression theory's criticism of both restorative justice social policy and so-called equal opportunity reform is that to overcome this denial of the transgenerational economic effects of historical oppression, equal opportunity advocates, restorative justice practitioners, and policy-makers must begin by incorporating into their policy-making discourse a worldview framework that accounts for systemic oppression to give both the terms *restorative* and *justice* more complete meaning.

The Role of Legitimation in Preserving Group-Based Inequality

In the earlier discussion of oppression as a cultural universal, it was asserted that culture, its institutions, its customs, its policies, its morality, and even its epistemology can function, at least in part, to legitimate a society's economic, social, and political hierarchy. In oppression theory, legitimation refers to those official justifications and explanations a society's dominant group promotes to rationalize its dominance and privilege. According to Berger (1965), the primary function of legitimation, and the institutions and practices it justifies, is to distract those who are at the bottom of an oppressive and unequal hierarchical arrangement from discovering the true source of their oppression: Those at the top. One of the goals of an oppression theory critique of restorative justice, therefore, is to examine restorative justice theory and practice to determine how, if at all, it legitimates the existing hierarchy.

To appreciate the coercive power of an effective oppression legitimation in modern times, it is useful to examine briefly how legitimation has been employed historically to support societal hierarchies. A sociologist of religion, Berger (1965) discovered that throughout history, hierarchical societies have most often used religion, its institutions, and its traditions to legitimate economic, social, and political hierarchies as the will of God. For instance, Jones (1998) chronicled how, during U.S. slavery, the slave masters were cautious to preach to enslaved Africans those particular biblical passages emphasizing unquestioning obedience to the slave master (e.g., in the New Testament, The Epistle of Paul to the Ephesians 6) and how, in the same sermons, they were equally careful to avoid biblical text promoting liberation (e.g., in the Old Testament, Leviticus 25). For the slave, who was indoctrinated to believe that salvation rested in obedience to this selective Scripture, protest of this arrangement in the face of divine omnipotence was not only fruitless, it was mortally and spiritually fatal.[6] The crucial psychological effect of successful religious legitimation, according to Jones (1998), was "quietism," or the individual's passive acceptance of one's subordination in a way that would minimize the economic and military cost of subjugation to the oppressor.

But, as the Age of Reason had challenged the primacy of religion in Western thought, scientific racism soon challenged religion as the major weapon in the arsenal of legitimation. By the late nineteenth century, the new social sciences had begun to provide the rational, scientific basis for ordering the races from superior to inferior as a means of legitimating the military, technological, and economic dominance of Northern Hemisphere societies over others (Gould, 1983). Just as religious legitimation had attempted to locate inequality in an immutable, eternal cosmic scheme, scientific racism justified group inequality as part of the eternal natural order of things and, therefore, beyond the machinations of human beings.

As a method of legitimating race-based inequality, scientific racism reached its zenith in the mid-twentieth century, falling into disrepute with the demise of Nazi Germany and employed only sporadically thereafter, most notably and recently by Herrnstein and Murray (1994) in the book *The Bell Curve*. Jones (1990a, 1990c, 1990d), however, warned of the insidious nature of oppression legitimation and its capacity to mutate to meet the exigencies of the "dominance agenda" of the oppressor group. Predictably, he proposed, a new and even more insidious form of legitimation has evolved to take the place of scientific racism, promoted, this time, not by social Darwinists or race supremacists, but by a politically liberal social reform establishment that blames neither God nor nature for race-based inequality, but rather places blame "within the victim" of historical inequality (Ryan, 1973, p. 8).

In his classic critique of modern social reform methodology, *Blaming the Victim*, Ryan (1973) described how the elite discourse of the social sciences has invoked blaming the victim legitimations to explain group-based, and particularly race-based, inequality.

[The] new ideology [of victim-blaming] is very different from the open prejudice and reactionary tactics of the old days. Its adherents include sympathetic social scientists with social consciences in good working order, and liberal politicians with a genuine commitment to reform [whose analysis of the source of poverty and deprivation is not the innate inferiority of the environs of the so-called "culture of poverty," but] . . . the malignant nature of poverty, injustice, slum life, and racial inequalities. . . . [To these adherents] the stigma that marks the victim and accounts for his victimization is an acquired stigma . . . of social origin. But, the stigma—*though derived in the past from environmental forces*—is still located *within* the victim [author's emphases], inside his skin. With such an elegant formulation, the humanitarian can have it both ways. He can, at the same time, concentrate his charitable interests on the defects of the victim, condemn the vague social and environmental forces that produced the defects (some time ago), and ignore the continuing effect of victimizing social forces (right now) (Ryan, 1973, pp. 7–8).

"With such an elegant formulation," let us now examine the restorative justice concept of reintegrative shaming to see how it fares in an oppressive societal context.

WHEN RESTORATIVE JUSTICE BECOMES BLAMING THE VICTIM JUSTICE: THE EXAMPLE OF REINTEGRATIVE SHAMING

A major difference between restorative justice and retributive justice is that restorative justice, in the ideal, places considerable value on teaching the offender to empathize with the plight of the victim and to comprehend the impact of the offender's behavior on the victim, the community, and the social fabric (Bazemore & Umbreit, 1998), whereas traditional retributive justice dispositions tend to be indifferent to the offender's moral sensibilities. Ideally, the process of building offender empathy occurs in a mediated environment in which the victim shares the consequences of his/her victimization with the offender. When confronted with the human toll of his/her behavior in a personal and emotional encounter with the victim, it is hoped the offender will correct his/her deficiency of conscience and lack of empathy and, consequently, be deterred from future criminal behavior (Bazemore & Umbreit, 1998; Braithewaite, 1989, Zehr, 1998).

Perhaps the most innovative expression of this strategy as a deliberate component of restorative justice is Braithwaite's (1989) notion of "reintegrative shaming." As distinguished from shame that stigmatizes individuals, reintegrative shaming does not degrade one's identity or self-esteem, but offers a path by which shame can be removed and individual self-respect restored, and the individual can be "reintegrated" into the community (Zehr, 1998). From a detailed examination of the role of shame in human history, Braithwaite (1993) concluded that reintegrative shaming of lawbreakers was a potential key to controlling crime. Separate studies by Strang (1996) and Leibrich (1996) supported Braithewaite's assertion with the conclusion that the most effective reintegrative approach was one that "shames while maintaining bonds of respect or love, that . . . terminates disapproval with forgiveness" (Leibrich, 1996, p. 297).

As a means of social control, however, reintegrative shaming has not been without its critics. Although Braithwaite (1994) acknowledged that injustice is an important part of systemic oppression, White (1994) noted reintegrative shaming theory's general preoccupation with changing the individual while remaining indifferent to the influences on behavior of contextual factors such as economic inequality, race- and gender-based political hierarchies, and access to resources, that is, in the parlance of oppression theory, reintegrative shaming tends to blame the victim without considering the effects of an oppressive historical context.

To appreciate how such a seemingly progressive idea can be a victim-blaming strategy, we need only refer to Ryan's recipe for blaming the victim social policy:

First, identify a social problem. Second, study those who are affected by the problem and discover in what ways they are different from the rest of us as a consequence of deprivation and injustice [while ignoring the causal connection to institutional deprivation and injustice]. Third, define the differences as the cause of the social problem itself. Finally, . . . invent a humanitarian action program to correct the differences (Ryan, 1973, p. 10).

Beginning with the proposition that the offender suffers from some deficit of conscience, social awareness, or empathy (i.e., the difference) that distinguishes him/her from civil society (i.e., the rest of us), it should be apparent that the ideal scenario of reintegrative shaming applies this recipe perfectly. Rather than exploring and substantively addressing additional economic, social, and political contextual explanations for this difference, the focus of analysis in a reintegrative shaming/restorative justice framework is only the difference itself rather than its contextual precursors, extending no further than the offender's deficit of conscience or lack of shame as the controlling causality of his/her criminal behavior. Consequently, in trying to instill in the offender empathy for the victim, advocates of restorative justice have not yet determined how to incorporate a sufficiently corrective, empathic response for that category of offender who is a predictable, necessary, and even a rational outcome of enforced inequality (Cornish & Clarke, 1987).

CONCLUSION

According to an oppression theory analysis, then, as currently conceived, the binary logic of restorative justice in general, and reintegrative shaming in particular, is one that tends to preserve an unequal, group-based, economic, social, and political status quo, at least, for some instances of offense perpetrated by offenders from historically disenfranchised minority contexts. A theory-based corrective for such a limitation would begin with an expansion of the interpretive framework of restorative justice to incorporate minority intellectual traditions and counter-discourse, such as oppression theory, that speak more directly to the reality of offenders who originate from historically oppressed group contexts. As to how such a reformulation could be constructed to deal equitably with the needs of the victim, the victim's community, and the economic, social, and political status of the offender in a victim/offender mediation, I would propose the following series of diagnostic questions:

1. What is the economic, social, and political context of the crime event from a dominant group perspective? From an oppression theory perspective?
2. Define the disequilibrium that has been introduced into the life of the victim and the community by the offender's behavior.
3. What must be done to restore equilibrium to the victim and to the community?
4. Define the disequilibrium of the offender's economic, social, and political context.
5. What specific correctives must be made to restore equilibrium to the offender in that context?
6. How can/should these correctives be implemented so as to validate and correct *both* disequilibria in a way that recognizes the victim/offender relationship in an oppression theory context?

According to oppression theory, when such a diagnostic is applied, especially the last three questions, restorative justice must either construct a "mechanism that can address and alter [i.e., correct] the existing social structures that are . . . the root cause of criminal conflict" (McCold, 1996, p. 95) or risk continued complicity with an oppressive societal arrangement. Fortunately, the binary logic thesis also circumscribes the parameters of the generic features of a corrective mechanism: That is, assuming a society of finite resources, any policy, program, and other corrective, no matter how local, must lead to a transfer of power and resources from the surplus side of the unequal societal power and resource equation to the deficit side.[7]

Oppression theory asserts that for minority offenders who are the victims of uncorrected historical oppression, it is this imbalance, not the individual deficiencies of the offender, that is the systemic root cause of criminal conflict. Oppression theory also predicts that until the dominant group is motivated by its own need for refuge from this conflict to restore economic, social, and political equilibrium to the disequilibrium that remains the shameful legacy of historical oppression, we will remain the conflicted society, racked by destructive crime and violence Frederick Douglass warned of more than a century ago, "a society in which neither persons nor property will ever be safe" (Douglass, 1992/1886, p. 7).

NOTES

1. The notion of *choice* may be misleading since it implies a conscious decision process. Jones asserts that oppressor group members tend to be in denial (i.e., psychologically unconscious) regarding a societal arrangement that favors their interests.

2. In *The Mis-education of the Negro*, Carter G. Woodson (1933) suggests that even a noble institution such as education "serves others so much better than it does the Negro." Thus, our institutions of education must be scrutinized for content and beliefs that would miseducate African Americans to accept their economic, social, and political subordination passively.

3. For some, it may be paradoxical that oppression theory demands that this level of scrutiny should also be applied to oppression theory, since one of its tenets is that the perspectives of minority individuals can be co-opted by the oppressive agenda of a group-based hierarchy through effective miseducation.

4. *Equality of result* refers to the notion that equal opportunity reforms should produce roughly equivalent demographic distributions by race at all economic levels.

5. Gordon (1995, p. 92) refers to this framework as "Angloconformity," or the worldview that promotes "English institutions (as modified by the American Revolution), the English language, and English-oriented cultural patterns as dominant and standard in American life" to the exclusion of other traditions.

6. In his book, *Is God a White Racist?*, Jones (1998) described how the mecha-

nisms of oppression and religious legitimation supported the enslavement of Africans by white North Americans.

7. On the order of societal magnitude McCold (1996) is referring to, aggressive, quota-based affirmative action would qualify as such a corrective policy. The challenge to restorative justice proponents armed with an oppression theory diagnostic is to determine how similar correctives can occur at the community level.

REFERENCES

Andrzejewski, J. (Ed.). (1996). *Oppression and social justice: Critical frameworks*. Needham Heights, MA: Simon & Schuster.

Bazemore, G. (1996). Three paradigms for juvenile justice. In B. Galaway & J. Hudson (Eds.), *Restorative justice: International perspectives* (pp. 37–68). Monsey, NY: Criminal Justice Press.

Bazemore, G., & Umbreit, M. (1998). *Conferences, circles, boards and mediations: Restorative justice and citizen involvement in the response to youth crime*. Fort Lauderdale, FL: Florida Atlantic University, the Balanced & Restorative Justice Project.

Berger, P. (1965). *The sacred canopy: Elements of a sociological theory of religion*. Garden City, NY: Doubleday & Co.

Braithewaite, J. (1989). *Crime, shame and reintegration*. New York: Cambridge University Press.

Braithewaite, J. (1993). Shame and modernity. *British Journal of Criminology, 33*, 1–18.

Braithewaite, J. (1994). Thinking harder about democratizing social control. In C. Alder & J. Wundersitz (Eds.), *Family conferencing and juvenile justice: The way forward or misplaced optimism?* (pp. 199–216). Canberra, Australia: Australian Institute of Criminology.

Close, B. (1997). *Towards a resolution of the discrimination/no discrimination debate in criminology and criminal justice: Revisiting black criminality and institutional racism*. Unpublished doctoral dissertation, Florida State University, Tallahassee, Florida.

Cornish, D., & Clarke, R. (1987). Understanding crime displacement: An application of rational choice theory. *Criminology, 25*, 933–949.

Douglass, F. (1992). Speech on the 24th anniversary of Emancipation, April 1886. In D. Baker (Ed.), *Power Quotes* (p. 7). Detroit: Visible Ink Press.

Dreyfus, H. (1983). *Beyond structuralism and hermeneutics*. Chicago: University of Chicago Press.

Freire, P. (1997). *Pedagogy of the oppressed* (rev. ed.). New York: Continuum Publishing.

Gordon, M. (1995). Assimilation in America: Theory and reality. In A. Aguirre & D. Baker (Eds.), *Sources: Notable sources in race and ethnicity* (pp. 91–102). Guilford, CT: Dushkin.

Gould, S. (1983). *The mismeasure of man*. New York: W.W. Norton.

Griffiths, C., & Hamilton, R. (1996). Sanctioning and healing: Restorative justice in Canadian aboriginal communities. In B. Galaway & J. Hudson (Eds.), *Restorative justice: International perspectives* (pp. 175–192). Monsey, NY: Criminal Justice Press.

Griffiths, C., & Patenaude, A. (1990). The use of community service orders and restitution in the Canadian North: The problems and processes of "localized" corrections. In B. Galaway & J. Hudson (Eds.), *Criminal justice, retribution and reconciliation* (pp. 145–153). Monsey, NY: Criminal Justice Press.

Herrnstein, R., & Murray, C. (1994). *The bell curve: Intelligence and class structure in American life.* New York: Free Press.

Howard, G. (1999). *We can't teach what we don't know.* New York: Teachers College Press of Columbia University.

Hudson, J., Galaway, B., Morris, A., & Maxwell, G. (1996). *Family group conferences: Perspectives on policy and practice.* Monsey, NY: Criminal Justice Press.

Jones, W. R. (1990a). *An anatomy of ESP oppression.* (Available from W. R. Jones, c/o Black Studies Program, Florida State University, Tallahassee, FL 32306-2520)

Jones, W. R. (1990b). *Institutional racism/oppression: Towards a new paradigm for uncovering neo-racism in the legal justice system.* (Available from W. R. Jones, c/o Black Studies Program, Florida State University, Tallahassee, FL 32306-2520)

Jones, W. R. (1990c). *Towards a definition of culture: Selected interpretations.* (Available from W. R. Jones, c/o Black Studies Program, Florida State University, Tallahassee, FL 32306-2520)

Jones, W. R. (1990d). *Towards a definition of culture II: Selected interpretations.* (Available from W. R. Jones, c/o Black Studies Program, Florida State University, Tallahassee, FL 32306-2520)

Jones, W. R. (1990e). *Towards a definition of worldview.* (Available from W. R. Jones, c/o Black Studies Program, Florida State University, Tallahassee, FL 32306-2520)

Jones, W. R. (1998). *Is God a white racist? A preamble to black theology* (rev. ed.). Boston: Beacon Press.

Leibrich, J. (1996). The role of shame in going straight: A study of former offenders. In B. Galaway & J. Hudson (Eds.), *Restorative justice: International perspectives* (pp. 283–302). Monsey, NY: Criminal Justice Press.

Littman, M. (Ed.). (1998). *Statistical portrait of the United States: Social conditions and trends.* Lanham, MD: Bernan Press.

McCold, P. (1996). Restorative justice and the role of community. In B. Galaway & J. Hudson (Eds.), *Restorative justice: International perspectives* (pp. 85–101). Monsey, NY: Criminal Justice Press.

McCold, P. (1997). *Restorative justice: An annotated bibliography.* Monsey, NY: Criminal Justice Press.

Nandy, A. (1987). *Tradition, tyranny and utopia: Essays in the politics of awareness.* New York: Oxford University Press.

Ryan, W. (1973). *Blaming the victim.* New York: Vintage Books.

Sidanius, J., & Pratto, F. (1990, March). *The inevitability of oppression and the dynamics of social dominance.* Paper presented at the Conference on Race and American Society and Politics, Berkeley, CA.

Strang, H. (1996, November). *Shaming conferences: Community policing and the victim's perspective.* Paper presented at the meeting of the American Society of Criminology, Chicago, IL.

Tetreault, M. (1993). Classrooms for diversity: Rethinking curriculum and pedagogy. In J. Banks & C. Banks (Eds.), *Multicultural education: Issues and perspectives* (2nd ed.) (pp. 129–148). Boston: Allyn & Bacon.

Umbreit, M. (1998a). *Multicultural implications of restorative justice: Potential pitfalls and dangers.* Washington, DC: Office for Victims of Crime.

Umbreit, M. (1998b, March). Workshop presented for Victim-Offender Mediation Training Program. Florida Atlantic University, Ft. Lauderdale, FL.

U. S. Bureau of the Census. (2000). *Statistical Abstract of the United States, 2000* (120th ed.). Washington, DC: U. S. Department of Commerce, Economics and Statistics Administration.

van Dijk, T. (1993). *Elite discourse and racism.* Newbury Park, CA: Sage.

Van Ness, D. (1993). A reply to Andrew Ashworth. *Criminal Law Forum, 5,* 251–276.

Van Ness, D., & Strong, K. (1997). *Restoring justice.* Cincinnati: Anderson.

West, C. (1982). *Prophesy deliverance! An Afro-American revolutionary Christianity.* Philadelphia: Westminster Press.

White, R. (1994). Shaming and reintegrative strategies: Individuals, state power and social interests. In C. Alder & J. Wundersitz (Eds.), *Family conferencing and juvenile justice: The way forward or misplaced optimism?* (pp. 181–196). Canberra, Australia: Australian Institute of Criminology.

Woodson, C. (1933). *The mis-education of the Negro.* Washington, DC: Associated Publishers.

Young, M. (1995). *Restorative community justice: A call to action.* Washington, DC: National Organization for Victim Assistance.

Zehr, H. (1990). *Changing lenses: A new focus for crime and justice.* Scott, PA: Herald Press.

Zehr, H. (1998, June). Seminar presented at Summer Peacebuilding Institute, Eastern Mennonite University, Harrisonburg, VA.

Index

About the Editor and Contributors

DAVID V. BAKER has a Ph.D. from the University of California–Riverside and a J.D. from California Southern Law School. He is an associate professor of sociology in the Behavioral Sciences Department at Riverside Community College. He has contributed works to several professional journals, including *Ethnic Studies, Social Justice, The Justice Professional, Social Science Journal, Women and Criminal Justice,* and *Criminal Justice Abstracts.* A coauthor of numerous books, Dr. Baker has received two National Endowment for the Humanities fellowships and is an associate editor for *The Justice Professional.*

PAUL J. BECKER is an assistant professor of sociology in the Department of Sociology, Anthropology, and Social Work at the University of Dayton, where he also is affiliated with the Criminal Justice Studies Program. Research interests include white racial extremist groups, hate crimes, state and corporate crime, and the Internet. Previous research has appeared in the *International Review of Law, Computers, and Technology, The Justice Professional, Teaching Sociology,* and the *American Journal of Criminal Justice.*

BRYAN D. BYERS holds a doctorate from the University of Notre Dame and is currently an associate professor of criminal justice and criminology at Ball State University. Dr. Byers' field experiences include positions as a prosecutor's special investigator, adult protective services investigator, deputy coroner, mental health liaison, juvenile corrections worker, criminal justice trainer, and researcher. He has published over twenty-five articles and book chapters and has written or edited five books.

ROBERT CONNERS, who holds a Ph.D. from Florida State University, is vice president for research and development with InfoWorks, Inc. During the 1990s he served as the director of Florida State University's Program in Multicultural Studies and Conflict Resolution, as a faculty member of the Black Studies Program, and as a principal coinvestigator of a U.S. Department of Justice research project that examined systemic sources of minority overrepresentation in Florida's juvenile justice system. Currently, he is writing a book, *The Ten Myths of Modern Racism*.

ROBERT ENGVALL holds J.D. and Ph.D. degrees from the University of Iowa and is an Associate Professor of Justice Studies at Roger Williams University in Bristol, Rhode Island. He is the author of two books and several articles concerning higher education issues.

SARAH ESCHHOLZ has a Ph.D. from Florida State University and is an assistant professor in the Department of Criminal Justice at Georgia State University. Her research has appeared recently in *Journal of Law & Public Policy, Journal of Research in Crime & Delinquency, Social Problems,* and *Critical Criminology.*

MARVIN D. FREE, JR. received his Ph.D. degree from the University of Denver and is an associate professor of sociology at the University of Wisconsin—Whitewater. His research interest centers on race and criminal justice. He has authored two previous books and over a dozen articles.

HIROSHI FUKURAI, who has his Ph.D.from the University of California—Riverside, is an associate professor of sociology at the University of California—Santa Cruz. Born in Japan, Dr. Fukurai's areas of expertise include the sociology of law, criminology, jury selection and jury trials, judicial systems of the world, the legal construction of race, advanced quantitative methods, and Pacific Rim issues. Book publications include *Common Destiny: Japan and the U.S. in the Global Age* (1990), *Race and the Jury: Racial Disenfranchisement and the Search for Justice* (1993), and *Anatomy of the McMartin Child Molestation Case* (2001). His 1993 book won the Outstanding Book Award on the Subject of Human Rights by the Gustavs Myers Center in 1994.

MICHAEL A. HALLETT, Ph.D., is an associate professor of criminal justice at the University of North Florida, where he is also director of the master of science program in criminal justice. He has worked extensively with labor unions and state legislatures on issues associated with prison privatization.

ELISSA KRAUSS has been a trial consultant with the National Jury Project since 1975. She has conducted jury research in twenty-three states and twenty-six federal districts.

MICHAEL J. LYNCH, who has a Ph.D. from State University of New York at Albany, is professor and director of the Ph.D. program in criminology at the University of South Florida. An author/editor of eight books, he has recently published articles in *The Archives of Pediatrics & Adolescent Medicine; Justice Quarterly; Social Science Quarterly; The British Journal of Criminology; Crime, Law and Social Change; Humanity & Society; Critical Criminology;* and *Theoretical Criminology.* Areas of research include the political economy of crime and justice, environmental justice, racial bias in criminal justice processes, and corporate crime.

KELLY J. OPIOLA is a student of criminal justice at Ball State University where she is completing honors work. Ms. Opiola has served as an officer of student organizations and has field experience in criminal justice and social services. Previous research experience includes an analysis of hate groups on the Internet and an examination of hate crime legal trends and issues.

KATHERYN K. RUSSELL has a Ph.D. from the University of Maryland where she is presently an associate professor of criminology and criminal justice. She also holds a J.D. degree from Hastings Law School. Her teaching and research have focused on criminal law, sociology of law, and race and crime.

AMIE M. SCHUCK received her doctoral degree from the State University of New York at Albany. She is an assistant professor in the Department of Criminology at the University of South Florida. Her research focuses on how neighborhood and community factors, particularly those processes that disproportionately affect racial and ethnic minorities, impact family and individual outcomes such as aggression and violence. Her interests specifically include how changes in neighborhood and community structure—such as capacity and empowerment—affect developmental outcomes for residents.

MARTHA SCHULMAN is a teacher and writer whose interests include juries and other legal issues. She is the daughter of the founder of the National Jury Project.

BECKY TATUM is assistant professor of criminology at the University of Houston—Clear Lake. She received her Ph.D. in criminal justice from the

State University of New York at Albany in 1995. Dr. Tatum is a recipient of the W.E.B. Du Bois Residential Fellowship sponsored by the National Institute of Justice and has held elected offices in the American Society of Criminology and the Academy of Criminal Justice Sciences. She has published in the areas of race and crime, juvenile crime and violence, and women and criminal justice education.

HELEN TAYLOR GREENE is associate professor in the Department of Sociology and Criminal Justice at Old Dominion University. She completed her Ph.D. in criminology at the University of Maryland. She is coeditor of *African American Classics in Criminology and Criminal Justice* (2002) with Shaun L. Gabbidon and Vernetta D. Young and is coauthor of *African American Criminological Thought* (2001) with Shaun L. Gabbidon. Research interests include policing and race and crime, with a special emphasis on blacks, crime, and justice.

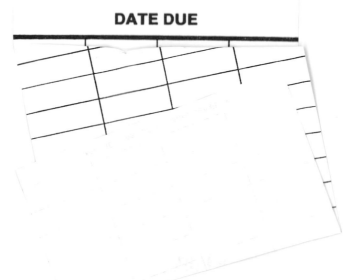
Please remember that this is a library book,
and that it belongs only temporarily to each
person who uses it. Be considerate. Do
not write in this, or any, library book.